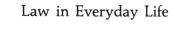

Law in Everyday Life

The Amherst Series in Law, Jurisprudence, and Social Thought

Each work included in The Amherst Series in Law, Jurisprudence, and Social Thought explores a theme crucial to an understanding of law as it confronts the changing social and intellectual currents of the late twentieth century.

Law in Everyday Life

Edited by Austin Sarat and Thomas R. Kearns

Ann Arbor

THE UNIVERSITY OF MICHIGAN PRESS

Copyright © by the University of Michigan 1993
All rights reserved
Published in the United States of America by
The University of Michigan Press
Manufactured in the United States of America

1996   1995   1994   1993   4   3   2   1

Library of Congress Cataloging-in-Publication Data

Law in everyday life / edited by Austin Sarat and Thomas R. Kearns.
        p.   cm. — (Amherst series in law, jurisprudence, and social
    thought)
    Includes bibliographical references and index.
    ISBN 0-472-10441-1 (alk. paper)
    1. Law—United States—Popular works. 2. Law—Philosophy.
I. Sarat, Austin.   II. Kearns, Thomas R.   III. Series.
KF387.L374   1993
340'.1—dc20   93-31233
                                                          CIP

A CIP catalogue record for this book is available from the British Library.

Acknowledgments

Law in Everyday Life is the third in a continuing series of books that emerge from, and reflect, the substantive interests in what was initially known as the Program in Law, Jurisprudence & Social Thought at Amherst College. Following a recent vote of the Faculty at Amherst, LJST has been accorded permanent departmental status with the right to offer a major, the first such entity at a liberal arts college in the United States. We are grateful to our colleagues at Amherst for their enthusiastic endorsement of our work. This department addresses itself to the historically and culturally specific ways in which legal institutions combine moral argument, distinctive rhetorical and hermeneutic practices, and the social organization of violence. Our everyday life has been particularly enriched by Lawrence Douglas and Victoria Saker, each of whom has made substantial contributions to the intellectual perspective reflected in these pages. We have been especially fortunate to enlist a group of distinguished scholars, whose contributions are included in this volume, to address themselves to issues central to the agenda of LJST. Finally, we would like to express special thanks to the Mellon, Keck, and Arthur Vining Davis Foundations without whose generous financial support LJST could not have come into being, and to Amherst's President, Peter Pouncey, for his friendship and enthusiastic engagement with our work.

Contents

Editorial Introduction

Austin Sarat and Thomas R. Kearns

The first two volumes of the Amherst Series in Law, Jurisprudence, and Social Thought surveyed the majesty and monstrosity of law and speculated about its future and its fate.[1] They considered the impact of feminism and postmodernism on law and legal theory and attended to the nature and consequences of law's violence. In so doing, they initiated this series with the dramatic and spectacular; they invited readers to see law through the eyes of philosophers, on the one hand, and of those who authorize and experience the force of law, on the other.[2] In *Law in Everyday Life*, the third volume in the series, we take up different questions and assume a different tone. We speak about routine, habit, convention, and the constraints and restraints that each imposes.[3] We confront law in its dailiness and as a virtually invisible factor in social life.[4]

---

1. See Austin Sarat and Thomas R. Kearns, eds., *The Fate of Law* (Ann Arbor: University of Michigan Press, 1991); and Austin Sarat and Thomas R. Kearns, eds., *Law's Violence* (Ann Arbor: University of Michigan Press, 1992).

2. As Robert Cover, "Violence and the Word," *Yale Law Journal* 95 (1986): 1601, reminds us, these are very different perspectives.

3. "The everyday implies on the one hand cycles, nights and days, seasons and harvests, activity and rest, hunger and satisfaction, desire and its fulfillment, life and death, and it implies on the other hand the repetitive gestures of work and consumption. . . . The everyday imposes its monotony. It is the invariable constant of the variations it envelops." See Henri Lefebvre, "The Everyday and Everydayness," *Yale French Studies* 76 (1987): 10.

4. Writing about social research on law, Austin Sarat and Susan Silbey argue that "by focusing upon law where it attempts to change social behavior, [researchers] divert attention from the ways in which law helps to constitute social practices; they direct attention away from the ways state law works to stifle resistance before it is voiced so that acquiescence becomes the norm. . . . Rarely do they look to where law is unproblematic, to instances of law-abidingness; sociolegal research seems for the

The essays collected in this volume describe law as it appears in various *places*, families, schools, communities, offices, and countless routine transactions,[5] and in various *forms*, including the law of separation and divorce, abortion, rape, sexual harassment, special education, international human rights, and torts. Yet each of the essays recognizes the ubiquity of law and the resentments that accompany its pervasive presence.[6] Each describes how law helps shape experiences, interpretations, and understandings of social life, and how legal rules are used in daily life.[7] Each suggests ways in which law itself is organized around and responds to images and representations of the everyday.

Throughout there is an awareness of the contingency and specificity of the relationship of law and everyday life. Thus the essays in *Law in Everyday Life* highlight different ways in which law makes its presence felt in the lives of men and women, whites and blacks, rich and poor.[8] They also remind us that the law of daily life is, in

---

most part to take for granted the fundamental values and rules which order daily life and which . . . are, at least partially, constituted through state legality." "The Pull of the Policy Audience," *Law and Policy* 10 (1988): 138. See also David Engel, "Legal Pluralism in an American Community," *American Bar Foundation Research Journal* 1980 (1980): 425.

There is, of course, considerable debate and discussion about how and when law is relevant in everyday life. Some believe that Sarat and Silbey radically overestimate the pervasiveness and significance of law. For them, the contribution of law to everyday life seems minimal and insignificant. See Stewart Macaulay, "Non-Contractual Relations in Business: A Preliminary Study," *American Sociological Review* 28 (1963): 55; and Robert Ellickson, *Order without Law: How Neighbors Settle Disputes* (Cambridge: Harvard University Press, 1991).

5. Usually, research that seeks to "understand the contribution of legal institutions to social processes, focuses primarily upon law." Susan Silbey and Austin Sarat, "Critical Traditions in Law and Society Research," *Law and Society Review* 21 (1987): 173. "To invert this aspect," Silbey and Sarat argue, "attention needs to be paid to social processes themselves. The risk has to be taken and the courage has to be mustered to immerse ourselves in the study of social transactions and social processes."

6. Jethro Lieberman, *The Litigious Society* (New York: Basic Books, 1981); and Lawrence Friedman, *Total Justice* (New York: Russell Sage, 1985).

7. For an interesting example of the place of law in the everyday life of a single community see Carol Greenhouse, *Praying for Justice: Faith, Order, and Community in an American Town* (Ithaca, N.Y.: Cornell University Press, 1986).

8. For a particularly powerful demonstration of this thesis see Patricia Williams, *The Alchemy of Race and Rights: Diary of a Law Professor* (Cambridge: Harvard University Press, 1991).

the late twentieth century (described in this volume by Patricia Williams, David Kennedy, and George Marcus), quite different from the law of daily life in the late eighteenth and early nineteenth century (described herein by Hendrik Hartog).[9] Taken together, the essays portray law in the lives of ordinary citizens and those who are otherwise implicated in the ordinary, nondramatic work of law, and they illustrate the possibilities and problems of law in everyday life.

But what does it mean to talk about everyday life? Is the very idea a remnant, a sign of nostalgia left behind in the twentieth (soon-to-be twenty-first) century? While the idea of the everyday appears episodically and variously in a range of research and theory, from the phenomenology of Alfred Shcutz to the critical Marxism of Henri Lefebvre,[10] it is not an ordinary and familiar concept in social and legal analysis.[11] In contemporary theory, feminism now carries the banner of the everyday, the everyday, on one understanding, being the world most often inhabited by women.[12] While in feminist scholarship the everyday is called the "private," elsewhere it is variously styled the "life-world," "the realm of the ordinary," or "the domain of the banal."

No matter what it is called, claims made about the everyday as a category of analysis and a grounds for theory are sometimes quite extravagant. As one example, Lefebvre argues that "[I]n so far as the science of man exists, it finds its material in the 'trivial,' the everyday."[13] Of course, it is precisely because the trivial is not trivial that it might, in Lefebvre's view, become the basis for a science of man.

Where such grand claims are not made, the everyday is nonetheless often used as a trope of authenticity and a standard of critique. The everyday is the domain of unalienated experience, the life-world

9. Some believe that the very idea of everyday life is called into question by the conditions of modern life. See David Harvey, *The Condition of Postmodernity: An Enquiry into the Origins of Cultural Change* (Oxford: Basil Blackwell, 1989), chap. 17.

10. See Alfred Schutz, *The Phenomenology of the Social World*, trans. George Walsh and Frederick Lehnert (Evanston, Ill.: Northwestern University Press, 1967); and Henri Lefebvre, *Critique of Everyday Life*, trans. John Moore (London: Verso, 1991).

11. See Jack Douglas, ed., *Understanding Everyday Life* (Chicago: Aldine, 1970).

12. See especially Catharine MacKinnon, *Feminism Unmodified: Discourses on Law and Life* (Cambridge: Harvard University Press, 1987).

13. Lefebvre, *Critique of Everyday Life*, 133.

that is contrasted to what Habermas calls the world of "communicative action," of discursive rationality, of instrumental action, choice, design, and project.[14] Praising the former, while understanding the inexorable pull of the latter, is one way of giving dignity to ordinary persons and the ordinary in all persons. The everyday is the domain of situated, bounded, local place and time; it is the domain of the human against the technological superhumanness of the modern, and it reminds us of the alienation and dangers of our era.[15] As Lefebvre asks,

> Is it not in everyday life that man should fulfill his life as a man? The theory of superhuman moments is inhuman. Is it not in day-to-day life . . . that the truth in a body and a soul must be grasped? If a higher life, the life of the "spirit," was to be attained in "another life" . . . it would be the end of mankind, the proof and proclamation of his failure. Man must be everyday, or he will not be at all.[16]

But, as Lefebvre also usefully points out, the search for the superhuman moment is not a random, unsituated event. It is the work of art, philosophy, and the "science of war" against the world of family, work, and leisure. It is thus the work of one class against another, of "particularly gifted, lucid and active individuals" against the masses.[17]

Thus Lefebvre and others see the defense and rehabilitation of everyday life as an essential political gesture, a gesture that begins in critique and ends in social transformation.[18] The everyday becomes the uncriticized critique, the here and now, the un(self)conscious

---

14. See, for example, Jürgen Habermas, *The Theory of Communicative Action*, vol. 1, *Reason and Rationalization in Society*, trans. Thomas McCarthy (Boston: Beacon Press, 1984), 337.

15. See Jürgen Habermas, *Legitimation Crisis*, trans. Thomas McCarthy (Boston: Beacon Press, 1975). See also George Simmel, *The Philosophy of Money*, trans. Tom Bottomore and Donald Frisby (London: Routledge and Kegan Paul, 1978). For a useful discussion of the way in which law contributes to the alienation of the modern age see Peter Gabel, "Reification in Legal Reasoning," *Research in Law and Sociology* 3 (1980): 28–29.

16. Lefebvre, *Critique of Everyday Life*, 127.

17. Id., 29.

18. See Agnes Heller, *Everyday Life*, trans. G. L. Campbell (London: Routledge, Chapman and Hall, 1984).

present, juxtaposed to the abstraction and artifice of the artistic, the bureaucratic, and the technological. The everyday is the immediate and the familiar juxtaposed to the distant, strange, and cosmopolitan.[19] The everyday is origin and home, point of departure and place of return.

In the work of Schutz and of Habermas among others, the so-called life-world is pretheoretical and prescientific.[20] It is the background for the projects of reason and science;[21] it is the world of the taken-for-granted, and

the reality which seems self evident to men. . . . This reality is the everyday life-world. It is the province of reality in which men continuously participate in ways which are inevitable and patterned. . . . The world of everyday life is consequently man's fundamental and paramount reality. . . . It is the unexamined ground of everything given in my experience . . . the taken-for-granted frame in which all the problems which I must overcome are placed.[22]

In the face of these claims one might ask whether any inquiry into everyday life is not, at best, a vain effort to rescue being from becoming, the past from the future. One might ask whether the everyday can survive what Harvey calls the "time-space compression" that characterizes the late modern era.[23] We think that the answer is

---

19. As Lefebvre puts it, "The programme we have sketched for a critique of everyday life can be summed up as follows: (a) It will involve a methodological confrontation of so called 'modern' life on the one hand, with the past, and on the other hand—and above all—with the *possible*. . . . (b) Studied from this point of view, human reality appears as an opposition and 'contrast' between a certain number of terms: everyday life and festival—mass moments and exceptional moments—triviality and splendour. . . . The critique of everyday life involves an investigation of the exact relations between these terms. It implies criticism of the trivial by the exceptional—*but at the same time* criticism of the exceptional by the trivial." *Critique of Everyday Life*, 251.

20. See Alfred Schutz and Thomas Luckmann, *The Structures of the Life World*, trans. Richard Zaner and H. Tristram Engelhardt (Evanston, Ill.: Northwestern University Press, 1973); and Habermas, *Theory of Communicative Action*.

21. For a different assessment of the relation of reason and the everyday see Slavoj Zizek, *The Sublime Object of Ideology* (Oxford: Verso, 1989), chap. 1.

22. Schutz and Luckmann, *Structures of the Life World*, 3–4.

23. Harvey, *Condition of Postmodernity*, 240. Harvey uses this term to "signal . . . processes that so revolutionize the objective qualities of space and time

to be found in the very self-evidence and taken-for-grantedness of the everyday. Both defy and undermine the localized, time-space reality of the everyday and its utility as an unproblematic grounding of experience.

Because it is self-evident and taken for granted, the everyday always sits just beyond the grasp of those who live in it and with it. It always contains the dim perception of a horizon, never reached. It thus contains its own compression of time and space, being at once an assurance and a suggestion, a present and an unknowable future. Thus the everyday is that which goes without saying because it cannot be said; it is the word on the tip of the tongue that never completely issues. As Maurice Blanchot puts it,

> Whatever its other aspects, the everyday has this essential trait: it allows no hold. It escapes. It belongs to insignificance, and the insignificant is without truth, without reality, without secret, but perhaps also the site of all possible signification. The everyday escapes. This makes its strangeness—the familiar showing itself . . . in the guise of the astonishing. It is unperceived, first in the sense that one has always looked past it . . . the everyday is always unrealized in its very actualization. . . . Nothing happens, that is the everyday.[24]

Blanchot helps plot a way of thinking about the everyday that frees it from its status as the always solid, always reliable other to modernity's alienating movement. The everyday, as Blanchot understands it, need be neither an object of nostalgia nor a remnant of the tranquil, quiet, locally contained life of some bygone, "Andy of Mayberry" place and time. It is and has always been a premonition of the modern experience, and it always partakes in the elusive known, but unknowable, quality of that experience.[25] Here Nietzsche

---

that we are forced to alter, sometimes in quite radical ways, how we represent the world to ourselves. I use the word 'compression' because a strong case can be made that the history of capitalism has been characterized by speed-up in the pace of life, while so overcoming spatial barriers that the world sometimes seems to collapse inwards upon us." See also Paul Virilio, *Speed and Politics*, trans. Mark Polizzotti (New York: Semiotext(e), 1986).

24. Maurice Blanchot, "Everyday Speech," *Yale French Studies* 76 (1987): 14–15.

25. As Blanchot puts it, "The everyday, where one lives as though outside the true and the false, is a level of life where what reigns is the refusal to be different,

might be thought of as a great, though seldom recognized, theorist of the everyday.

> And do you know what "the world" is to me? Shall I show it to you in my mirror? This world: a monster of energy, without beginning, without end; . . . enclosed by "nothingness" as by a boundary; not something blurry or wasted, not something endlessly extended, but set in a definite space as a definite force, and not a space that might be "empty" here or there, but rather as force throughout . . . a sea of forces flowing and rushing together, eternally changing, eternally flooding back . . . ; out of the simplest forms striving toward the most complex, out of the stillest, most rigid, coldest forms toward the hottest, most turbulent, most self-contradictory, and then again returning home to the simple out of this abundance, out of the play of contradictions back to the joy of concord, still affirming itself in this uniformity of its courses and years, blessing itself as that which must return eternally, as a becoming that knows no satiety, no disgust, no weariness.[26]

Seen in this way the everyday is a domain of action as well as events, and of production as well as consumption. Because it is a scene of action and production, we can turn to the everyday to see the way law is reenacted and remade far from its well-recognized, well-marked official sites.[27] Law seeks to colonize everyday life and give it substance, to capture it and hold it in its grasp, to attach itself to the solidity of the everyday and, in so doing, to solidify it further. But because everyday life is a force in motion and a clash of forces that never fully reveal themselves, law can never fully capture or organize the everyday.[28] Law does not just happen *to* the

---

a yet undetermined stir: without responsibility and without authority, without direction and without decision, a storehouse of anarchy, since casting aside all beginning and dismissing all end. This is the everyday." "Everyday Speech," p. 17. See also Harvey, *Condition of Postmodernity*, 285–88.

26. See Friedrich Nietzsche, *The Will to Power*, trans. Walter Kaufman and R. J. Hollingsdale (New York: Vintage Books, 1968).

27. See Clifford Geertz, *Local Knowledge: Further Essays in Interpretive Anthropology* (New York: Basic Books, 1983).

28. For a useful example see Carol Greenhouse, "Courting Difference: Issues of Interpretation and Comparison in the Study of Legal Ideologies," *Law and Society Review* 22 (1988): 687; and also Barbara Yngvesson, "Inventing Law in Local Settings: Rethinking Popular Legal Culture," *Yale Law Journal* 98 (1989): 1689.

everyday; it is produced and reproduced *in* everyday encounters.[29] As de Certeau argues, citizens and consumers make of the "rituals, representations and laws imposed on them something quite different from what their . . . (originators) had in mind."[30]

In the productions and reproductions of law in everyday life, law is appropriated for purposes that its authors and administrators often neither completely foresee nor completely understand. If, as Schutz and others suggest, the everyday is the domain of lived experience, then it always affords an escape route, a way of evading that which law identifies as proper and necessary.[31] The everyday defines its own rules and knows its own law. Law does not descend on the everyday as an all-powerful outsider without encountering a lively resistance. From the perspective of state law, the everyday is "the suspect (and the oblique) that always escapes the clear decision of the law, even when the law seeks by suspicion, to track down every indeterminate manner of being: everyday indifference."[32] Without the everyday, law is a voice never heard, a memory never known. Without the everyday, law is a living impossibility.

So we turn to the everyday to get a better fix on the ways of law, on what law is and what it can be. The essays in this volume turn to the everyday to try to grasp both law's awesome power and its frustrating inadequacies. They turn to the everyday to see how law becomes part of the taken-for-granted world. Each speaks about the everyday in its own way and in its own voice. Some find it both a useful and unproblematic concept and have no difficulties in finding the traces of law in the everyday. Others are more doubtful. Some emphasize law as ideology, as a system of knowledge, and as a code that gives meaning to social relations and to its constitutive effects.[33] Others investigate law as a set of rules and resources that people use in their daily lives.

---

29. As Yngvesson puts it, "'[T]he spirit of the law,' while embodying the concerns of a powerful and dominant professional elite, is not simply invented at the top but is transformed, challenged, and reinvented in local practices." "Inventing Law," 1693.

30. Michel de Certeau, *The Practice of Everyday Life*, trans. Steven Rendall (Berkeley and Los Angeles: University of California Press, 1984), xiii.

31. Blanchot, "Everyday Speech," 13.

32. Id.

33. See Alan Hunt, "The Ideology of Law: Advances and Problems in Recent Applications of the Concept of Ideology to the Analysis of Law," *Law and Society Review* 19 (1985): 11.

Despite this diversity of perspective, *Law in Everyday Life* illustrates how law's consumers produce their own law and, in so doing, transform and reproduce state law. This book describes what happens to state law and to the law of everyday life—what some would call custom—in their varied confrontations and collaborations.[34] We have already suggested one possibility, resistance as a form of reproduction.[35] Others would argue that the confrontation of law and everyday life provides the occasion for the proliferation of legalities and the development of legal pluralism.[36]

The essays in this book examine the varied ways in which law and everyday life come together, and in which law both constitutes and is constituted in the everyday. They highlight variation across time and in the different domains of the everyday. They remind us that the play of law in the everyday world is stratified and culturally specific. They take us from the domestic life of a married woman in eighteenth-century America to the scene of mass injuries and international politics in the late twentieth century. In so doing, they attend to the ways everyday life makes its presence felt in law, as well as to the ways law comes alive in the everyday world. And they deploy a wide variety of conceptual frameworks to explore the rich and varied configurations of law and everyday life. Together these essays chart new directions for scholarship and help us understand law "not as something removed from social life, occasionally operating upon and struggling to regulate and shape social forms, but as fused with an inseparable from all the activities of living and knowing."[37]

The first essay, by Austin Sarat and Thomas R. Kearns, provides an analytic framework for understanding law and everyday life, and it explores some of the major issues and debates that are present in the other essays. It does so by describing two different understandings

---

34. See Stanley Diamond, "The Rule of Law versus the Order of Custom," in *The Rule of Law*, ed. Robert Paul Wolff (New York: Touchstone Books, 1971); and Paul Bohannan, "Law," *International Encyclopedia of the Social Sciences* (New York: Macmillan, 1968), 73–78.

35. See Peter Fitzpatrick, "Law and Societies," *Osgoode Hall Law Journal* 22 (1984): 115.

36. See Boaventura de Sousa Santos, "The Postmodern Transition: Law and Politics," in Sarat and Kearns, *Fate of Law*; and also Boaventura de Sousa Santos, "Law: A Map of Misreading, Toward a Postmodern Conception of Law," *Journal of Law and Society* 14 (1987): 279; and Sally Merry, "Legal Pluralism," *Law and Society Review* 22 (1988): 869.

37. Silbey and Sarat, "Critical Traditions," 173.

of the relationship of law and the everyday and by arguing that any adequate conception of that relationship has to come to terms with both. The first, what we call the "instrumentalist" understanding, treats the everyday as a site of interests, preferences, and patterns of behavior that operate on and in legal processes. Law, correlatively, is seen as standing outside of and separate from social relations. Law intervenes occasionally to order and reorder those relations. While law can be dramatic in its impact, it is in this view neglected, ignored, or evaded as often as not. The continuity of everyday practices is rarely disrupted and seldom rearranged by anything that law does.

The second, or "constitutive" view, sees the everyday as providing a grounding set of tacit assumptions in legal life. For example, the everyday assumption that people often forget what they agree to or lie to preserve a position of advantage provides, in this view, the normative basis for the parol evidence rule in contracts. The everyday understanding that the prospect of death brings penance is, on this account, what gives substance to the dying declaration exception to the hearsay rule. And there are many other examples of the way everyday understandings, conventions, and assumptions structure legal thinking and practice.

But the constitutive view also suggests that those understandings, conventions, and assumptions are themselves produced and shaped by legal rules and practices. The way people think about promises is, for example, constituted in part by the regime of contract. Thus,

> [A]s a rule "one pays one's debts and renders to one's employer the performance that is due"; one pays the shopkeeper for a packet of toothpaste, and the title is thereby transferred. It is neither the threat of adjudication nor compulsion by the state that routinely induces a person to perform these duties, although that is certainly part of the situation. More is at stake than the performance of legal obligations. . . . [L]aw is embedded in those relations and practices so much so that it is virtually invisible to those involved.[38]

Thus law is always already inseparably a part of the everyday. In

---

38. Sarat and Silbey, "Pull of the Policy Audience," 139.

this sense law's efficacy is not in what it can get people to agree to do, but in what they will think and do un-self-consciously.

We argue that the instrumentalist view tends to overestimate the impact of the everyday in law and legal processes and to underestimate the power of law in society. The constitutive view, on the other hand, underestimates the normative import and impact of the quotidian and overestimates the effectivity of law in setting the terms of everyday life. We conclude by suggesting that the instrumentalist and the constitutive views can be reconciled and the meanings of law for everyday life and everyday life for law be apprehended only by attending to particular practices and concrete, historically situated examples of law and social relations.

The remaining essays in *Law in Everyday Life* take up that challenge and provide close attention to such practices and such examples. Thus Hendrik Hartog and Catharine MacKinnon begin our exploration of law in everyday life in the realm of the domestic, and in the varied interplay of men and women, husbands and wives, and parents and children. Though Hartog writes about the late eighteenth century and MacKinnon about the late twentieth century, both draw attention to the specificity of law's everydayness. Both explore that specificity in the context of the complex interplay between law and gender. Both Hartog and MacKinnon demonstrate the pervasive, though often unnoticed, ways in which law is gendered and the way law gives meaning to gender in American society.

Hartog takes us back to the 1790s to chart the role of law in the struggle of a married woman, Abigail Bailey, to come to terms with her husband's sexual abuse of one of their daughters. As Hartog reads Bailey's story, it is a story of conformity and conflict, and of acquiescence and assertion in which the law of coverture,[39] and the normative order of which it was a part, inspired conflict and assertion as well as conformity and acquiescence. Hartog urges that close attention be paid to individuals like Abigail Bailey and to their life stories. In such stories we can see how law both sustains individuals during years of private and public struggle and helps resolve that struggle.

The struggle in Abigail's life began when she learned of the incestuous abuse by her husband, Asa, a prosperous, respected merchant,

---

39. The law of coverture provided that married women "could neither contract nor manage any property. In many situations they would have no standing in court. Their domicile was, in legal theory, their husbands'." See Hartog, below.

of their daughter Phoebe. Hartog notes that while Abigail had a right
to a legal separation from the moment she found out about the incest,
she waited and prayed for four years before taking any action. For
Abigail the law of coverture might have meant that she had no legal
identity separate from her husband, but it did not mean that she had
no self. Her self was formed in and through her religious devotion;
marriage did nothing to alter that fact. It was through her religious
devotion that she was able to respond to Asa's crime. As Hartog
argues,

> Rather than a woman transformed by marriage into a feme co-
> vert, we would do better to think of Abigail Bailey as a self
> "covered" by her husband during marriage. Being covered by
> her husband, being submissive to him, was not a denial of her
> self. On the contrary, it constituted the central test of her self
> and of the strength of her religious identity.

The sexual abuse of her daughter brought an end to Abigail's
submission and a start to her search for autonomy. Hartog describes
the role law played in both. He notes that Abigail and her husband
were aware of their legal rights and duties and that both tried to use
the law to negotiate the terms of their separation and gain advantage
in so doing. As Hartog notes, here echoing de Certeau's reminder
that the everyday world is a world of production and reproduction,[40]
"They constantly referred to law as an external force shaping their
conduct. Yet the legal shadow within which they bargained was in
large part the product of their own interpretations, interpretations
constructed out of mixed images of legal and religious and local
authority, as well as of structures of formal law."
Eventually Abigail and Asa separated. That separation, Hartog
argues, would not have been possible had not Abigail learned to use
law tactically.[41] Yet for Abigail separation did not terminate the obli-

---

40. de Certeau, *Practice of Everyday Life*.
41. Again Hartog reminds us of de Certeau. See the discussion of "tactics" in
Practice of Everyday Life, xviii. See also Sally Merry, *Getting Justice and Getting
Even: Legal Consciousness among Working-Class Americans* (Chicago: University of
Chicago Press, 1990); and Austin Sarat, "'The Law Is All Over': Power, Resistance,
and the Legal Consciousness of the Welfare Poor," *Yale Journal of Law and the
Humanities* 2 (1990): 343.

gations of marriage; instead, it made it possible for her to live up to those obligations.

Throughout his reading of Abigail's life, Hartog illustrates the complex and often unpredictable impact of law, how law helped shape her consciousness and both constrained and propelled her actions. He suggests that law played contradictory roles in Abigail's struggles— for example, in first reinforcing submission and then providing justification for acts of resistance. Moreover, by describing the way the law of Abigail Bailey's life was inextricably bound up with religion and religious ideas, Hartog reminds us of the way law both works with, and works against, other normative orders. As Hartog puts it, "For Abigail Bailey, as for many others throughout American history, law was inescapably, at times overwhelmingly, present yet at the same time not the most important determinant of her moral situation."

A similar interest in the power and limits of law and in the complex and contradictory roles of law in everyday life informs Catharine MacKinnon's "Reflections on Law in the Everyday Lives of Women." The law about which MacKinnon writes, while no less pervasive in the lives of twentieth-century women than was law in the life of Abigail Bailey, seems less available to them than was law to her. MacKinnon notes that while law—whether the law of sex discrimination, of pornography, or of rape—deeply shapes women's lives, women seldom have a say in shaping it.

MacKinnon argues that law is complicit in the political subordination of women and in the harms inflicted on them at home, at work, and in every other domain of daily life. For her, the law of the late twentieth century expresses in somewhat more subtle forms the prejudices and power of the eighteenth century's law of coverture. All too often, in her view, law abdicates its responsibility to protect women in their daily lives.

She is particularly critical of the idea of privacy, which reflects and perpetuates an ideology that trivializes and ignores the tedious world of daily life to which most women are confined. That ideology, left unchallenged, divides law from everyday life and calls that division freedom. In truth, MacKinnon argues, this ideology serves those who prefer to use their secluded freedom to injure women. Recognizing the inescapable involvement of law in everyday life is, for her, a necessary first step in protecting women and in maintaining their dignity.

MacKinnon notes that when law can be made to notice the realities of the everyday lives of women, as it has in the area of sexual harassment, it can be a powerful tool in altering those realities. She argues that similar progress could be made in responding to the everyday, ordinary sexual abuse of women, abuse of the kind that happened to Abigail Bailey's daugher Phoebe, were law to notice the effects of pornography.[42] But she cautions that here, as in other areas, taking the everyday lives of women seriously requires alteration of fundamental values and traditional ways of doing things.

MacKinnon's essay ends with a caution. She warns against the increasing tendency of progressive scholars to urge women and others to turn away from law and rights.[43] For her, the undeniable power of law in shaping everyday life requires an active, confrontational engagement with it. As she puts it,

> Women's experience makes us suspicious of those who seek to make women's legal exclusion and marginalization and invisibility into a radical virtue. . . . Our everyday lives make us suspicious of those who tell us rights don't matter. . . . Those who say law cannot make change, so we should not try, should explain why the law should be exempt in the struggle for social change. Some of us suspect that women, in particular, are being told that not much can be done with law because a lot can be.

The question of what can be done with law, of how it can be used to alter and transform everyday realities, is taken up in quite a different context in the next essay, "Law in the Domains of Everyday Life: The Construction of Community and Difference." There David Engel examines the role of law, in particular the Education for All Handicapped Children Act of 1975 (EHA), in shaping the experiences of parents, children with disabilities, and school officials. That act requires school officials to work with parents in developing individualized educational programs for their disabled children and to integrate those children, as much as possible, into the regular school environment. The EHA sought to change the categories and behaviors

---

42. For a more complete discussion of her views about pornography see MacKinnon, *Feminism Unmodified* (Cambridge: Harvard University Press, 1987).

43. For an example of such an argument see Carol Smart, *Feminism and the Power of Law* (London: Routledge, 1989).

of everyday life that stigmatize persons with disabilities and give professionals power over parents. Thus this law attempted to rearrange the everyday realities of identity and power for disabled children and their families.

Engel's analysis of the EHA is not, however, confined to a one-way, top-down, instrumentalist look at the intervention of state law and at its effects. His is a rich portrait of the way legal rules, categories, and interpretations are used and transformed both by parents and school officials. Engel argues that law is dependent on such everyday uses to give it meaning. For him law and everyday life do not, and cannot, stand in opposition; as he puts it, "Everyday life is not opposed to law, nor does it exist merely by insinuating itself into the interstices of the law. Everyday life constitutes law and is constituted by it."[44]

Engel's analysis highlights the importance of a contextual analysis of law and everyday life. Indeed, he argues that the law of everyday life is "domain" specific. For him the various domains of social life are constructed and reconstructed through unique and shifting combinations of law and what Engel calls the "culture of common sense."[45] Thus what is true about the role of law in the lives of women generally may not be true about relations between mothers and children; what is true for the family in isolation may not be true in the interaction of families and schools.

To give some concreteness to his argument about the mutually constitutive effects of law and everyday life, Engel describes the experience of six families with handicapped children. In the context of developing the individualized educational plans mandated by EHA, Engel shows how those families struggle to avoid categorizing their children as different but are required by law to do so in order to qualify for the special educational benefits mandated by the act. Law provides one arena to challenge stigmatizing definitions of handicap, but, as Engel argues, it is not immune from the impact of those definitions.

---

44. Here Engel criticizes de Certeau for developing what Engel believes is a one-sided and imbalanced view of everyday life. He rejects the view that law dominates and that everyday life is simply a source of resistance to legal hegemony.

45. Law and the culture of common sense combine in each social domain to define the identities, roles, and statuses of *actors* within that domain, to give meaning to ideas of *time and space*, to identify who belongs and who does not (this involves what Engel calls the *community*), and to generate *norms*.

In addition, Engel shows how the legal treatment of children with disabilities invites a radical individuation among those children, where the needs of one child would be set against the needs of others. Engel notes the efforts of some parents to resist this individuation by developing mutually supportive relations with others. Here he shows how parents take advantage of the opportunities provided by EHA and reshape the concepts and procedures through which that act was implemented. He concludes that law and everyday life "are mutually defining in the sense that neither could exist or have meaning without the other. . . . [L]aw and everyday life interact to define social actors, to construct understandings of time and space, to make and unmake communities, and to shape norms."

Patricia Williams's contribution to *Law in Everyday Life* further illustrates the complex interactions and dependencies of law and everyday life. Indeed, reading Williams, one can find no clear boundary where law ends and everyday life begins. Just as law is a symbolic site for representations of the everyday, so law in its power and signification is constituted in the everyday.

The scene of law in the everyday exhibits itself at the beginning of her essay, as Williams recounts the experience of reading a sign hung on the FBI building in Washington, D.C. Williams reads the sign—"A Drug Free America: The Right Choice"—through the window of a taxi on her way down Pennsylvania Avenue. Here law presents a public signification with double meaning. Freedom and choice are set against the architectural embodiment of America's best-known law-enforcement agency. This encounter, an in-motion reading of the paradox of law and of the availability of its complex symbolization, captures the spirit of Williams's representation of the law of everyday life and the law in everyday life.

Her reading of the everyday signification of law begins at the level of the body, of women's bodies, and, more particularly, of black women's bodies. Williams shows that the language of choice is used to justify surveillance, regulation, and invasion of those bodies. From the right-to-die case of Nancy Cruzan to the fetal-protection policies challenged in *Johnson Controls* to the drug-addicted pregnant woman, Jennifer Johnson, convicted of drug dealing through her umbilical cord, Williams writes of choices, imputed, imagined, and denied in the embodied beings of real women. When the ideology of choice is not justifying control, it is used to rationalize the neglect of women's bodies. In all of this Williams sees law's complicity in what she calls "the bizarre, even hallucinatory self-partialization that afflicts these times."

Williams presents an evocative personal narrative of the kind that Abigail Bailey might have produced had she lived two hundred years later. Unlike the late eighteenth-century Abigail, Williams is constantly in motion, displaced in time and space, searching for the "histories and experiences that propel most of us in our daily lives." In a taxi or settled in her home watching television, the everyday life of Patricia Williams, whether temporarily situated in Washington, D.C., or Madison, Wisconsin, or Kraków, Poland, crosses boundaries and establishes new connections. Thus Williams reminds us that the scene of the everyday in the late twentieth century has been transformed by the market, the state, and the globalization of capital and its relentless logic of accumulation. What was once, like Abigail Bailey's marrige, seemingly quite local and disconnected from larger events, is now clearly interconnected with persons, places, and events on the global level. Things are constantly in motion, transmitted physically and symbolically at astonishing, but by now taken-for-granted, speeds. To comprehend the relationship of law and everyday life one must expand the sweep of the narrative and link scenes of domesticity and the technology that connects those persons, places, and events across national boundaries.

The motif of crossing boundaries and establishing connections provides the background for another personal narrative in the sixth essay in this volume. This essay, "Autumn Weekends," by David Kennedy, locates the intersection of law and everyday life in the engagements and activities of an academic/international lawyer attending conferences in Lisbon and Madrid. This essay has Kennedy going and coming to and from Lisbon, and then off again to Madrid. He crosses international boundaries with greater ease and less cultural strain than it took Abigail Bailey to go from New Hampshire to New York.

In the movement to the international arena, to the idealism of the quest for international human rights, and to the establishment of connections among "cosmopolitan elites," Kennedy hopes law might rise above the everyday; here the habits, petty jealousy, and competitiveness of everyday life might be displaced in the service of justice and international understanding. Yet, Kennedy suggests, we must remember that

> [l]awyers remain divided between the transcendent idealism of their normative vision and the institutional grind of legal practice, as well as between the programmatic institutional aspirations of legal institutions and the tedium of doctrinal interpretation. . . . And like other professionals, the international lawyer earns his keep as a ventriloquist, throwing his legal idealism forward from the realism of his everyday.

Kennedy's essay, while it holds out the hope that law can assert itself against the everyday, continuously cautions about the pull of the routine, the habitual, the everyday. Away from home and displaced, new familiarities are, nonetheless, quickly created. On a stage of hope for international legality, the daily realities of drafting documents, planning strategy, and implementing resolutions set the real agenda.

The meaning of these various entanglements of law and everyday life, of hope and realism, is only disentangled in transit. Like Williams, Kennedy reminds us of the mobility of all readings of the relationship of law and everyday life. He does so by presenting his readings and interpretations as a recollection of his flight home from Lisbon. There he first longs for the continuing power of the "old Warren Court dream" that law, whether in the international arena or the lives of women and minorities in the United States, can make the everyday a little more just and livable. Quickly, however, he joins with the other authors in this volume in "wanting to rebuke the autonomy of law and the bounded identifiability of the everyday." In the end, he urges us to reject law and everyday life as "the great narrative stabilizers" in favor of "rhetorical, tactical invocations" in stories of power and change, resistance and restoration.

Like Kennedy, George Marcus doubts that the everyday can be a narrative stabilizer in legal discourse. However, unlike most of the other authors in this collection, Marcus is not interested in law's contribution to either the instrumental or ideological constitution of everyday life. Instead, he is interested in the way the everyday is represented in law.

Marcus's essay, "Mass Toxic Torts and the End of Everyday Life," demonstrates the failure of images of everyday life to organize legal doctrine in an era of mass injuries and invisible toxic disasters. Tort law, Marcus contends, has traditionally been committed to sustaining the human scale of everyday life, and it has been grounded in conventional images of the everyday. The law of torts has depended on images of everyday life in which injuries result from intentional or negligent acts done by identifiable persons in identifiable ways to other identifiable persons. Today, however, the rise of so-called mass toxic torts undermines the capacity of such images to organize, rationalize, and legitimate the law.

Marcus is concerned that the scene of the everyday might be out of place in the late modern era. Disjunctive, fragmented, simultaneous place-time combinations, he claims, know no everyday. The speed and motion so characteristic of our era undermine the stability of the quotidian. The inadequacy of the everyday as a figure in law and in organizing legal thinking is seen in the Agent Orange case, in which massive numbers of persons were injured and in which it is impossible to know what caused their injuries and who, if anyone, is responsible.

Marcus is less optimistic than we are about the adaptability of the everyday and about its continuing validity in law and legal theory. In his view, if the everyday is to survive as a grounding for legal thinking, it will have to be radically rethought. New meanings will have to be identified and assigned. New assumptions about persons and their social relations will have to be brought to bear. Today, Marcus contends, the most global, systemic forces operate in the most intimate, familiar surroundings. The everyday provides no escape from the cosmopolitan world. And law can organize neither until more adequate representations of the elusive, heterogeneous character of everyday life are made available to law.

Whether the everyday is as adaptable as we hope or as fragile as Marcus believes cannot be resolved in these pages. It is our hope, however, that by collecting essays that attend to specific legal practices and that provide concrete examples of law in everyday life this book

will help to overcome the sterile divide of instrumentalist and constitutive views. We hope that *Law in Everyday Life* will provide the
basis for further inquiry into the routine and undramatic, but nonetheless powerful, attractions and combinations of law and the world
that we all inhabit everyday.

Beyond the Great Divide:
Forms of Legal Scholarship and
Everyday Life

Austin Sarat and Thomas R. Kearns

Studies of law and society in general and of law and everyday life in particular divide fairly sharply into two distinct perspectives, the instrumental and the constitutive.[1] They differ from each other largely in what they take to be the principal means by which law affects society: whether (roughly) by imposing external sanctions and inducements or by shaping internal meanings and creating new statuses. But, despite this considerable difference, the two perspectives are alike in privileging law in studying society. As a result, they tend to overlook the variety of ways in which society responds to law, sometimes by ignoring it, reconstructing it, or using it in novel, unanticipated ways. In this essay, we explore the possibility that a focus on everyday life would encourage legal scholarship to bridge the separation between the instrumental and the constitutive perspectives and to recognize more fully the interactive character of law's relation to society.

We begin by clarifying the distinction between the two dominant perspectives in scholarship on law and society. One of the views, instrumentalism, takes an external stance. It posits a relatively sharp distinction between legal standards, on the one hand, and nonlegal human activities, on the other. It then explores the effects of the

---

1. For a useful discussion of the nature of these divergent perspectives see David Trubek, "Where the Action Is: Critical Legal Studies and Empiricism," *Stanford Law Review* 36 (1984): 575; and also Robert Gordon, "Critical Legal Histories," *Stanford Law Review* 36 (1984): 57.

former on the latter.[2] By contrast, the constitutive perspective contends that social life is run through with law, so much so that the
relevant category for the scholar is not the external one of causality
(as the reference to effects would suggest) but the internal one of
meaning.[3] In bold outline, the constitutive view suggests that law
shapes society from the inside out, by providing the principal categories that make social life seem natural, normal, cohesive, and
coherent.

This paper advances the thesis that both perspectives tend to
adopt a "law-first" procedure in analyzing law in everyday life. The
effect, we think, is to mute the interactive nature of the relationship
between law and everyday life, to exaggerate the importance of state
law and to discount society's nonlegal normative resources. By focusing on law in everyday life rather than on society generally, one is
reminded that the everyday is elaborately constituted by a variety
of normative relationships that, if not entirely separate from law, are
by no means exhausted by it.[4] Examples might include the institution
of marriage, colleagueship in a firm or other organization, or the
practice of promising.

To clarify our thesis, we begin by elaborating more fully the
contrast between instrumental and constitutive perspectives, citing
instances of legal scholarship that appear to be dominated by one or

---

2. Trubek, "Where the Action Is."

3. See Gordon, "Critical Legal Histories." See also Christine Harrington and
Barbara Yngvesson, "Interpretive Sociolegal Research," *Law and Social Inquiry* 15
(1990): 141. We should emphasize at the outset that there are considerable differences
between and among those we have lumped together as taking the constitutive view.
For example, Barbara Yngvesson's study, "Making Law at the Doorway: The Clerk,
the Court and the Construction of Community in a New England Town," *Law and
Society Review* 22 (1988): 409, draws attention to the power of legal officials in
shaping the (social) meanings of "good neighbor" or "dutiful parent"; but this effect
of law on social meaning seems quite different from what, say, Gabel and Feinman
have in mind when they contend that contract law encodes an invasive ideology, an
idealized (and generally unarticulated and unexamined) way of thinking about conflicts and agreements that tends to legitimate (as natural and necessary) various
oppressive socioeconomic realities. See Peter Gabel and Jay M. Feinman, "Contract
Law as Ideology," in *The Politics of Law: A Progressive Critique*, ed. David Kairys
(New York: Pantheon Books, 1982). In the first case, the law's effect on social meaning
is relatively transparent and explicit; in the other, social meaning is engendered
systemically and is, as a result, less easily detected.

4. See Henri Lefebvre, *Critique of Everyday Life*, trans. John Moore (London:
Verso, 1991); also Jack Douglas, ed., *Understanding Everyday Life* (Chicago: Aldine,
1970).

the other of these views. We try as well to clarify our claim that both are law-first perspectives and to point out that this commitment narrows the analyses of legal as well as social phenomena. Along the way, we suggest that a common ancestry in legal realism explains why instrumental and constitutive perspectives tend to detach social phenomena from their larger social moorings. Toward the end of the paper we indicate how a focus on the everyday might soften the separation between instrumental and constitutive perspectives and, at the same time, help us to see law's effects as consequences of its interactions with other normative schemes and commitments.

Instrumentalism

As we are characterizing it, instrumentalism conceives of law as a tool for sustaining or changing aspects of social life. We need not ascribe to instrumentalism any particular view about the mechanisms by which law affects social life. However it does its work, law's job is to regulate effectively the activities of legal subjects, what they do or abstain from doing. Legal regulation might be directly observable in the behavior of persons (e.g., driving faster on the interstate after speed limits are raised from 55 to 65 mph) or only indirectly detectible by inferring beliefs from practices (e.g., the increased confidence in banks following the creation of the Federal Deposit Insurance Corporation). Again, instrumentalists need not share any particular view about the kinds of mechanisms deployed by law to shape or sustain various social arrangements—these might include brute force, the threat or fear of force, or, very differently, the creation of new legal meanings or statuses.[5] The crucial point is that instrumentalists are centrally interested in law's effectiveness (roughly, in the extent to which a law is observed or not observed, used or ignored)—and not in law's effects more broadly conceived.[6]

---

5. By making a "wolf whistle" legally actionable, the law confers new meaning (say, as sexual harassment) on conduct that might previously have been regarded as merely annoying or socially offensive. At the same time, the law also makes those who persist in such conduct eligible for a new status, namely, that of defendant in a civil action.

6. See Bruce Ackerman, *Reconstructing American Law* (Cambridge: Harvard University Press, 1984); see also Austin Sarat and Susan Silbey, "The Pull of the Policy Audience," *Law and Policy* 10 (1988): 97.

But what is the distinction between effects and effectiveness? The distinction might initially seem suspect since it is impossible to determine a law's effectiveness without knowing its effects, or some of them. But the appended phrase, "or some of them," makes all the difference. To the extent that instrumentalism views laws as tools for promoting antecedently identified policies or purposes, then the relevant effects are just those that advance or imperil these aimed-at outcomes.[7] These (and only these) are the effects that matter. These (and only these) determine a law's effectiveness and so its instrumental value.[8]

Of course, instrumentalism need not be blind to the ways that the effects of some particular law may conflict with the intended effects of some other law. For example, enforcement of the laws against the consumption of alcohol might conflict with rules meant to increase tax revenues or to protect privacy. Plainly, a rational system of laws would want to be aware of such secondary effects and decide how warring interests might be accommodated. Nothing in the instrumental conception discourages such attention to law's consequences. But it is one thing to attend to a law's effects on other laws, another to attend to a law's *nonlegal* effects. The law-first focus of the instrumentalist perspective tends to restrict scholarship to law's legal effects; society is looked to only to determine these legal effects, not to consider more general social ramifications.

Historically, instrumentalists have not only begun their inquiry from the perspective of legal materials, they have favored some legal materials (namely, rules)[9] over others, focusing on the way these particular carriers of legal direction are used, violated, or ignored.

---

7. Or, what might, in the writings of Lon Fuller or John Dewey, be termed ends-in-view. For useful discussions of law as purposeful directives aimed at the eradication of some "evil," see John Dewey, *A Theory of Valuation* (Chicago: University of Chicago Press, 1939) and Lon Fuller, *The Morality of Law* (New Haven: Yale University Press, 1963).

8. See Malcolm Feeley, "The Concept of Law in Social Science: A Critique and Notes on an Expanded View," *Law and Society Review* 10 (1976): 497; and also Jonathan Casper and David Brereton, "Evaluating Criminal Justice Reforms," *Law and Society Review* 18 (1984): 121. As Gordon puts it, this view "almost unconsciously reserves even what it believes to be the very marginal opportunities for legal influence on the direction of social change to an elite of policymakers." See "Critical Legal Histories," 70.

9. See H. L. A. Hart, *The Concept of Law* (Oxford: Clarendon Press, 1961), 54–59, for a discussion of the distinction between rules and mere social habits.

Instrumentalist legal scholarship both encourages and benefits by such a focus. Rules compartmentalize social phenomena and operate on those aspects of social life most amenable to all-or-nothing normative ordering. The effect of a focus on rules is to make a law's immediate consequences more apparent. Scholarship that correspondingly centers on rules is likely to absorb their logic and, like the rules themselves, detach the regulated activities from their full social setting.

Instrumentalists, as we have indicated, treat rules as tools used (or avoided) in the everyday world to facilitate the accomplishment of various goals, whose origins are substantially independent of law itself.[10] Law, in the instrumentalist account, mirrors society. Changes in law tend to follow social changes and often intend to do no more than make those changes permanent.[11] Legal rules are used to maintain, reproduce, and alter the everyday in conscious, rational, and planned ways. Instrumentalism denies that law is already an integral part of that which it regulates.

Perhaps the key to the instrumentalist understanding is the belief that there is a fairly firm division between the legal and the social, with law being an important influence on society, but standing outside of it. As Gordon has observed, writers in this tradition

> divide the world into two spheres, one social and one legal. Society is the primary realm of social experience. It is "real life": What's immediately and truly important to people . . . goes on there. . . . "Law" or "the legal system," on the other hand, is a distinctly secondary body of phenomena. It is a specialized realm of state and professional activity that is called into being by the primary social world in order to serve that world's needs. Law

---

10. For an important discussion of this conception of legal rules as purposive instrumentalities, see Susan Silbey and Egon Bitner, "The Availability of Law," *Law and Policy Quarterly* 4 (1982): 399. As these authors write, "Neither the purposes nor the uses of any specific law are fully inscribed upon it. Therefore, the meaning of any specific law, and of law as a social institution, can only be understood by examining the ways it is actually used" (400).

11. Lawrence Friedman, *The Legal System: A Social Science Perspective* (New York: Russell Sage Foundation, 1975). Grant Gilmore argues, "Law reflects but in no sense determines the moral wisdom of a society. The values of a reasonably just society will reflect themselves in a reasonably just law. . . . The values of an unjust society will reflect themselves in an unjust law." *The Age of American Law* (New Haven: Yale University Press, 1977), 110–11.

is auxiliary—an excrescence on social life, even if sometimes a useful excrescence.[12]

Law, then, is pictured as a residual category whose role in the everyday is episodic, artificial, and often disruptive.[13]

So conceived, legal scholarship begins and ends with a specifically legal focus: it begins with legal rules (or with cognate legal standards) and ends in an examination of their effectiveness in regulating or changing everyday life, that is, in a study of the extent to which this law has, or has failed to have, *the intended role* in shaping the domain of activity in question.[14] The view of legal rules as discrete, purposive devices thus tends to narrow the instrumentalists' concern from the general category of *effects* to the considerably more limited one of *effectiveness*.[15] Of course, this narrowing of the concerns of instrumentalism comports nicely with the positivistic commitments of legal realism, with which instrumentalism is associated, a point we discuss more fully below.[16]

To recapitulate, the history of social research on law is closely tied to the search for the conditions under which law is effective, that

---

12. See Gordon, "Critical Legal Histories," 60.

13. David Engel and Eric Steele, "Civil Cases and Society: Process and Order in the Civil Justice System," *American Bar Research Journal* (1979): 295.

14. Instrumentalists speak about the success or failure of law and measure success by the ways legal rules are used and resisted. See Austin Sarat, "Legal Effectiveness and Social Studies of Law: On the Unfortunate Persistence of a Research Tradition," *Legal Studies Forum* 9 (1985): 23. See also Richard Abel, "Law Books and Books about Law," *Stanford Law Review* 26 (1973): 175.

15. Sometimes, it appears, this view rather narrowly links the operations of law to coercion and constraint and so purports to measure legal effectiveness by looking for "conforming conduct."

> The "instrumental theory" integrates notions of action and law. Once created by human beings, laws and legal institutions appear as objective constraints on behavior. Citizens perceive the legal system as a constraint and orient their behavior accordingly. Therefore, if the law is effective, the actual behavior of citizens will correspond to the behavior prescribed by legal doctrine.

See David Trubek and John Esser, "'Critical Empiricism' in American Legal Studies: Paradox, Program, or Pandora's Box?" *Law and Social Inquiry* 14 (1989): 15.

16. The point here is that the legal realist movement was generally ill-disposed to take up large normative issues. For example, questions of justice tended to be put aside; law was conceived of as reflecting the free play of self-interested ambition; it was to be studied from a correspondingly value-neutral perspective. Messy, open-ended questions concerning the nature of the good were addressed, if at all, at the level of institutional design and procedure.

is, when legislation or judicial decisions can be counted on to guide behavior or produce social changes in desired ways. "Legal effectiveness research" (as it is sometimes called)[17] begins by identifying the goals of legal policy and moves to assess its success by comparing those goals with the results produced. Where, as is almost invariably the case, the results do not match the goals, attention typically shifts to the factors that might explain the gap between law on the books and law in action.[18] Understanding the causes of discrepancies keeps alive the hope of reducing or eliminating such gaps and thus increasing law's effectiveness. But legal scholarship might be focused less on the study of gaps and (in)effectiveness and more on the variety of relations in which law and other normative systems stand. Such a focus would, we think, be encouraged by adopting the perspective of everyday life (rather than law), as the point of departure for law and society studies.

The Constitutive Perspective

As we emphasized above, instrumentalism conceives of law as largely external to the social practices it regulates. For the most part it is assumed that these practices precede the law that pertains to them. They already exist, and law comes later to cull, clarify, and coordinate.[19] But presumably no instrumentalist would deny that law occasionally constructs new practices, if not from whole cloth, then from unfamiliar weaves. Thus, the idea of ownership and the status of tenant, while not utterly unrelated to prior notions of possession and long-standing occupancy, import new rights, meanings, and roles. Laws affecting ownership and tenancy might be said not merely to regulate what was already in place, but to bring into being something new, to constitute new relations and meanings. Here, then, we depart from the wholly external, instrumental conception of law and move toward the internal, constitutive view, where law's effects are seen in meanings and self-understandings rather than in the results of sanctions.

---

17. See Sarat, "Legal Effectiveness."

18. Id.

19. We do not suggest, however, that law's aims are always modest and merely ministerial; still, instrumentalists seem to think of law as something that mostly intervenes on already established, on-going operations and practices.

Perhaps the most stunning example of law's constitutive powers is the willingness of persons to conceive of themselves as legal subjects, as the kind of beings the law implies they are—and needs them to be. Legal subjects think of themselves as competent, self-directing persons who, for example, enter bargained-for exchanges as free and equal agents.[20] In thus thinking about law's constitutive effects, the scholar tends to see the links between law and society at the level of networks of legal practices, on the one hand, and clusters of beliefs and systems of meaning, on the other. Sociolegal associations tend, therefore, to be relatively diffuse, especially in comparison to the effects of laws as tools, which tend to be both determinate and rule specific.[21]

Of course, to acknowledge that law has meaning-making power is to acknowledge, contrary to the instrumentalists' general view, that some social practices are not logically separable from, or intelligible apart from, the laws that shape them. Arguably, marriage is such a practice, assuming for the moment that it differs from similar bonds of affection of indefinite duration because it can be instituted and terminated only with the law's blessings. A more diffuse example of law's constructive powers is the general similarity between legal and nonlegal ascriptions of praise and blame.[22] Thus, even where people are not familiar in detail with legal rules and doctrines, their habits of mind and social practices will tend to be highly legal in character.[23] Constructivism of this kind, however, need not be rejected by instrumentalists as falling entirely outside their ken. To the extent that legal regulations modify not just conduct but also the way persons view themselves and their relations with one another, the distinction

---

20. See, for example, Gabel and Feinman, "Contract Law as Ideology," 172–84.

21. For a discussion of law's constitutive powers at the level of "clusters of beliefs," see Robert W. Gordon, "New Developments in Legal Theory," in Kairys, *Politics of Law,* 287.

22. See Max Gluckman, ed., *The Allocation of Responsibility* (Manchester: Manchester University Press, 1972).

23. As Tocqueville put it in his description of the "constitutive" effect of law in America, "[A]ll parties are obliged to borrow, in their daily controversies, the ideas, and even the language, peculiar to judicial proceedings. . . . The language of the law thus becomes, in some measure, a vulgar tongue; the spirit of the law, which is produced in the schools and courts of justice, gradually permeates beyond their walls into the bosom of society, where it descends to the lowest classes, so that at last the whole people contract the habits and tastes of the judicial magistrate." *Democracy in America*, vol. 1, trans. Henry Reeve (Boston: John Allyn, 1876), 358–59.

between instrumentalist and constitutive perspectives tends to collapse. Perhaps, then, the distinction is more a matter of degree than
proponents are prepared to grant, but the central contrasts—between
external and internal influences and between sanctions and meaning—
are still sufficiently powerful to keep alive the distinction between
instrumental and constitutive views of law.

Thus, those who adopt the constitutive perspective believe that
law permeates social life and that its influence is not adequately
grasped when law is treated as an external, normative missile
launched at independent, ongoing activities. And their point is not
merely the quantitative one that law is more ubiquitous than the law-
as-tool model would suggest. Law *is* ubiquitous, but more than that,
law affects social life in ways that the instrumental view tends to
overlook. Law-thought and legal relations (or emanations from such
thought and relations) dominate self-understanding and one's understanding of one's relations to others. We are not, as instrumentalists
suggest, merely pushed and pulled by laws that impinge on us from
the outside. Rather, we have internalized law's meanings and its representations of us, so much so that our own purposes and understandings can no longer be extricated from them. We are not merely
the inert recipients of law's external pressures. Rather, we have
imbibed law's images and meanings so that they seem our own. As
a consequence, law's demands seem natural and necessary, hardly
like demands at all. According to the constitutive perspective, law
has "colonized our souls," making its demands ours at the same time
that it reinforces the illusion of independence from law.[24]

In *Local Knowledge*, Clifford Geertz suggested that

> law, rather than a mere technical add-on to a morally (or immor-
> ally) finished society, is, along of course with a whole range of
> other cultural realities, . . . an active part of it. . . . Law . . . is, in
> a word, constructive; in another constitutive; in a third,
> formational. . . . Law, with its power to place particular things
> that happen . . . in a general frame in such a way that rules for
> the principled management of them seem to arise naturally from

---

24. Nietzsche proffered a similar account of the operations of morality in our
lives. See Friedrich Nietzsche, *The Birth of Tragedy* and *The Genealogy of Morals*,
trans. Francis Golffing (Garden City, N.Y.: Doubleday, 1956).

the essentials of their character, is rather more than a reflection of received wisdom or a technology of dispute-settlement.[25]

Geertz's observations help one understand why instrumentalists are naturally inclined to think of legal systems as "struggling to retain what seems like a tenuous grasp on the social order"[26] But for someone like Geertz, the apparent frailty of law's hold on social life derives from the mistaken assumption that individuals are "autonomous and self-constituting,"[27] when in fact "the values, knowledge, and evaluative criteria embodied in the subjectivity of actors are not individually held units of meaning but rather are the threads or traces of a collectively held fabric of social relations."[28]

Meaning is perhaps the key word in the vocabulary of those who speak about law in constitutive terms. "Our gaze focuses on meaning, on the ways [people] make sense of what they do—practically, morally, expressively, . . . juridically—by setting it within larger frames of signification, and how they keep those larger frames in place or try to, by organizing what they do in terms of them."[29] So conceived, law is inseparable from the interests, goals, and understandings that comprise social life. Law is part of the everyday world, contributing powerfully to the apparently stable, taken-for-granted quality of that world and to the generally shared sense that as things *are*, so *must* they be. "[T]he power exerted by a legal regime consists less in the force that it can bring to bear against violators of its rules than in its capacity to persuade people that the world described in its images and categories is the only attainable world in which a sane person would want to live."[30]

The contrast between the constitutive and instrumental per-

---

25. See Clifford Geertz, *Local Knowledge: Further Essays in Interpretive Anthropology* (New York: Basic Books, 1983), 218, 230.

26. Susan Silbey, "Law and the Order of Our Life Together: A Sociological Interpretation of the Relationship Between Law and Society," in *Law and the Order of Our Life Together*, ed. Richard Neuhaus (Grand Rapids, Mich.: William Eerdmans Publishing, 1990), 20.

27. See Trubek and Esser, "Critical Empiricism," 17.

28. Id. The standard critique of instrumentalism also rejects the "radical distinction between ideas and behavior" and the conception of "action as responding to external sanctions, legal or otherwise." Id.

29. Geertz, *Local Knowledge*, 232.

30. Gordon, "Critical Legal Histories," 108.

spectives may now seem tolerably clear. To say, as defenders of the constitutive view do, that law is a continuous part of social practice means several things: first, law is *internal* to the constitution of those practices, linked by meaning to the affairs it controls;[31] second, and correlatively, law largely influences modes of thought rather than conduct in any specific case.[32] Law enters social practices and is, indeed, imbricated in them, by shaping consciousness, by making law's concepts and commands seem, if not invisible, then perfectly natural and benign. As Trubek writes:

> [S]ocial order depends in a nontrivial way on a society's shared "world view." Those world views are basic notions about human and social relations that give meaning to the lives of society's members. Ideals about the law—what it is, what it does, why it exists—are part of the world view of any complex society. . . . Law, like other aspects of belief systems, helps to define the role of an individual in society and the relations with others that make sense. At the same time that law is a system of belief, it is also a basis of organization, a part of the structure in which action is embedded.[33]

So conceived, it is understandable that law's demands might be either invisible (as part of the frame in terms of which actions are formulated) or seemingly necessary and natural (as part of what it means to be an agent or actor at all). As a result, law in the minds of legal

---

31. Gordon argues that "the 'interests' in the instrumental account that make demands are not self-constituting prelegal entities. They owe important aspects of their identities, traits, organizational forms, and sometimes their very existence to their legal constitution." "Critical Legal Histories," 106. See also Harrington and Yngvesson, "Interpretive Sociolegal Research," 140: the constitutive approach "rejects . . . dualistic ways of framing the sociolegal world, moving away from the positivist distinction between ideas and experience, consent and coercion, and between subjective and objective 'realities.'"

32. See Alan Hunt, "Rights and Social Movements: Counter-Hegemonic Strategies," *Journal of Law and Society* 17 (1990): 310–13.

33. Trubek, "Where the Action Is," 589–604. As Gordon suggests, "[L]awmaking and law-interpreting institutions have been among the primary sources of the pictures of order and disorder, virtue and vice, reasonableness and craziness, realism and visionary naivete and some of the most commonplace aspects of social reality that ordinary people carry around with them and use in ordering their lives" ("Critical Legal Histories," 109). See also W. V. O. Quine and Joseph Ullian, *The Web of Belief* (New York: Random House, 1970).

subjects tends to "get separated from the material life—from its own role in creating the relations of material life."[34]

But here a certain difficulty arises for the constitutive view, since (as a matter of fact) it seems that many legal subjects view the law precisely as instrumentalists do, namely, as external to social practices (not definitive of them) and as a relatively changeable force (neither natural nor necessary). But defenders of the constitutive view have a plausible reply: for the most part, only those laws that have yet to become operative at the level of meaning and definition remain visible—and these, assuming them to have any effect at all, must operate instrumentally. It is therefore unsurprising that "the plain man" tends to think of law as the instrumentalist does. This "difficulty," then, has the virtue of bringing to light the following important point: on the constitutive view, commonplace opinions about law cannot be taken at face value since, *ex hypothesi*, law's most powerful effects may be unnoticed. And their being unnoticed may partially explain the source of their power. Just so, law sometimes makes itself "appear to stand apart from social relations and to be of a different and separate order, rather than a continuous part of social practice."[35]

It seems, then, that the constitutive perspective can have it both ways: it can contend that law strongly constructs legal subjects and at the same time generates the impression that law-infused social relations might readily be changed under the pressure of sufficient reasons emerging from ordinary life. That such pressures almost never arise is itself made to seem a contingent matter when, in fact (if constructivist legal scholars are right), this appearance is itself an expression of law's hegemonic hold on social life.

---

34. Harrington and Yngvesson, "Interpretive Sociolegal Research," 141. As Harrington and Yngvesson put it, those who advocate a constitutive view of law see law as

> a form of power that also creates a peculiar kind of world, specifically, a liberal-legal world constituted as separate spheres of 'law' and 'community' with 'practice' or 'process' located uneasily between the two. In such a world, acts impose ideologies or persuade others to take them on as 'voluntary.'. . . (The constitutive view) is based on an interest in questions about the way law gets separated from material life—from its own role in creating the relations of material life. This question draws attention to practices of law that are taken for granted, practices that make law appear to stand apart from social relations and to be of a different and separate order, rather than a continuous part of social practice. (141)

35. Id.

Instrumentalism, the Constitutive Perspective, and the Legacy of Legal Realism

In light of the great differences between the instrumentalist and the constitutive perspectives, it may seem implausible to suggest that the roots of both may be found in a single intellectual antecedent—legal realism. Instrumentalism might be said to take the operation of rules too seriously to be congenial to legal realism, since many of the realists regarded rules as mere insubstantial playthings, easily avoided should they happen to get in the way of anyone, particularly legal officials.[36] On the other hand, few legal realists had patience with anything as ethereal as meanings—they tended to be interested in behavior, not shadowy ideas in someone's head[37]—so constitutivists and realists would seem improbable bedfellows as well. But these incongruities dissolve when one remembers the diverse agenda— impatience with speculative metaphysics, an affinity for the practical over the theoretical, and liberal political commitments—that tended to characterize legal realism.

The possibility, then, of tracing both instrumental and constitutive legal scholarship back to legal realism arises in part because of the diffuse character of a "movement" that incorporated three fairly distinct strands.[38] First, it included a critical, oppositional strand that sought to expose the contradictions of classical legal formalism.[39] Here realism suggested that legal doctrine was not hermetically sealed, self-contained, and self-sustaining; law could not be understood apart from it social context. Second, realism also included a brand of scientific naturalism whose proponents attempted to advance a more enlightened, rational, and efficient social order by using the methods

---

36. See Jerome Frank, *Law and the Modern Mind* (New York: Brentano's, 1930).

37. John Brigham and Christine Harrington, "Realism and Its Consequences: An Inquiry into Contemporary Sociological Research," *International Journal of the Sociology of Law* 17 (1989): 41.

38. See Laura Kalman, *Legal Realism at Yale, 1927–1960* (Chapel Hill: University of North Carolina Press, 1986); Edward Purcell, *The Crisis of Democratic Theory* (Lexington: University of Kentucky Press, 1973).

39. For an analysis of the distinction between formalism and realism see Elizabeth Mensch, "The History of Mainstream Legal Thought," in *The Politics of Rights*, 2d ed., ed. David Kairys (New York: Pantheon, 1990). See also Duncan Kennedy, "Toward an Historical Understanding of Legal Consciousness: The Case of Classical Legal Thought in America 1850–1940," *Research in Law and Sociology* 3 (1980): 3.

of the empirical sciences to understand a wide range of human, political, and social phenomena. In this view, law's effects could be measured scientifically and used by policymakers to alter legal policy. Third, realism was a practical political effort that was embraced by officials in charge of making and reforming policy. These officials promoted "the conscious espousal of policy-oriented intervention by the state."[40]

By attacking the classical conception of law, with its assumptions about the independent and objective movement from preexisting rights to decisions in specific cases,[41] realists opened the way for a vision of law as policy, as a tool that could be used to maintain or alter existing social practices, or, as in the regime of contract, that could be used by private parties to regulate rationally their own affairs. In this vision, law could and should be guided by pragmatic, utilitarian considerations.[42] By exposing the difference between law on the books and law in action, realists established the need to approach lawmaking and adjudication with an eye toward how law could and would be used in society. As Ackerman argues in *Reconstructing American Law*,

> [T]he Realist's view of the common law . . . [recognized] that the lawyers' common law was far more complex and subtle than the common law abstractions bandied about in political talk. Rather than losing themselves in a fog of abstract political rhetoric about contract, property, and the like, the aim of legal craftsmen was to pierce the emptiness of such rhetoric. The so-called organizing concepts of the common law should be recognized as empty boxes concealing a host of distinct fact situations. . . .[43]

By exploring the ways law in action was often deeply entangled in

---

40. See Alan Hunt, *The Sociological Movement in Law* (Philadelphia: Temple University Press, 1978), 39.

41. Felix Cohen, "Transcendental Nonsense and the Functional Approach," *Columbia Law Review* 34 (1935): 809; Karl Llewellyn, "Some Realism about Realism," *Harvard Law Review* 44 (1931): 1222.

42. See Karl Llewellyn, "On Reading and Using the Newer Jurisprudence," *Columbia Law Review* 40 (1940): 581. Kenneth Casebeer argues that the realist attachment to empiricism was part of a broader embrace of pragmatism. See "Escape from Liberalism: Fact and Value in Karl Llewellyn," *Duke Law Journal* 1977 (1977): 671.

43. Ackerman, *Reconstructing American Law*, 15–16.

politics, realists provided the energy to reform the legal process and restore its integrity.[44] Exploring, exposing, and attacking, realism sought to sweep away the last vestiges of an idealist conception of law and reorient legal thought toward what we have called instrumentalism. Realism opened up an agenda for those concerned with figuring out the conditions under which legal rules would be translated into effective regulation.

But instrumentalism required more than a new way of thinking about law; it required new understandings about the generation and use of social knowledge. Realists saw the twentieth century as a period of the explosion and the transformation of knowledge.[45] In both the natural and emerging social sciences, rationality triumphed over tradition, inquiry over faith, and the human mind over its environment.[46] Realists took, as one of many projects, the task of opening law to this explosion and transformation.

Moreover, some realists argued that law's rationality and efficiency ultimately depended upon an overt alliance of law and science.[47] "Underlying any scientific study of law," Cook argued, "will lie one fundamental postulate, viz., that human laws are devices, tools which society uses as one of its methods to regulate human conduct and to promote those types of it which are regarded as desirable."[48] Using the methods of science to assess the consequences of legal decisions, realists claimed that what law *could* do would help establish what law *should* do.[49] As Yntema put it,

> Ultimately, the object of the more recent movements in legal science . . . is to direct the constant efforts which are made to reform the legal system by objective analysis of its operation.

---

44. See Brigham and Harrington, "Realism and Its Consequences."

45. See David Reisman, "Law and Social Science," *Yale Law Journal* 50 (1941): 636.

46. Myres McDougal, "Fuller v. The American Legal Realists," *Yale Law Journal* 50 (1941): 827.

47. John Schlegel, "American Legal Realism and Empirical Social Science," *Buffalo Law Review* 28 (1979): 459. Gordon argues that "Instrumentalist theories of law . . . generally aspire to a positivist style of explanation" ("Critical Legal Histories," 75).

48. W. W. Cook, "Scientific Method and the Law," *American Bar Association Journal* 13 (1927): 232.

49. See Llewellyn, "Some Realism about Realism."

Whether such analysis be in terms of a calculus of pleasures and pains, of the evaluation of interests, of pragmatic means and ends, of human behavior, is not so significant as that law is regarded in all these and like analyses as an instrumental procedure to achieve purposes beyond itself, defined by the conditions to which it is directed.[50]

It is difficult to imagine a stronger formulation of law's potential as an independent, objective instrument of social regulation.

The realist aspired to make law scientific and to employ it to rationally manage human affairs. Making law scientific was, in part, the process of eradicating "legal theology" and replacing it with policy planning and research on legal effectiveness.[51] Many writers of the day believed that social science could make available to legal decision makers an accurate and relatively undistorted portrait of social processes. Science, in their view, would unearth the positive, determinative realities, "the tangibles which can be got at beneath the words."[52] According to Cook, "Lawyers, like the physical scientists, are engaged in the study of objective physical phenomena.... As lawyers we are interested in knowing how certain officials of society... have behaved in the past in order that we may make a prediction of their probable behavior in the future."[53] And Llewellyn wrote that the realists "want to check ideas and rules and formulas by facts, to keep them close to the facts."[54] For law to be usable as an instrument, it had to recognize and conform to such definite, tangible, and observable facts; to ignore the facts of social life was folly.

Some realists went beyond the assertion of faith in the observability of fact and the possibility of value-neutral inquiry into the conditions of law's effectiveness to argue for the priority of context

---

50. Henry Yntema, "Legal Science and Reform," *Columbia Law Review* 34 (1934): 209.

51. Harold Lasswell and Myres McDougal, "Legal Education and Public Policy," *Yale Law Journal* 52 (1943): 203.

52. Llewellyn, "Some Realism about Realism," 1223.

53. W. W. Cook, "The Logical and Legal Basis of the Conflict of Laws," *Yale Law Journal* 33 (1924): 475.

54. Llewellyn, "Some Realism about Realism," 1222.

and structure in explaining behavior. They tried to look beyond idio-syncratic or individualistic explanations to analyze the social context within which decisions were made and within which receivers of legal decisions acted. In this move, realists inverted the determinism of classical legal formalism. Instead of arguing for the autonomy of law, these realists believed that it was possible to identify "significant, predictable, social determinants" of decision and action.[55] Social sci-ence could aid legal decision making by identifying the factors that limited the choices available to officials and, more importantly, by identifying the determinants of responses to those decisions.[56] Aware of those determining conditions, the informed decision-maker should take account of what was possible in a given situation.[57] For many realists, building a new legal science "modeled on the natural sciences . . . would restore the law's ability to serve as a central yet autonomous social 'steering mechanism.'"[58]

Not all strands of the realist movement, however, were com-fortable with the instrumentalist conception of law and its insistent

---

55. See Cohen, "Transcendental Nonsense," 809.

56. By pointing to the scientific impulse in realism and to the way this impulse propelled an instrumentalist understanding of law, we do not want to suggest that there was only one model of empirical social science available for adoption by those who pursued an instrumental approach. Institutionalists attacked the metaphysics and psychological abstractions of classical economics and organization theory; they produced detailed histories and analyses of organizational behavior and legal doctrine. See W. Hamilton and H. R. Wright, *The Case of Bituminous Coal* (New York: Macmillan, 1926); J. R. Commons, *The Legal Foundations of Capitalism* (New York: Macmillan, 1924). Indeed, "Only a small number of scholars went so far as to embrace a full-fledged operationalism," i.e., defining concepts in terms of a set of physical operations, external to and removed from the human mind, and "probably half of the active social scientists of the period accepted the outlines of (a) broader quan-titative behaviorism" (Purcell, *Crisis of Democratic Theory*, 39). The work of the largest majority of realists was even more particularist and functional without sharing the tenets of extreme objectivism.

57. Lasswell and McDougal, "Legal Education and Public Policy," 203. This strand of realism was "less threatening to the legal world because its implication of a determinate, objective discourse for the representation of social life was amenable to the notion of a neutral and determinate rule of law. Under this conception deter-minacy existed in consequences rather than antecedents. Objective consequentialist analysis, it was imagined, could ground law as an instrumentalist discourse which could carry out purposes and policies provided by elective bodies or made apparent by the social field itself." Gary Peller, "The Metaphysics of American Law," *California Law Review* 73 (1985): 1226.

58. See Trubek and Esser, "Critical Empiricism," 9–10.

alliance of law and science. Some saw in that alliance an attempt to rationalize and stabilize law,[59] thereby freezing in place as "eternal, objective truths" the contingent (and often illiberal) arrangements of the day. They worried, moreover, that the instrumental conception of law tended to hide from view the pervasive role of law in social life. Exclusive concern with the problem of "effective legal regulation" made it difficult to see a broader range of law's effects on society.

Within the realist movement, some saw law as powerful in shaping the consciousness of society. They tried to expose the indeterminacy, contingency, and contradictions of the consciousness thus shaped. According to Peller,

> This deconstructive, debunking strand of realism seemed inconsistent with any liberal notion of the rule of law distinct from politics, or indeed any mode of rational thought distinct from ideology. . . . This approach emphasized contingency and openended possibilities as it exposed the exercises of social power behind what appeared to be the neutral work of reason.[60]

Here, among these critics, it is possible to find the precursors of the constitutive perspective on law.

Exposing the "exercises of social power" meant more than noting what happened when a particular legal policy was enacted and applied. It meant taking a broader and more encompassing look at the way law was implicated in the transactions of everyday life. While this strand of realism opposed the effort to disconnect law from the world, it also opposed the effort to treat law as mere policy and to make the study of law subservient to science. In this view, because law is embedded in history and culture, it cannot be divorced from social practices and from the ways it shapes consciousness, not merely conduct. To treat law deductively as if it were a closed system was, in Cohen's famous phrase, "transcendental nonsense."[61] While Llewellyn claimed that legal concepts could only be understood in and through their impact in the world,[62] Cohen suggested that

---

59. For an interesting exploration of this tendency in realist thinking see Brigham and Harrington, "Realism and Its Consequences."
60. Peller, "Metaphysics of American Law," 1223.
61. See Cohen, "Transcendental Nonsense."
62. Llewellyn, "Some Realism about Realism"; see also Casebeer, "Escape from Liberalism."

[l]egal concepts ... are supernatural entities which do not have a verifiable existence except to the eyes of faith. Rules of Law, which refer to these concepts, are not descriptions of empirical social facts (such as the customs of men or the customs of judges) nor yet statements of moral ideals, but are rather theorems in an independent system. It follows that a legal argument can never be refuted by moral principle nor by any empirical fact. Jurisprudence, as an autonomous system of legal concepts, rules and arguments, must be independent of ethics and of ... positive sciences.[63]

In an important paper analyzing the legal concept of the corporation, William Douglas made a particularly compelling case regarding law's constitutive powers. He maintained that a corporation's liability could not finally depend on the status and acts of its subsidiaries as if those "agents," "tools," or "alter egos," were determining.[64] Those concepts themselves were legal creations, consequences of, rather than sources for, legal reasoning and judicial decisions.[65] Douglas's analysis was important because it indicated the difficulty of drawing on the everyday as a way to settle uncertain legal issues. If Douglas's claim was to be credited, the "private sphere," the world of the everyday, had already been penetrated and partially constituted by the very legal notions that required filling in.

Another powerful statement of law's constitutive consequences for everyday life was Hale's famous analysis of property, published in 1923.[66] Hale argued that what is commonly believed to be free, private action is always thoroughly permeated by law. Even contracts

---

63. Cohen, "Transcendental Nonsense," 821.

64. See William Douglas, "A Functional Approach to the Law of Business Associations," *Illinois Law Review* 23 (1929): 673; see also William Douglas and Charles Shanks, "Insulation from Liability through Subsidiary Corporations," *Yale Law Journal* 29 (1929): 195.

65. Of course, one might argue that the concepts in question could be *both* determining and deductions from prior legal rules, but this misses the point. What is at issue is whether "independent" grounds could be found for extending a corporation's liability. To invoke the catgories of "agent," "alter ego," and so on is simply to *assert* (what is actually in issue) that the corporation is responsible for the conduct in question.

66. See Robert Hale, "Coercion and Distribution in a Supposedly Non-Coercive State," *Political Science Quarterly* 38 (1923): 470; see also Felix Cohen, "Property and Sovereignty," *Cornell Law Quarterly* 13 (1927): 8.

were not properly the products of individual actions whose source existed outside law. Individuals made contracts, Hale suggested, in the context of a preexisting regime of property rules that determined the relative bargaining power of the parties. Property itself is, in turn, a legally created category. "According to Hale, property was prior to contract, public prior to private, and context was prior to intent."[67]

As Peller expresses the point, realists like Douglas and Hale insisted that

> the bargaining power which influenced . . . contractual consent was itself not private, but the result of public power manifest in legal rules defining property and granting owners the power of exclusion. The property rights themselves reflected contingent and social decisions as to what to protect as property. They thus could not themselves be rationalized as flowing from and matching something "out there." The dichotomization and prior-itization of free will and coercion in the liberty of contract discourse . . . were merely relational in that free will was created by coercion.[68]

Realists, in Peller's view, recognized the way legal doctrine constituted the very rights it had, in the classical conception, been thought merely to acknowledge. "'Rights' or 'rules,' it was argued, do not exist as things with positive content separate from the legal discourse, but rather are the result of judicial decisions and thus cannot be the ground for the decisions."[69] Some realists sought to demonstrate the contingent and varied ways that law called into being and favored some social practices and relations while it inhibited others. For them, this was the essence of the political character of law.

Yet realism was a thoroughly legalist doctrine that, in all of its strands, took law as the point of departure and, in so doing, laid the intellectual foundation for the law-first tendencies of both the instrumental and constitutive perspectives. Law was the invariable, uniform starting point of all realist inquiry, whether it examined some

---

67. Peller, "Metaphysics of American Law," 1233.
68. Id., 1222.
69. Id., 1223.

specific piece of legislation or the entire regime of property. The idea of beginning with a social practice—with the very activities whose existence would seem necessary *to give law meaning*—and studying law's often turbulent life in connection with that practice, seems not to have occurred to legal realists. Thus, despite its seeming radicalism, there is reason to agree with Brigham and Harrington that legal realism is "lawyer's law and has become the self conception of the legal profession itself," an intellectual movement designed to appropriate modern understandings "in the interest of maintaining established legal authority."[70] In any case, it plainly did not energize legal scholarship to become more genuinely sociological, for example, to begin inquiry with the practices of everyday life.

Exemplifying Instrumentalism and the Constitutive Perspective

The origins in legal realism of both instrumental and constitutive perspectives on law are manifested, as we have argued, in the tendency of both to allow legal materials to dictate the domain of inquiry. For the instrumentalists, study begins with a body of doctrine or rules coupled with an intent to determine their effectiveness in the regulation of social life, to determine, that is, whether the world conforms to or deviates from the expectations those legal materials create. In the case of the constitutive perspective, the starting point is again a law, a body of laws, or a set of legal practices, though this time that material itself is subjected to a kind of "deep reading," to adduce the underlying structures and meanings these materials contain or imply for the persons whose lives they govern.

In both cases, the approach is broadly empirical in character, though the evidence attended to differs in the two cases. Instrumentalists will be interested in "raw" behavior, in the extent to which the relevant legal actors are encouraged to act (or abstain from acting) in the indicated or intended ways. By contrast, adherents of the constitutive view will be more interested in the ways in which the law has generally shaped the beliefs, attitudes, and understandings of legal subjects, in the ways they imagine their own capacities and their relations with one another. To be sure, the behavior of

---

70. Brigham and Harrington, "Realism and Its Consequences," 44, 56.

legal subjects will be relevant in detecting the effects that interest
the constitutive view, but that behavior will itself have to be "read"
for its meaning in the lives of legal subjects. Moreover, there is
no particular reason to suppose that those subjects occupy a privileged position with respect to its meaning for them. Like a skilled
psychotherapist, a practitioner of the constitutive view may uncover
meanings of which the legal subject is substantially or even wholly
unaware.[71]

But despite these differences, both kinds of studies are themselves
shaped by an exclusively legal agenda, namely, a desire to understand
the extent of law's hold on society, either in terms of sanctions or
meanings. There are reasons to believe, however, that the relationships
between law and everyday life are far more complex than either of
these perspectives, or any combination of them, can accommodate.
That this is so emerges in even a cursory review of some of the
leading examples of both kinds of studies.

Some Examples of Instrumentalism

Instrumentalism has played an important role in the efforts of the
modern law and society movement to advance the scientific, empirical, policy-focused aspect of legal realism.[72] Study after study measures the impact of legal rules and assesses the gap between law on
the books and law in action.[73] A smaller number examine empirically
the way particular persons or groups use or ignore legal rules in their
day-to-day practices. Three such studies exemplify the instrumentalist
conception. Each of these studies attempts to identify where law is
present and where it is absent, where law is used and where it is
ignored, where law is effective and where it is ineffective.

The first of these studies—Stewart Macaulay's "Non-Contractual
Relations in Business"—was an important precursor to contemporary

---

71. For example, presumably the real meaning of contract ideology is to encourage acceptance of the false belief, of the illusion, that contracting parties are free
and essentially equal bargainers. See Roberto Unger, *False Necessity: Anti-
Necessitarian Social Theory in the Service of Radical Democracy* (Cambridge: Cambridge University Press, 1987).

72. See Lawrence Friedman, "The Law and Society Movement," *Stanford Law
Review* 38 (1980): 805.

73. See Sarat, "Legal Effectiveness."

efforts to chart the role of law in everyday life. It is a classic example of a "gap" study, which sought to identify the "gap between the academic model of contract law and the system as it works."[74] In the academic model, contractual relations are pervasive because they are indispensable to market transactions. That model thus suggests that contracts will be relied on extensively in the business world, that contract law elaborately and effectively structures business relations.

Macaulay begins his study as an agnostic in relation to the academic model of contract. He does not just assume the value or pervasiveness of contractual devices in everyday business relations. For him those are empirical issues rather than matters of academic theorizing. Here he echoes the legal realist faith in scientific observation to provide usable knowledge of the legal world.[75] Thus he begins his article with the deceptively simple questions, "What good is contract law? Who uses it? When and how?"[76]

Contracts involve two elements for Macaulay; first, planning transactions and specifying duties, requirements, and expectations, and, second, the threat or use of legal sanctions to induce performance.[77] With this understanding it was possible for him to treat contract as a variable and to argue that contracts can be used to a greater or lesser degree in any business relationship or transaction. Testing that argument required measuring the degree to which contract was present in the business world by observing the extent of planning and of reliance on legal sanctions.

Macaulay found that most routine transactions are handled by what he called "standardized planning,"[78] that is, by boilerplate language that is only marginally adjusted to fit the details of any particular transaction. Yet often the terms buyers and sellers used to describe a transaction are inconsistent with this language. This does not get in the way of the completion of transactions because "[e]ven

---

74. Stewart Macaulay, "An Empirical View of Contract," *Wisconsin Law Review* 1985 (1985): 477.

75. As Macaulay later wrote about his 1963 article, "The challenge is to find a way to avoid cynicism, recognize the value of classic views of law, and rationalize a dispute processing system that does not turn on litigation and doctrine. . . . [T]his is the challenge of an empirical perspective on law." ("Empirical View of Contract," 482).

76. Stewart Macaulay, "Non-Contractual Relations in Business: A Preliminary Study," *American Sociological Review* 28 (1963): 55.

77. Id.

78. Id.

when a purchase order and an acknowledgement have conflicting provisions printed on the back, almost always the buyer and the seller will be in agreement on what is to be sold and how much is to be paid for it."[79]

In the day-to-day work of businessmen there is, according to Macaulay's findings, little or no planning concerning "legal sanctions and the effect of defective performances."[80] Contract as a tool for doing business stands in the background but is neither uniformly nor predictably used. "Contract planning and contract law," Macaulay contends, "at best, stand at the margin of important long-term continuing business relations."[81]

This means that there are many chances for misunderstandings or disputes about performance. While misunderstandings and disputes do arise, Macaulay found that

> [d]isputes are frequently settled without reference to the contract or potential or actual legal sanctions. There is a hesitancy to speak of legal rights or to threaten to sue in these negotiations. Even where parties have a detailed and carefully planned agreement which indicates what is to happen if, say, the seller fails to deliver on time, often they will never refer to their agreement but will negotiate a solution when the problem arises apparently as if there had never been any original contract.[82]

In Macaulay's view contract is much less a part of the everyday world of business practice than one would assume if one simply examined contract doctrine. "Contract and contract-law are often thought unnecessary because there are many effective non-legal sanctions."[83] Business transactions are, in fact, governed by informal norms that dictate that one ought to stand behind one's products and honor agreements. The key sanction should such norms be breached is termination of the business relationship.[84] The expectation of, and

79. Id., 147.
80. Id., 148.
81. See "Empirical View of Contract," 467.
82. Macaulay, "Non-Contractual Relations," 149.
83. Id., 150.
84. See Ian Macneil, "Relational Contracts: What We Do and Do Not Know," *Wisconsin Law Review* 1985 (1985): 483. See also Robert Gordon, "Macaulay, Macneil, and the Discovery of Solidarity and Power in Contract Law," *Wisconsin Law Review* 1985 (1985): 565.

desire for, continuing relations serves to support a structure of interaction that pushes contract into the background such that "contract
and contract law are not needed."[85] As Yngvesson says about Macaulay's study,

> It showed that social control processes in the market, the stereo-
> type of a social sphere in which law is needed to limit the
> behavior of self-interested individuals, cannot be explained sim-
> ply by reference to official legal rules. The market, like the family,
> is pervaded by self-regulating processes so often found when
> relationships extend in social space and endure in time. This
> insight challenged fundamental assumptions about appropriate
> settings for informality and about the significance of formal rules
> and formal legal processes in an area at the core of American
> cultural and economic life.[86]

The question remains, however, whether contract law does not
have effects to which Macaulay's instrumentalism remained systematically inattentive.

It is, we think, both odd and troublesome that Macaulay's work
seems not to have caused scholars to explore more fully the extent
to which the *availability* of contract law makes possible reliance on
arrangements and negotiations that are not explicitly or formally
legal. Thus, it seems reasonable to ask: what are the implications of
negotiating and working out elaborate business arrangements *in the
shadow* of, rather than in the total absence of, law?[87] That instrumentalists seem not to be moved to ask such a question is, we suggest,
a predictable consequence of their focus, namely, the direct (all-or-
nothing) effectiveness of specific legal rules. The effects of a legal
shadow would seem to be too ethereal a phenomenon to attract the
attention of a committed instrumentalist.[88]

---

85. Macaulay, "Non-Contractual Relations," 154.

86. Barbara Yngvesson, "Re-Examining Continuing Relations and the Law,"
Wisconsin Law Review 1985 (1985): 624.

87. See Robert Mnookin and Lewis Kornhauser, "Bargaining in the Shadow of
the Law: The Case of Divorce," *Yale Law Journal* 88 (1979): 950.

88. On the other hand, it is of passing interest to note that despite the ideological
effect of the legal institution of contracting, Macaulay's subjects—at least at some
level—seem to have effectively resisted the full contractualization of their relationship,
insisting on informal practices, even if, as the text suggests, these were "underwritten"
on the relatively firm expectations or framework that the law of contracts provided
them.

More recently, Robert Ellickson has produced an instrumentalist account of law in another important area of American cultural and economic life, namely, property.[89] Ellickson's is an ethnographic study of disputes and their resolution among ranchers and cattle farmers in Shasta County, California. He studied what happened under statutory schemes that allocate responsibilities in disputes arising when cattle stray off farms. He concluded "that legal rules hardly ever influence the settlement of cattle-trespass disputes in Shasta County." Instead Ellickson found that most residents resolve animal trespass disputes according to what he calls "workaday norms" that support the idea that neighbors should be cooperative.[90]

Neighbors ignore the law even though they have a relatively reliable grasp of what the law provides and what the rules say. Whatever the rules say, in Shasta County the operative norms are that "an owner of livestock is responsible for the acts of his animals," and that "a rural resident should put up with ('lump') minor damage stemming from isolated trespass incidents."[91] Ellickson contends, again displaying his instrumentalist conception of law, that "allegiance to [these norms seems] wholly independent of formal legal entitlements."[92] The idea of mapping law's presence and absence is replaced with another spatial metaphor, namely the idea that while some domains of everyday life are inside the realm of law, others remain outside it.

Like Macaulay, Ellickson finds that law is seldom used when social relations are, as they are between neighbors, "continuing."[93] The continuing-relations hypothesis is also used by Ellickson to explain how the costs of fencing are allocated. Here too ranchers and farmers have a basic grasp of the legal regime, which states that landowners who put up fences have no legal right to restitution from adjoining landowners. In daily practice, however, adjoining landowners in Shasta County "share fencing costs in rough proportion to the average density of livestock present on the respective sides of the boundary line."[94]

---

89. See Robert Ellickson, *Order without Law: How Neighbors Settle Disputes* (Cambridge: Harvard University Press, 1991).

90. Id., 40, 48.

91. Id., 53.

92. Id., 53.

93. Id., 55.

94. Id., 71.

Where there are no continuing relations, as is the case in highway accidents involving livestock, law is used. As Ellickson puts it, "Compared with trespass and fence-financing disputes, which almost never result in litigation, collision disputes . . . seem to be resolved relatively 'legalistically.'"[95] But the overall thrust of Ellickson's argument is to identify social spaces in which order is produced "without law." As he puts it, there is a

> growing library of evidence that large segments of social life are located and shaped beyond the reach of law. Despite this mounting evidence, the limits of law remain too little appreciated. . . . An alert observer can find in everyday life abundant evidence of the workings of nonhierarchical processes of coordination.[96]

But as with Macaulay's conclusions, one who is not wholly the captive of a narrow instrumentalism is apt to catch more than a fleeting glimpse of law's presence in the putatively alegal responses Ellickson describes. Thus, the mannerly ways of good neighbors might well prevail because both parties know that "if things got ugly" there are clear (and comforting) limits to what either side could gain. Where this is so, it seems, the law might be quite effective even when rarely invoked and when agreed-on outcomes are rarely what the law itself would have prescribed. Whether one would regard such resolutions as legalistic or not perhaps matters less than that one remain attentive to law's effects, even when law is "ignored."

A third study of the role of law in everyday life moves us from the everyday life of citizens to the day-to-day world of those charged with administering legal rules. Yet the essential question remains the same: namely, are the practices of those persons organized by, or are they external to, the world of legal rules? This study, by Abraham Blumberg, describes the daily practices of criminal courts.[97]

Like Macaulay and Ellickson, Blumberg's work emphasizes the power of continuing relations to override legal norms, in this case to circumvent legal rules protecting the rights of criminal defendants.

---

95. Id., 94.
96. Id., 4–5.
97. Abraham Blumberg, "The Practice of Law as a Confidence Game," *Law and Society Review* 1 (1967): 15.

In the course of their ongoing work, judges, prosecutors, and defense attorneys interact repeatedly and regularly. Networks of reciprocal deference and obligation develop that simultaneously bind them together and constitute the practice of criminal prosecution and defense. They form a relatively coherent group of courthouse regulars. In this setting the defendant, paradoxically, is the odd man out. As a transient who passes through the organization rather than as a continuing member, his rights are regarded as peripheral to the activities that sustain the court as a productive and efficient organization.

Blumberg insists that when legal officials work to undercut defendants' legal rights, they act reasonably rather than malevolently. He highlights the contradictions between the needs of the court as an organization and the due-process rights of criminal defendants. He describes his work, in classically instrumentalist terms, as an effort to examine whether important Supreme Court decisions effectively regulate the institutional practices of lower criminal courts. As he puts it,

> [V]ery little sociological effort is expended to ascertain the validity and viability of important court decisions which may rest wholly on erroneous assumptions about the complex realities of social structure. A particular decision may rest upon a legally impeccable rationale; at the same time it may be rendered nugatory or self-defeating by contingencies imposed by aspects of social reality of which lawmakers are themselves unaware.[98]

Blumberg takes as his point of departure "important court decisions," and while he wants to ascertain the validity of those decisions, validity is limited to viability; that is, a court decision is valid only if consistent with the relevant social facts and thus capable of altering behavior. Specifically, court decisions are valid only if they actually make a difference in the behavior of those to whom they are addressed.

The particular decisions with which Blumberg was concerned involved the rights of criminal defendants.[99] He read Supreme Court

---

98. Id., 16.
99. See Gideon v. Wainwright, 372 U.S. 335 (1963); Escobedo v. Illinois, 378 U.S. 478 (1964), and Miranda v. Illinois, 384 U.S. 436 (1966).

decisions to identify mandates for the behavior of criminal defense lawyers and to determine whether "the Supreme Court's conception of the role of counsel in a criminal case squares with social reality."[100] On the basis of his empirical observations, he found defense lawyers and prosecutors conspiring to induce defendants to waive their legal rights and plead guilty. Organizational pressures require that most defendants enter guilty pleas; those pressures, not legal rules, govern the everyday world of the criminal courts. The consequence, Blumberg warns, is that "recent Supreme Court decisions may have a long range effect which is radically different from that intended or anticipated."[101]

In at least one crucial respect, Blumberg's analysis is similar to those of Macaulay and Ellickson: legal material that does not issue in its anticipated or intended results is, from the instrumental perspective, ipso facto inoperative or ineffective. But in all of the cases cited so far, it seem tolerably clear that the law has had (or may have had) important effects even if they are not always as direct and predictable as might have been supposed, imagined, or intended. Thus, there is nothing in Blumberg's study indicating that the balances struck between defendants, defense attorneys, judges, and prosecutors in criminal cases are not deeply affected by Supreme Court rulings. Contrary to Blumberg, that a judicial decision does not "work" in the world in the sense of achieving fully conforming behavior by the parties involved by no means entails that such a decision is without legally important effects.[102] Only a legal scholar with an extremely

---

100. Blumberg, "Practice of Law," 18.

101. Id., 39.

102. Not all instrumentalist research documents law's "failures," the places where it is ineffective or is simply ignored. For example, H. Laurence Ross, *Deterring the Drinking Driver* (Lexington, Mass.: D. C. Heath, 1984), describes several ways in which attempts to deter drinking and driving have been at least marginally successful. Following the Scandinavian model of control, using very specific and technically defined criteria of impairment, Ross argues that contemporary regulations can closely approximate the conditions for effective deterrence. By specifically defining the criteria of offense, providing the technical means of determining when someone is under the influence of alcohol, and increasing surveillance of drivers, law enforcement increases the perceived certainty of apprehension and thus the likelihood that citizens will take law into account.

Yet by conceiving law in narrowly instrumental terms, Ross is forced to construct a mystifying paradox—to regard drinking and driving, a pervasive social activity, as socially unsituated. Ross argues that because drinking and driving involves offenses "less anchored in morality and other nonlegal systems of rules" than more traditional

narrow view of effectiveness could suppose this to be the case. Regrettably, such a view tends to be standard equipment for many instrumentalists.

Some Studies of Law's Constitutive Effects

Constitutive theories of law reject the instrumentalist picture of law as external to social practices and as displaceable by systems of norms and relations that exist beyond the reach of law.[103] They seek to trace the way legal power and legal forms exist in social relations. They claim that "in actual historical societies the law governing social relations—even when never invoked, alluded to, or even consciously much thought about—has been such a key element in the constitution of productive relations that it is difficult to see the value . . . of trying to describe those relations apart from law."[104]

Constitutive theories claim that instrumentalism produces a distorted picture of the role of law in everyday life. By focusing on law as a discrete tool, or on the efforts of law to change behavior, instrumentalism diverts attention from the deep, often invisible, but pervasive effects of legal concepts on social practices. Moreover, it diverts attention from the ways law stifles resistance and shapes consciousness, so that contingent social practices are regarded as necessary. Most of those who advance a constitutive view of law in everyday life seek to examine law where it is least recognizable and least problematic, where, to use Gramsci's phrase, law is "hegemonic."[105]

---

crimes, legal regulation can be studied in relative isolation from other social processes. His research demonstrates, however, that law has only slight effects in controlling drunken driving. Most drinking and driving behavior is untouched by law; on the other hand, he suggests that this behavior is relatively unconnected to nonlegal rules or conventions. Unlike Macaulay, Ellickson, and Blumberg, Ross ends up with a description of a widespread social behavior that he implies is without normative ordering and cultural signification.

103. See Gordon, "Critical Legal Histories" and Harrington and Yngvesson, "Interpretive Sociolegal Research." Also see Alan Hunt, "The Ideology of Law: Advances and Problems in Recent Applications of the Concept of Ideology to the Analysis of Law," *Law and Society Review* 19 (1985): 11. As Hunt says, "The creation of legal subjects involves the recognition of 'the law' as the active 'subject' that calls them into being. It is by transforming the human subject into a legal subject that law influences the way participants experience and perceive their relations with others" (15).

104. See Gordon, "Critical Legal Histories," 105.

105. See Antonio Gramsci, *Selections from the Prison Notebooks* (London:

The hegemonic character of law in everyday life cannot be seen in those instances in which law actively intervenes in people's lives to change behavior, or where some discrete legal mechanism is available for use. Law is hegemonic in everyday life where it works unobtrusively, inseparably from social practices themselves. "Law is omnipresent in the very marrow of society. . . . [T]he legal forms we use set limits on what we can imagine as practical options."[106] Here law may be hardest to see and to differentiate from the social norms by which people go about their daily lives. By helping to constitute routine life, law is associated with particular visions of order, justice, goodness, and so forth.

And because people generally go along with legal prescriptions, law's vision becomes ordinary practice. Law establishes its moral, political, and cultural values as conventional. This means, for example, that, as a rule, "one pays one's debts and renders to one's employer the performance that is due."[107] It is neither the threat of adjudication nor compulsion by the state that routinely induces a person to perform those duties. More is at stake than the use of law or the performance of legal obligations. Because law is constitutive of the very forms that social relations and practices take, it is embedded in them, so much so that it is virtually invisible to those involved. This invisibility, this taken-for-grantedness, makes legality and legal forms extremely powerful.

Gordon's "New Developments in Legal Theory" explains the turn away from instrumentalism and the appropriation of the constitutive strand of legal realism in Critical Legal Studies and in what Trubek and Esser call "critical empiricism."[108] Gordon argues that the turn toward a constitutive approach was a product of the Vietnam era's disillusionment with the "vision of law as a technocratic policy science administered by a disinterested elite." That disillusionment led to the rejection of both the liberal and orthodox Marxist versions of instrumentalism; both versions, Gordon claims, "assume that legal systems

---

Lawrence and Wishart, 1977), 377. See also Maureen Cain, "Gramsci, the State, and the Place of Law," in *Legality, Ideology and the State,* ed. David Sugarman (London: Academic Press, 1983).

106. See Gordon, "Critical Legal Histories," 109–10.

107. S. Vago, *Law and Society* (Englewood Cliffs, N.J.: Prentice Hall, 1981), 40.

108. See Gordon, "New Developments"; and Trubek and Esser, "Critical Empiricism."

go through different stages that are necessary functions of prevailing economic organization."[109] Both versions claim that particular groups benefit from and manipulate, use, or ignore law to serve particular interests.

Gordon suggests that the turn toward a constitutive view grows out of an interest in seeing the way law functions to "'legitimate' the existing social order." Constitutive views of law argue that it is "one of those clusters of belief—and it ties in with a lot of other nonlegal but similar clusters—that convince people that all the many hierarchical relations in which they live and work are natural and necessary."[110] Gordon gives the example of a person who owns a small business. His claim to ownership as the basis for his right to dictate the terms and conditions of work is unlikely to be challenged by his employees because of the pervasiveness of the idea of ownership—a legally constituted idea—in organizing the social experience of workers, who as parents, for example, adjudicating a dispute between their child and a neighbor about a bicycle, themselves readily ask the question of whose bike is it. "[E]mployers are not likely to think that they can challenge that [claim] because to do so would jeopardize their sense of the rights of ownership, which they themselves exercise in other aspects of life . . . ; they are locked into a belief cluster that abstracts and generalizes the ownership claim."[111]

Few studies actually show *how* the constitutive and hegemonic effects of law operate in society, while many examine the ideological dimension of law and the way it portrays social relations and naturalizes relations of power. Few scholars have mapped "the relationships among elite ideological production, the social definition of meaning, and the history of social relations."[112] Among the best work exemplifying a constitutive perspective on law are Brigham's examination of the role of law in social movements, Gordon's study of elite lawyers in the late nineteenth and early twentieth century, and Cain's research on civil litigation.[113] Brigham shows the way legal forms are evident

---

109. See Gordon, "New Developments," 415, 416.
110. Id., 418.
111. Id., 419.
112. Trubek, "Where the Action Is." 612.
113. See John Brigham, "Right, Rage, and Remedy: Forms of Law in Political Discourse," *Studies in American Political Development* 2 (1987): 306; Robert Gordon, "Legal Thought and Legal Practice in the Age of American Enterprise, 1870–1920,"

in the language, purposes, and strategies of movement activity, while Gordon demonstrates that "every legal practice—from drafting a complaint for simple debt to writing a constitution—[makes] a contribution to building a general ideological scheme or political language out of such explaining and rationalizing conceptions."[114] Cain, like Gordon, shows how general practice lawyering is "conceptive ideological work: (it uses) old rules to generate new ways of thinking, of making sense of, and thereby constituting ideologically new and emergent material forms."[115]

One other study may be used to describe how law's constitutive power works. This is Yngvesson's research on the handling of complaints in a lower criminal court.[116] Yngvesson is neither interested in the conditions under which people bring their disputes to court, nor whether court decisions are implemented and obeyed, that is, whether they effectively regulate the social world. Instead she describes the conduct of "show cause" hearings as a way of understanding how "exchanges between clerk and citizens produce legal and moral frameworks that justify a decision to handle a case a particular way [and how] court and community are mutually shaped." Yngvesson describes the "interpenetration of our most fundamental cultural assumptions with legal ones." She argues that "complaint hearings reproduce the paradox at the heart of modern law: that it is characterized by an independence achieved in and through dependence. It is neither 'from above' nor 'from below' but simultaneously separate and immanent, imposed and participatory."[117]

In complaint hearings, community is constituted as clerks categorize legal disputes. Some disputes are characterized as "garbage" cases or "kidstuff," yet even they become "vehicles for talking about legal rights and local morality, joining the language of law with the 'common sense' of custom to shape notions of the good neighbor, the bad daughter, and the dutiful parent." Complaint hearings pull

in *Professional Ideologies in America,* ed. G. Gordon (Chapel Hill: University of North Carolina Press, 1983), 72; and Maureen Cain, "The General Practice Lawyer and the Client: Towards a Radical Conception," *International Journal of the Sociology of Law* 4 (1983): 13.

114. Brigham, "Right, Rage, and Remedy," 306; Gordon, "Legal Thought and Legal Practice," 72.

115. Cain, "General Practice Lawyer," 13.

116. Yngvesson, "Making Law at the Doorway," 409.

117. Id., 410, 410–11, 411–12.

the court "into the most mundane areas of daily life" and "become forums for . . . 'thinking the community,' for constituting what the local community is and who is not of it."[118]

Yngvesson finds that clerks use two distinct images of order and relationship in constituting the meaning of community. One is based on the "interconnections of neighbors," the other on the balancing of claims "between individuals whose relationship is defined by rights to property, privacy, and to live in peace."[119] She finds that the ideas developed in these legal forums become part of the community's taken-for-granted norms, and she argues that the normative order of the community and the world of legal procedures cannot be separated.

In this she disagrees with Macaulay and Ellickson, both of whom treat local and legal norms as separate rather than as mutually constitutive. In her account, as in others that advance a constitutive perspective, "law creates the social world by 'naming' it; legal professionals are empowered by their capacity to reveal rights and define wrongs, to construct the meaning of everyday events (as just or unjust, as crime or normal trouble, as private nuisance or public grievance) and thus to shape cultural understandings of fairness, of justice, and of morality."[120] Yngvesson's work illustrates that

> in practice it is just about impossible to describe any set of "basic" social practices without describing the legal relations among the people involved—legal relations that don't simply condition how the people relate to each other but to an important extent define the constitutive terms of the relationship, relations such as lord and peasant, master and slave, employer and employee, ratepayer and utility, and taxpayer and municipality.[121]

Conclusion: Everyday Life in Legal Scholarship

Instrumental and constitutive approaches to the study of law in everyday life share a common commitment to what we have called the law-first perspective. The former emphasizes effectiveness to the exclu-

---

118. Id., 414, 420.
119. Id., 444.
120. See Barbara Yngvesson, "Inventing Law in Local Settings: Rethinking Popular Legal Culture," *Yale Law Journal* 98 (1989): 1691.
121. Gordon, "Critical Legal Histories," 103.

sion of broader effects, the latter focuses on law's role in constituting social meanings and excludes law's more focused regulatory effects. Because law is enacted in regular, seemingly uneventful experiences, the law-first perspective misses much of the richness and complexity of the interactions of the legal and the everyday. Law is continuously shaped and reshaped by the ways it is used, even as law's constitutive power constrains patterns of usage.[122] Law in everyday life is, in this sense, both constitutive and instrumental. The possible variations in practice are situationally circumscribed; there are, for example, a limited number of available meanings within any setting. Thus, "[W]hile the law may be a resource, a tool available for all sorts of uses, the ways in which it is put to use are constrained by ... conventions, ways of doing things that relate to courts, lawyers, litigation, claims of right, precedent, evidence, judgment.... [W]hat is done in the name of the law is constrained by a world of its own creation."[123]

In our view, scholarship on law in everyday life should abandon the law-first perspective and should proceed, paradoxically, with its eye not on law, but on events or practices that seem on the face of things, removed from law, or at least not dominated by law from the outset. As Silbey puts it, "[L]aw is located in concrete and particular circumstances where the relations of ends and means are governed by situational rather than abstract or general criteria."[124] By beginning with such circumstances, it is possible to see that more is at stake than law, that motives, needs, emotions, anxieties, aspirations that are not entirely fixed by legal meanings or by legal forces operate throughout without totally losing their identity to law. In fact, it is law that regularly buckles and is resisted, or reinterpreted, or distorted. It is awareness of this kind of multiplicity in interactions that is gained by relocating legal scholarship in the everyday; persons, relatively whole and complex persons, reemerge in the story of law in a way that is unlikely under either instrumentalism or the constitutive perspective.[125]

---

122. See Yngvesson, "Inventing Law."

123. See Susan Silbey, "Ideals and Practices in the Study of Law," *Legal Studies Forum* 9 (1985): 20.

124. Silbey, "Ideals and Practices," 15.

125. There is some encouragement for the perspective we are advocating in the recent popularity of the story-telling, or narrative, perspective in legal scholarship.

Everyday life, as we conceive of it, is a mélange of social practices and normative commitments that stand, no doubt, in a wide variety of relations to law and legal materials. But to call a practice a social practice is to direct attention to its underlying intelligibility, even if its connection with law and legal concepts were nonexistent. Thus, for example, it might be argued that the institution of giving and accepting promises is a social practice no matter how much it may, *as a purely contingent matter*, be shaped by contract doctrine.[126] The crucial point is this: the institution of promising does not conceptually depend on anything drawn from the law of contracts.[127] Similarly, though more contentiously, the institution of marriage as a wide-ranging commitment to another for a lifetime might be extricated from its legal accompaniments and still retain its nonlegal significance as a powerful normative enterprise. Finally, there is little reason to suppose that the belief that one should respond to beneficent acts in kind is a conviction that owes its existence to law.

By inviting legal scholarship to focus on everyday life, rather than on legal doctrine, we seek to bring into view, if not give primacy to, the lively normative resources of the everyday. These, no doubt, are resources powerfully shaped by law; but they are also resources on which law itself deeply depends, or so we are inclined to suppose. On such a view, if there is a single defect common to the constitutive and instrumental perspectives, it is the unargued postulate that law's story can be told in terms of the effects of legal doctrine or practices on a relatively stable, placid, nonlegal "other." But, in fact, the other that law seeks to affect has its own normative direction and momentum, even when it is obliged to accommodate law's presence. It is unlikely, then, that law's influence can accurately be portrayed in a static tale of fixed effects or displaced meanings. If everyday life is the normatively resourceful place we believe it to be, then a more plausible conjecture is that law's story will be an ongoing one;[128] it

See, for example, "Symposium on Legal Storytelling," *Michigan Law Review* 87 (1989).

126. See A. I. Melden, *Rights and Persons* (Berkeley and Los Angeles: University of California Press, 1977).

127. By contrast, it might be argued that the very concept of a contract does borrow from the informal practice of promising. See Charles Fried, *Contract as Promise: A Theory of Contractual Obligation* (Cambridge: Harvard University Press, 1981).

128. Yngvesson's study suggests (with an uncertain degree of self-consciousness)

will have more the feel of a narrative account than the lawlike presentations we have come to expect from empirically minded social
scientists. On the other hand, such accounts will be decidedly empirical in character, if by this one means they will be grounded in
extensive observations, rigorously assembled—and imaginatively
"read," of course.[129]

Several studies in recent years, prominent among them Kristin
Bumiller's "victims study,"[130] have documented the widespread existence of self-conceptions that battle the model of legal protection and
powerfully resist law's attempt to construct the persons it seeks to
assist as "helpless" or "hapless" victims. Bumiller's study indicates
that the intended beneficiaries of such legislation have a variety of
reasons for not taking advantage of it—and thus greatly reducing the

---

a kind of continuous, interactive relationship between legal and nonlegal domains.
Yngvesson emphasizes the power of court clerks in "show cause" hearings "to shape
the notions of the good neighbor, the bad daughter, and the dutiful parent." See
"Making Law at the Doorway," 409. As we have suggested, her emphasis appears
to be on the law's power to influence social conceptions and judgments. But at least
of equal interest in this paper is the implied power of a community's judgments,
categories, and commitments to shape legal outcomes and to "control" the application
of legal notions. Thus, as Yngvesson points out, some disputes are disposed of with
a "legal" analysis that hardly goes beyond the observation that the matter is a
"garbage" case or that it is "kidstuff." In those cases, it appears that a shared, rough-
and-ready sense of what is a "serious" or "passing" problem, a community perception
more than a legal doctrine, puts the legal matter to rest.

It is true, as Yngvesson notes, that "show cause" hearings can draw the court
"into the most mundane areas of daily life" (see 420), but her study suggests as well
that a community's sense of "the private" can circumscribe law's intrusive tendencies.
Perhaps then, at the interface of relatively minor human quarrels and the blunt
apparatus of law, the relationship between law and other normative practices and
commitments is fated to an ongoing battle. Here the law's "effects" will tend to be
reversible and its impact on social meanings uncertain and negotiable. And in the
context of such exchanges, it seems that the value of instrumental and constitutive
styles of legal scholarship will be minimal at best.

129. The essays in the present volume comprise perhaps the most relevant test
of our thesis regarding the usefulness of the everyday to evoke a new kind of legal
scholarship, one that might finally abandon the limiting (and we think, distorting)
perspectives of both the instrumental and constitutive views.

130. See Kristin Bumiller, "Victims in the Shadow of the Law: A Critique of
the Model of Legal Protection," *Signs* 12 (1987): 421. Another forceful study of this
kind was conducted by David Engel. See "Oven Bird's Song: Insiders, Outsiders,
and Personal Injuries in an American Community," *Law and Society Review* 18 (1984):
551. Engel's study documents the power of the "work ethic" in a small Illinois town
and uncovers deep resentment against those who would use the law to "profit" from
injuries they had sustained at the hands of others.

"effectiveness" of the law in question—including, for example, the belief that to complain would only worsen the situation or in any case would not improve it. Sometimes they do not complain because they believe they would not be able to prove their case. But often, Bumiller observes, such apparently objective reasons mask more substantial though psychological impediments to pursuing a legal remedy, namely, an unwillingness to relinquish "a positive self-image," an unwillingness to accept "the image of the victim as powerless and defeated."[131]

But Bumiller's analysis does not end with the observation that there is a "natural" resistance to perceiving oneself as a victim, as a person who, without the assistance of others, is powerless to respond to a source of injury. Especially in the context of antidiscrimination law, "victims" must accept a second, further kind of depersonalization; in addition to their powerlessness, potential claimants must acknowledge that their right to recovery depends in part on their *group* identity. Their purely private, personal pain and injury does not qualify them for protection; they must also be members of a damaged group. Understandably, such dual depersonalization diminishes the psychic availability of the proposed remedy.

Here, it seems, law contributes to its own ineffectiveness. The image of self-sufficiency is one that pervades our legal system,[132] yet it powerfully inhibits injured persons from availing themselves of legal remedies in response to racial discrimination. Indeed, one might see here a perfect example of law's constitutive powers, of its capacity to induce in legal subjects self-images that are then projected back onto law, masquerading as an independent kind of moral evaluation and acceptance. So construed, Bumiller's study provides an example of the effectiveness of a law being diminished as a result of a social ideology that is itself a consequence of a pervasive legal model of self-sufficient persons. Perhaps it is a case, then, of law's instrumental value being diminished in one place because of its constitutive successes elsewhere.

But those who recognize that society's normative resources are not exhausted by legal ideology may be reminded by Bumiller's study

---

131. Id., 433.
132. See, for example, Gabel and Feinman, "Contract as Ideology." See also Yania v. Begin, 155 A.2d 343 (1959).

that visions of self-sufficiency often go hand in hand with expressions of autonomy and a refusal to take lying down the patently wrongful action of another. One might suppose, then, that the legislation in question would engage normative resources that sound in the language of dignity, honor, and self-respect, and would ignite sentiments of indignation in the presence of abuses that even the law has declared to be intolerable and wrong. In short, law's constitutive powers with respect to images of self-sufficiency cannot be fully credited unless we also suppose that those same powers have sponsored commitments to dignity and self-respect as well. And this is because, *in social morality*, though not (particularly) in law, images of dignity and self-respect are part and parcel of the commitment to self-help. Thus, following constitutive theories of law, legal images of self-sufficiency might indeed embed themselves in the social psyche, but it is doubtful they could do so in *this* society without bringing along with them antecedently established affinities with images of dignity and self-respect. There is reason to think, then, that society's normative resources are not entirely dictated by law; on the contrary, law's constitutive powers might easily awaken nonlegal commitments that will prove to be law's undoing.

To trace these complex connections between law and everyday life it is necessary to begin with the detailed observation of concrete relations, or transactions, with what has been called the "practice of everyday life."[133] By practices we mean "[a]ny coherent and complex form of socially established cooperative human activity through which goods internal to that form of activity are realized."[134] Attention to the practices of everyday life can, as Silbey suggests, "bridge apparently conflicting literatures and approaches to legal phenomena: The research . . . tradition describing law as a system of interaction relying upon ordinary, non-legal categories [what we call constitutive approaches], and the . . . literature identifying law as a unique mode of action and thought different from ordinary action," what we call instrumentalism.[135] We need "thickly described accounts of how law

133. See Michel de Certeau, *The Practice of Everyday Life*, trans. Steven Rendall (Berkeley and Los Angeles: University of California Press, 1984).
134. Alasdair MacIntyre, *After Virtue* (Notre Dame, Ind.: University of Notre Dame Press 1981), 175. See also Pierre Bordieu, *Outline of a Theory of Practice* (Cambridge: Cambridge University Press, 1977).
135. Silbey, "Ideals and Practices," 17.

has been imbricated in and has helped to structure the most routine practices of social life."[136]

Studies of law in everyday life must be intensive rather than extensive; they must describe the world of the quotidian in its singularity rather than assimilating it to general categories. They must be open to the multiple ways law is present. Thus there is no "order without law" among ranchers and farmers whose status as landowners is already inscribed within a system of law. People can use or ignore law as they seek to regulate their relations, but that does not "alter the fact that the bundle of legal endowments they start out with positions them for the struggle, and may make all the difference as to whether they win, lose, or get a good compromise deal. The new deal, when sufficiently stabilized in practice, will simply be the new legal constitution of their relationship."[137] Similarly it is not enough to examine the way law constitutes the meanings of community without also observing the ways members of the community deploy their legal entitlements.[138]

Studying law in the practices of everyday life emphasizes particularity and specificity, something that might be called the "authenticity of dailiness."[139] To see law in everyday life means going to small towns, to rural places, and to urban neighborhoods and looking at the way people in those places come to terms with, use, or ignore law as they construct their own local universe of legal values and behavior.[140] The risk has to be taken to immerse ourselves in the study of the everyday world that at first glance has no legal content. We must study families, schools, workplaces, and even academic conferences; we will find instances where law both constitutes practice and is a tool for changing practice. We will find law shaping relations and interceding to alter relations.

---

136. Gordon, "Critical Legal Histories," 125.

137. Id., 106.

138. See Sally Merry, *Getting Justice and Getting Even: Legal Consciousness among Working-Class Americans* (Chicago: University of Chicago Press, 1990).

139. See Susan Silbey and Austin Sarat, "Critical Traditions in Law and Society Research," *Law and Society Review* 21 (1987): 173.

140. Yngvesson argues that "law is 'invented,' negotiated, or 'made' in local settings. This approach to legal culture suggests that it is only as 'popular' culture, as local 'common' sense that informs the ways people view and act upon the world, that any sense can be made of law. . . . [T]he production of law [is] an ongoing process dialectically linked to the production of community, which is both a vehicle for and an outcome of the invention of law." "Inventing Law," 1690.

In all of this, it is as dangerous to overstate the penetration of law into everyday life as to underestimate its presence. While both law and norms work to produce order, to relegate relations to the realm of the taken for granted, neither is nor can be completely successful. The way people use or ignore law is itself a sign of their resistance to the constitutive effects of law.[141] The constitutive power of law, with the characteristic habits, skills, and cultures it enables, always provides room for challenge even as it imposes constraints.[142] Such opposition is itself manifest in the ways people use or ignore the legal facilities available to them.

Instrumental and constitutive approaches have largely talked past each other. Their different views of the role of law in everyday life are a result of differences in theory and method. If they are going to talk to each other, and if we are to understand the dailiness of law, we cannot choose abstractly one or another of these theories and methods. Law plays a constitutive role in the world of the everyday, yet it is also available as a tool to people as they seek to maintain or alter their daily lives. While it is a mistake to claim that law is absent in those instances where people eschew legal forms or resolve disputes without recourse to law, so too it is a mistake to suppose that law's presence is only ideological. Law is in everyday life as both constituent and instrument. Only if we can find ways to bridge the great divide between instrumental and constitutive approaches in legal scholarship can we begin to appreciate the richness and complexity of the way law makes its presence felt in everyday life.

---

141. As Michel Foucault puts it, "[W]here there is power there is resistance. . . . [P]ower relationships . . . depend on a multiplicity of points of resistance. These play the role of adversary, target, support or handle." Although contained within power, resistances are "inscribed . . . as an irreducible opposite." See *The History of Sexuality*, vol. 1, trans. Robert Hurley (New York: Random House, 1978), 95–96.

142. See Peter Fitzpatrick, "Law, Power, and Resistance" (University of Kent, photocopy); and also Martha Minow, "'Forming underneath Everything That Grows': Toward a History of Family Law," *Wisconsin Law Review* 1985 (1985): 819. As Trubek and Esser put it, "In this new model, changes in ideas do not cause changes in behavior nor do changes in behavior cause changes in ideas. Rather social actors apply dispositions or meaningful patterns of action in changing situations. . . . [S]ince dispositions are open to adaptation, and since they may be more or less suited to dealing with a new type of situation, the resulting interaction may produce changes in actors' habits. Hence, while dispositions provide an initial structuring of life activity, they are subject to change." "Critical Empiricism," 18.

Abigail Bailey's Coverture: Law in a Married Woman's Consciousness

Hendrik Hartog

It is now nearly forty-five years since the publication of Mary Beard's neglected classic, *Woman as Force in History*. In that time the field of women's history has grown up, a field whose reason for being is to challenge, as Beard did, "the haunting idea" of conventional history:

> It is the image of woman throughout long ages of the past as a being always and everywhere subject to man or as a ghostly creature too shadowy to be even that real. . . . As for centuries the Ptolemaic conception of the astrophysical universe dominated discussions and "reasonings" in astronomy, so the theory of woman's subjection to man, the obliteration of her personality from consideration, governs innumerable discussions and reasonings in relation to human affairs. Here, there, and almost everywhere, it gives animus, tendency, and opinionative assurance to the man-woman controversies of our day.[1]

Research for this chapter was supported by the American Council of Learned Societies, the University of Wisconsin Graduate School, and the Smongeski Bequest of the University of Wisconsin Law School. Early versions were given to workshops at Cornell Law School and the University of Toronto Law School and as a Mellon Lecture at Amherst College. I have benefited from the comments and criticisms of Gregory Alexander, Elizabeth Clark, Nancy Cott, Charles Cohen, Michael Grossberg, Nancy Hartog, Nancy Isenberg, Linda Kerber, Mary Beth Norton, William Novak, Marky Rath, Vicki Schultz, and Barbara Yngvesson.

1. Mary R. Beard, *Woman as Force in History* (New York, 1946), 77.

Beard regarded with particular scorn the Anglo-American legal historical assumption that the "very being" of married women was "suspended during the marriage, or at least . . . incorporated and consolidated into that of the husband."[2] Nothing, she thought, was further from the truth as a description of the ordinary lives of most women. And she blamed the survival of that notion into the present day on the rhetorical skill of nineteenth-century feminists and law reformers, who had used the formula for polemical purposes.[3]

In historical writing, at least, Mary Beard's perspective has won the day. Today, there are scores of studies of women as architects of their own lives, as active participants in human history, as makers and breakers of communities and marriages and political alliances. Yet, at the end of the historian's day, after he or she has finished unfolding yet another paean to human agency, structures of submission and docility still remain, if only as contexts and markers against which we measure our subjects' lives. They are monuments to the intractability of habit and the continuing reality of sexual and domestic power in human history.[4]

Of course, Mary Beard was right. At all times in human history, women had identities and personalities. Even married women, subject in the Anglo-American world to the strictures of common-law coverture, were never just feme coverts—women whose identities had been merged into those of their husbands.[5] As Beard argued, many found in alternative legal regimes, notably that of equity law, legal means for establishing separate legal identities. Still, most wives—meaning most women for a large portion of their lives—were feme coverts. Legally, that meant they could neither contract nor manage

---

2. William Blackstone, *Commentaries on the Laws of England* (Oxford: Clarendon, 1765), 1:442.

3. Beard, *Woman as Force*, 113–21; see generally, the retrospective critical essay by Suzanne Lebsock, "Reading Mary Beard," *Reviews in American History* 17 (June 1989): 324–39.

4. See generally Gerda Lerner, *The Creation of Patriarchy* (New York: Oxford University Press, 1986), Martha Fineman, "Dominant Discourse, Professional Language, and Legal Change in Child Custody Decisionmaking," *Harvard Law Review* 101 (1988): 727–74.

5. Coverture was the term given at common law to the legal condition or state of a married woman, who, as a feme covert, was covered by her husband. As a matter of conventional legal theory, a married woman no longer had a legal identity— neither legal rights nor legal personality. And thus, legal understanding of coverture always began with husbands' rights.

any property. In many situations, they would have no standing in court. Their domicile was, in legal theory, their husbands', as was the exclusive right to their sexuality. It is true that the connections between these rules and the practices of everyday life were complex and difficult. Wives, we know, often contracted, managed property, testified in court, sued and were sued, had affairs. A variety of norms and cultural understandings restrained husbands from exercising legal power over their wives. Yet, the fact that the relationship between the rules of coverture and everyday life was complex and difficult, that life did not conform to the art of the legal imagination, does not mean that the art of the legal imagination did not shape those lives.

What difference did such legal constructs make? What can we say about the roles legal structures played in the life and identity of a married woman? What can we learn from a close reading of one woman's autobiography?

In this essay, I will use the memoirs of Abigail Bailey, an eighteenth-century American wife, to illustrate two claims: first, that the terms of wifely submission in the common law, coverture, did find reflection in one woman's expressed beliefs and values, and second, that the normative order of which coverture was a part also provided Abigail Bailey with the moral and political authority to free herself from her husband as oppressor. Neither of these claims are in the least novel or controversial, stated abstractly. Only in the details—in the exploration of voice and the particularities of situation—do they become interesting or important. That is why those of us interested in understanding the role of legal values and legal institutions in the shaping of ordinary social identities attend to autobiographies and memoirs like those of Abigail Bailey.

Bailey's narrative, first published posthumously in 1815 and just now reprinted in a superb edition edited by Ann Taves,[6] focused on events that occurred in the late 1780s and early 1790s. It tells a story

---

6. Ann Taves, ed., *Religion and Domestic Violence in Early New England: The Memoirs of Abigail Abbot Bailey* (Bloomington: Indiana University Press, 1989). All citations in the rest of this essay are to this edition and are given in the text. Earlier references to Bailey's memoirs can be found in Mary Beth Norton, *Liberty's Daughters: The Revolutionary Experience of American Women, 1750–1800* (Boston: Little, Brown, 1980), 49–50; and Nancy Cott, "Divorce and the Changing Status of Women in Eighteenth-century Massachusetts," *William and Mary Quarterly*, 3d ser., 33 (1976): 586–614.

about the discovery of autonomy and rebellion by a deeply submissive, self-consciously conservative woman. Abigail Bailey, born in 1746, lived in New Hampshire and was married to a violent and hard man who, after twenty years of marriage and the birth of fourteen children, sexually abused one of their daughters. The bulk of her memoirs details her struggle to separate herself from that husband after she became aware of the incest. Eventually, she learned to think of him as her "enemy," and from that time on the modern reader can begin to see her as an individual in modern dress. But that transformation of husband into otherness occurs quite late in the story, and even then incompletely, as we shall see. Her struggle, for what in the nineteenth century would be called "self-ownership," occurred entirely within a legal and religious culture that made her identity contingent and dependent on that of her husband.

Abigail Bailey's memoirs illuminate a central interpretive difficulty in the history of individualism and individual identity. As Natalie Davis has written, the exploration of the self in early modern Europe (and America) could only have occurred in conscious relation to the groups to which one belonged. Women and men worked out strategies of self-expression and autonomy within the boundaries of structures of authority and domination and ascribed status. Davis suggests that in sixteenth-century France women and men often experienced themselves as physically continuous with parents, children, husbands, and wives. Only with difficulty could they identify themselves as separate selves at all. And they could never free themselves from an awareness of identity within a structured hierarchy. Yet, even so, aspects of that hierarchical, patriarchal order still led some of its members toward self-discovery and self-presentation. They found effective "strategies for achieving some personal autonomy in a world where in principle parents and husbands ruled and where, because of openings into other bodies and minds, it was not always certain where one person ended and another began."[7]

What were Abigail Bailey's strategies for achieving personal autonomy? How did she (tentatively and partially) break the habit of submission? Most importantly, for our purposes, what, if anything, did law have to do with the habits and changes that marked her life?

---

7. Natalie Z. Davis, "Boundaries and the Sense of Self in Sixteenth-Century France," in *Reconstructing Individualism*, ed. Thomas C. Heller, Morton Sosna, and David E. Wellbery (Stanford: Stanford University Press, 1986), 53–63.

Some Problems of Method

Cultural representations of marriage do not reflect actual relations of power and dependence as organized by marital instability. They reflect what people say in the process of claiming, justifying, contesting, and manipulating the privileges that power relations make possible.[8]

This chapter means to be a contribution to the study of law in everyday life. But Abigail Bailey's memoirs are not for the most part a description of what she thought of as her everyday life. Nor is her book about law. Her memoirs are, rather, a reconstruction of the "great trials, and wonderful mercies," that were her "lot" at the hands of her "Heavenly Father" (178). The narrative describes the extraordinary events that disrupted her ordinary life as a wife and mother. But little in the text describes her everyday life as a wife and mother. The problem the narrative poses is how she, as a Christian, ought to respond to extraordinary events.[9]

Abigail Bailey's unswerving focus throughout the memoirs is on her conversations with and monologues about her husband. The work represents an intense reflection on her marital relations. She carefully reconstructs arguments, prayers, invocations of religious authority. She constantly monitors the changing discourse of her marriage.

In that discourse law played an apparently prominent role. The book is filled with assertions about legal rights, legal remedies, and the sanctions of public institutions. Talk about rights and remedies—

---

8. Jane Collier, *Marriage and Inequality in Classless Societies* (Stanford: Stanford University Press, 1988), 231–32.

9. There are a variety of responses a social historian or ethnographer might make to the question of how this narrative connects to the study of everyday life. One possible response: nothing in this paper is inconsistent with George Marcus's conclusion that "while law is certainly part of everyday culture and society, it tends not to be intimately present in this life except in very banal ways" (see Marcus in this volume). Other responses: incest and domestic violence, we know today, are hardly so unusual as they seemed to her to be. More, the process of separation from husband is and was a relatively ordinary aspect of human experience. Many women did it then, just as many do it now. Likewise, Abigail's husband's resistance to her separation hardly marks him as distinctive or unusual. Nor, as we shall see, were the weapons he used in resisting her that much out of the ordinary. Finally, the very construction of "the exceptional," conceived as an antinomic category, may help us to understand the mundane and the everyday. Even without intending to do so, Abigail Bailey may have told us much about her everyday life.

about what she could do to him, if he would not abide by her wishes,
about what he had a right to do to her, if she would not abide by
his—appear to have been the foundation of their relationship, particularly in its latter days. Those conversations reproduced power
relations and notions of the self within marriage. Those conversations
also justified and explained her need for rebellion and autonomy.

Did Abigail Bailey accurately reproduce the talk of her marital
life? Although the memoir was first published posthumously, nearly
a quarter century after the events it recorded, the memoir reads as
if it were constructed from a diary written at the time of those events.
Yet the reader has no way of knowing if that is in fact the case; there
is no way of knowing whether she accurately reproduced her conversations with her husband, let alone her monologues. Ann Taves,
the modern editor of the new edition, has exhaustively and scru-
pulously established the accuracy of most of the facts recorded in
the text. Bailey's story is, in its essentials, a true story. Yet Bailey
was unquestionably telling a story with a particular message, a story
that used her life, as she understood it, to illustrate the mysteries of
God's love (and along the way how she, a dutiful and good wife,
became a divorced woman). Her memoirs also conformed in important ways to contemporary fictional genres of "captivity narratives"
and of the "pilgrim's progress."

We cannot treat Abigail Bailey's memoirs as a clear window onto
the talk of her marriage. Still, for the purposes of this paper, we can
use the memoirs as a text about marriage and the changing identity
of a married woman. I am reading her memoirs in search of the
commonsense assumptions about law and marital power and personal
transformation that informed her description of her marriage. Given
those goals, it does not matter to me that, by the time she sat down
to write her memoirs, she may have forgotten precisely what he had
said to her, or who had won which argument. I am relatively unin-
terested in the extent to which she shaped her memoirs to conform
to contemporary genres. What is important, for me, is that Abigail
Bailey reproduced the pivotal events of her married life as a set of
conversations and monologues about power and legal right.[10]

---

10. "I focus on discourses because it is in discourse that culture and power are
joined. Power relations provide the necessity for, and the contexts of, ongoing and
recurring conversations. At the same time, such conversations, by requiring and
producing particular understandings of the social world, presume unexamined

The discourse of power and legal right that Bailey described was only intermittently connected to an objective, established body of legal doctrine. The Baileys' law, as she described it, had little to do with lawyers' law. Asa and Abigail were sometimes objectively wrong in the things they said to one another about what public institutions would actually do if confronted by the Baileys' situation.[11] At other times their uncertain knowledge reflected ambiguities present in doctrinal law as well.[12]

It would be relatively easy (although not that easy!) to discover what legal doctrine and legal institutions of the time allowed each of them to do with regard to the other. Their legal assertions and claims are important to me, however, not for their truth as law, but for their roles in giving meaning to actions. My goal is to examine how legal power structured "the contexts in which people negotiate the consequences of actions and events."[13] It is to recover something of the meanings Abigail Bailey gave to the events of her life through her use of the language and the symbols of law.[14]

In important ways, Abigail and Asa made (up) the law to which

---

assumptions that grant power to some and not to others." Collier, *Marriage and Inequality*, 6–7.

11. She gave, for example, an exhaustive description of how she was tricked by her husband into traveling with him across Vermont into New York, because he believed that in New York, unlike New Hampshire, the laws were far more protective of husband's prerogatives. When they got there, "He told me, we are now in the State of New York, and now you must be governed by the laws of this State, which are far more suitable to govern such women as you, than are the laws of New Hampshire" (124). Was Asa Bailey right? Was New York's general law of husband-wife relations significantly more patriarchal than that of New Hampshire? Probably not. In fact, it is hard to judge the truth of his (and her) belief in the relative efficacy of eighteenth-century laws in different jurisdictions. New York did not grant divorces through most of the eighteenth century, while New Hampshire did. But at the time that Mr. Bailey coerced Mrs. Bailey into traveling with him, she was only contemplating an informal separation, not a full divorce. Given the localized quality of justice in the eighteenth century, moreover, generalizations about state law would be of limited relevance in predicting the availability of remedies from particular courts. Of much greater importance than the formal legal regime would have been her separation in New York from friends and relations, her isolation among strangers.

12. As we will see, their negotiations over separation were framed both by their (particularly her) uncertainties about the legal import of a separation and also by the legal ambiguity of the status of marital separation.

13. Collier, *Marriage and Inequality*, 6.

14. Here and throughout most of the rest of this paper, I focus on Abigail's normative universe, rather than that of Asa, whom we see only through her eyes. For a suggestion of the terms of his world, see n. 51.

they referred. The relevant legal context for their negotiations was one that they produced through their interpretations and reconstructions of their normative universe.

How then can one talk about Abigail Bailey's realizing herself as a more autonomous self within the legal context of her eighteenth-century marriage? What is the legal context? The problem is real. Yet the problem is more frightening stated abstractly, in terms of a schematized "self" and a theoretical "context," than when confronted in terms of historical particularities and descriptions. Relevant contexts are created through interpretations, yet interpretations are constrained and limited by historically specific structures that restrict the range of available interpretive postures. The Baileys may have interpreted or understood law wrongly. They could not interpret it in ways that would not find support and reinforcement in the cultural and institutional structures that surrounded them. When they were wrong in their statements about legal rights and remedies, they were wrong in ways that were plausible and coherent with available understandings about marriage and moral identity.

The central normative structure in Abigail Bailey's life—a structure that radically constrained her interpretive options—was that of eighteenth-century evangelical Christianity.[15] To understand the relationship of legal context to moral identity, we need first to understand the structural significance of religious belief in her life (that is, I suppose, something like the relationship of moral context to legal identity). Legal rules, rights, and remedies would be interpreted, would be recognized by her within that order. For Abigail Bailey, human law was always secondary to God and his "wonderful" plan. Legal power was ultimately ineffectual against the power of prayer and submission to God's will.[16]

Unless one appreciates the distinctive parallax of her Christianity, there is no way to make historical sense of the pivotal problem in her narrative: that is, knowing when it would become right for her to act separately from and in opposition to her husband. From the

---

15. On evangelical Protestantism, see Philip Greven, *The Protestant Temperament* (New York: Knopf, 1980), Charles Cohen, *God's Caress: The Psychology of Puritan Religious Experience* (New York: Oxford University Press, 1986), and the introduction to Bailey's memoirs by Ann Taves.

16. As we shall see, there were moments when Asa evidently agreed with her on this.

time she first became aware of the incest in 1788, she theoretically possessed formal legal rights against her husband. She might have had a right to a full divorce. She certainly had a right to a separation from bed and board (a court-ordered limited divorce), including an equitable distribution of marital property. She had a right to have articles of the peace drawn up against him. She could always threaten her husband with indictment for a capital crime. Yet, she waited and prayed and suffered for the better part of four years before invoking formal legal processes. In Taves's slightly anachronistic reading, Bailey's long hesitance and apparent passivity exemplifies the "battered wife" syndrome of modern social policy. She should have acted much sooner, although Taves would understand and forgive her reluctance, because today we understand that reluctance as constituted by a structure of sexual power (28).[17]

Surprisingly, the anonymous clerical editor of the 1815 publication of Bailey's memoirs apparently shared Taves's judgment. He too felt that Abigail Bailey was wrong to wait so long. Like Taves, he also saw her weakness as the explanation for her misjudgment:

The discreet reader will repeatedly wonder that this pious sufferer did not look abroad for help for so vile a son of Beliel, and avail herself of the law of the land, by swearing the peace against him. Her forbearance does indeed seem to have been carried to excess. But when we consider her delicate situation at this time; her peaceable habits from youth; her native tenderness of mind; her long fears of a tyrannical cruel husband; her having no time of her sufferings seen all that we now see of his abominable character as a reason why he should have been brought to justice; her wishes and hopes that he might be brought to reformation; her desires not to have the family honor sacrificed; and the difficulty of exhibiting sufficient evidence against a popular subtle man, to prove such horrid crimes;—these things plead much in her behalf. After all, it will be difficult to resist the

---

17. There has been a good deal of work recently critical of the conventional portrait of the battered wife. See Linda Gordon, *Heroes of Their Own Lives* (New York: Penguin, 1988); Donileen R. Loseke and Spencer E. Cahill, "The Social Construction of Deviance: Experts on Battered Women," *Social Problems* 31 (1984): 284; and Martha Mahoney, "Legal Images of Battered Women: Redefining the Issue of Separation," *Michigan Law Review* 90 (1991): 1–94.

conviction which will be excited in the course of these memoirs that Mrs. B. did truly err, in not having her husband brought to justice. The law is made for the lawless and disobedient. (72)

What both editors miss is Abigail Bailey's understanding of prayer as active and primary, and of legal rights as secondary and derivative. Both also assume that her prolonged passivity reflected a personal weakness, an absence, if you will, of personal identity and strength. Patience is for them (and probably for most of us) not much of a virtue.[18] For Bailey, by contrast, waiting for the moment when public action was requisite was essential for her moral identity. She could not act until she knew and understood God's will for her; yet, she recognized that God's will would not be revealed in easy fashion. She knew that she could learn what she ought to do about her husband only at the end of a long spiritual journey. And her memoirs are, in the first place, a detailed description of that journey.

The Submissive Self

> ... for all tame animals there is an advantage in being under human control, as this secures their survival. And as regards the relationship between male and female, the former is naturally superior, the latter inferior, the former rules and the latter is subject.
>
> —Aristotle, *Politics*

Abigail Bailey lived in the second half of the eighteenth century, a time unmarked by evidence of significant change in the legal status of married women. There is today a lively and unsettled debate among historians about whether women's lives altered during this era of political revolution.[19] And we are gradually coming to realize the degree of variation from jurisdiction to jurisdiction (both as colonies

---

18. See Jane Tompkins, *Sensational Designs: The Cultural Works of American Fiction* (New York: Oxford University Press, 1985).

19. See Mary Beth Norton, "The Evolution of White Women's Experience in Early America," *American Historical Review* 89 (1984): 593-619; Linda Kerber, *Women of the Republic* (Chapel Hill: University of North Carolina Press, 1980); Linda Kerber et al., "Forum: Beyond Roles, Beyond Spheres: Thinking about Gender in the Early Republic," *William and Mary Quarterly*, 3d ser., 46 (1989): 565-85.

and as states) in marital legal relations and property rights.[20] But Abigail Bailey ended her life a full generation before public challenges to the legal structure of wifely submission.[21] She, like all other American wives in every state, remained, in unquestioned legal theory, a woman in a state of coverture.[22]

For Abigail Bailey, as for other women of her time, marriage meant moving from the domain of her parents to that of her new husband, exchanging one dependence for another. "As, while I lived with my parents, I esteemed it my happiness to be in subjection to them; so now I thought it must be a still greater benefit to be under the aid of a judicious companion, who would rule his own house" (56). It would be a mistake to characterize that move as an alienation of the self, using alienation in either its legal or its psychoanalytic senses. Unlike nineteenth-century young women, who often viewed the transition to marriage as one involving an exchange of a life of freedom for one of bondage and separation, she did not describe her

---

20. Marylynn Salmon, *Women and the Law of Property in Early America* (Chapel Hill: University of North Carolina Press, 1986).

21. Voices sometimes regarded as rebellious, like the Abigail Adams of the "Remember the Ladies" letter, were fully ensconced within domestic identities. See Edith B. Gelles, "The Abigail Industry," *William and Mary Quarterly*, 3d ser., 45 (1988): 656–83. Early English feminists, like Mary Astell and Mary Wollstonecraft, took the power relations of marriage as given and unchangeable; instead of emphasizing the possibilities of legal or secular reform, they cautioned women against entering into marriages. See Ruth Perry, *The Celebrated Mary Astell, An Early English Feminist* (Chicago: University of Chicago Press, 1986); Bridget Hill, ed., *The First English Feminist: Reflections upon Marriage and Other Writings by Mary Astell* (New York: St. Martin's Press, 1986); and Mary Wollstonecraft, *A Vindication of the Rights of Woman* (1792; reprint, New York: Norton, 1967).

22. This is, of course, true, whether or not a wife had a separate estate protected by trustees and by the rules of equity. Today, legal historians typically treat coverture as nothing more than an earlier regime of marital property, one that disappeared sometime during the nineteenth century. I want, in a large project just beginning, to explore the extent to which coverture remained descriptive of general nineteenth-century (and, to a surprising extent, twentieth-century) political understandings about marriage, husband-wife relations, and domestic rights (including ostensibly personal rights). The reading I have done so far in a variety of corners of American domestic relations legal doctrine—custody law, criminal conversation cases, marital property cases, separation and divorce law—convinces me that through the nineteenth century the patriarchal symbols of coverture remained of central (although contested) significance. But that conviction remains both controversial and, I should add, subject to revision and reconsideration. That marriage in the late eighteenth century was, legally speaking, described by coverture is, by contrast, neither controversial nor interesting.

marriage as requiring the loss of a prior self.[23] Indeed, we might
better think of her as finding herself through her hierarchical relationships. She was, at least as she described herself in her memoir,
fulfilling her destiny, being true to her nature.

Although she longed for a relationship with her husband founded
on friendship, she soon learned that he would only intermittently
offer that. Yet, she insisted, she could be happy as his wife. God
had, she believed, given her "a heart to resolve never to be obstinate,
or disobedient" to her husband. Rather, she would "be always kind,
obedient, and obliging in all things not contrary to the word of God."
She thought, "[I]f Mr. B. were sometimes unreasonable, I would be
reasonable, and would rather suffer wrong than do wrong." She would
be so because it was her nature so to be. When he treated her badly,
as he did from the first, she hoped that it resulted "not from ill will,"
but "from the usual depravity of the human heart." She felt, during
a good period in their marriage, "the tenderest affection for him as
my head and husband. I ever rejoiced when he returned from abroad.
Nor did I see him come in from his daily business without sensible
delight. Much pleasure I took in waiting upon him, and in doing all
in my power to make him happy" (57–58, 66).[24]

Abigail Bailey's stated willingness to subsume her identity into
that of her husband, to live as a dependent within his household,
might seem to reflect the normative vision of common-law coverture.
She knew that she was "under his legal control," and that "he could
overrule all my plans as he pleased." She knew, as she told him in
one of their many conversations after the discovery of the incest, "I
well knew I had been placed under his lawful government and authority, and likewise under his care and protection. And most delightful
would it have been to me, to have been able quietly and safely to
remain there as long as I lived. Gladly would I have remained a kind
faithful, obedient wife to him, as I had even been" (77–78).

Her description of her marriage as a natural fate conforms, moreover, to the conventional legal understanding, as presented in an
eighteenth-century legal text, "that all Women, in the Eye of the Law,

---

23. See Ellen Rothman, *Hands and Hearts: A History of Courtship in America*
(Cambridge: Harvard University Press, 1984).

24. As one might expect, he was quite dependent on her in their daily lives.
He trusted her with his money and his property. And with "prudent management,"
she could sometimes keep him in "a pleasant mode" for weeks (65).

are either married or to be married; and their Desires are Subject to their Husbands."[25] Like other wives, her place within her husband's household, subject to his control and power, left her dependent on his honor and restraint.[26]

And yet, to connect Abigail Bailey with Mary Beard, marital submission did not mean a loss of personal identity, on the order of the apparent prescriptions of law and theology. Abigail Bailey may have been "covered" by her husband, according to common-law doctrine. The consequence of their marriage was not, however, that they became "one flesh" in anything other than the most formal legal sense. She knew herself as a distinct and separate child of God. Her identity and her ultimate interests always remained her own.

Her relationship with God was primary; her relationship with her husband never more than secondary. She implicitly but absolutely rejected the Pauline admonition: "He [the husband] [lives] for God; she for God in him."[27] Indeed, moments in the text when she longs for emotional connection with Asa Bailey are immediately followed by admonitions against the sin of idolatry. "On a certain day," for example, something she had said had infuriated him, leading him to abuse her verbally and then to leave the room. She grieved "to see him in so wicked a frame; and the more, as I had been (though without design) the cause of it. I mourned, and longed for his return, and for his friendship, as a hungry child longs for the breast." Yet,

---

25. *A Treatise of Feme Coverts: Or, The Lady's Law* (1732; South Hackensack, N.J.: Rothman Reprints, 1974), v.

26. As James Wilson said in law lectures delivered in the 1790s, while in "very pressing emergencies" it might be necessary for public authority to intervene in the relations of husband and wife, in general, "[t]he rights, the enjoyments, the obligations, and the infelicities of the matrimonial state" are removed from legal attention. Towards a married couple, the law "will not appear as an arbitress; but, like a candid and benevolent neighbour, will presume . . . all to be well." Instead of "municipal regulations," women would have to rely on "the influence of that legitimate honour, which we have described as the inseparable friend and companion of virtue." Robert Green McCloskey, ed., *The Works of James Wilson* (Cambridge: Harvard University Press, 1967), 1:599–602.

27. In her study, *Good Wives* (New York: Knopf, 1982), Laurel Ulrich writes that for seventeenth-century New England women, "Submission to God and submission to one's husband were part of the same religious duty" (6). For Abigail Bailey, by contrast, both submissions were religious duties, but they were certainly not the same religious duty. One would like to know whether the Pauline admonition was a part of the religious teachings of the late eighteenth century New England community in which Abigail Bailey lived, but I have been unable to find evidence on the question.

no sooner did she write this than she stopped and noted that she quickly "recollected, that in all my troubles, Christ was my hiding place." She, the memorialist, was telling the reader that she, the wife, was wrong to look to her husband for succor that only God could provide (68).

Rather than a woman transformed by marriage into a feme covert, we would do better to think of Abigail Bailey as a self "covered" by her husband during marriage.[28] Being covered by her husband, being submissive to him, was not a denial of her self. On the contrary, it constituted the central test of her self and of the strength of her religious identity. It is a mistake to think that marriage made a woman like Abigail Bailey into an absence of self, as nineteenth-century women's right advocates and law reformers argued.[29] For Abigail Bailey, by contrast, marriage was both destiny and achievement. "[I]t had ever been my greatest care and pleasure (among my earthly comforts) to obey and please him." What she called "the habit of obedience" was a learned and practiced habit, crucial to her because in it she would find her salvation. She had hoped, when she married, "to find a companion of meek, peaceable temper; a lover of truth; discreet and pleasant.... But the allwise God, who has made all things for himself, has a right, and knows how to govern all things for his own glory." It was, she quickly learned, "the sovereign pleasure" of that same "allwise God to try me with afflictions in that relation from which I had hoped to receive the greatest of my earthly comforts" (78, 69, 56–57).

Thinking of submission as a test helps to suggest some of the complexity in the eighteenth-century idea of a feme covert. To men, perhaps, coverture suggested simple merger and unity.[30] To Abigail Bailey and, presumably, to other women, it suggested the task for a lifetime, a way of establishing credentials as a worthy Christian. Coverture was hard work for the self. It was also necessary work for a self that would realize her own salvation through submission.[31]

28. See Alan Macfarlane, *Marriage and Love in England* (Oxford: Oxford University Press, 1986), for a similar claim.

29. See Beard, *Woman as Force*.

30. Mike Grossberg suggests in conversation that there was probably a more complex and religiously based male conception of the meaning of marriage, one tied to the idea of duties toward subordinates and of Christian charity to the weak and dependent. Such a conception might provide a measure against which she judged her husband's acts.

31. Greven points to the feminine and submissive quality of the saved Christian in evangelical discourses. See *Protestant Temperament*, 62–151.

To understand Abigail Bailey's legal identity, the reader must work through paragraph after paragraph in which she reflects on God's goodness in testing her through the affliction of her husband. It was God's wondrous way to make her life so miserable. When her friends and relatives told her that Asa was "a cunning, crafty man" who was likely to leave his family destitute if she did not take legal action against him, she replied that "there is a time to speak; and a time to keep silence, and that, at the present time, the latter was my duty" (111–12). Like Job, the difficulty of her situation came close to providing a measure of the strength and quality of her faith:

> The preacher says, "Surely oppression maketh a wise man mad." If so, what must become of me, a poor simple woman, under distressing oppression? But O, it is no matter of discouragement, though much matter of humility, to behold my own weakness, while God enables me by faith to behold at the same time his allsufficiency, and the fulness of grace in the Captain of our salvation. It is with inexpressible delight that I contemplate the power, wisdom, goodness and faithfulness of God; that he does regard his people; that he has a tender care for all his chosen in Christ. Now, "when I am weak, then am I strong." Even divine corrections are in love and faithfulness. "All things shall work together for good to them that love God." I see such safety in trusting in him, that though the earth be removed, such as confide in him need not fear. There is the greatest satisfaction in casting our burdens on such a God. Unworthy as I am, I am sure God careth for me. For it has been his supporting mercy, that has held me up under the trials I have endured, and has given me a patient resignation to the divine will, and a confidence in God of deliverance. (106–7)

And yet, the test God had given her was more difficult even than simply bearing up under the burdens of an oppressive husband. She knew that there would come a time when she must "henceforth look out, and take care of" herself, when she must rid herself of her husband, when the habit of obedience would no longer be a virtue (135). There was a time when the test of marital submission had been passed, to be replaced by a test of separation.

But when would that point occur? And how would she recognize it? And what kinds of actions would be appropriate? Her husband's oppression, as such, would never justify resistance and rebellion. Nor would his sinful conduct alone. All these were little else than the markers of God's wonderful (and totally inscrutable) plan for her. As she wrote, in describing her reaction to her first suspicions of her husband's incestuous behavior, "I saw that it was as much my duty to submit to God under one trial, as under another." How could she know when change was requisite and, more difficult yet, what forms of change would be obligatory in her legal and moral situation?

Those questions established the terms of her narrative of change and transformation.

The Story of Change

The Narrative

Abigail Bailey's memoirs tell of her marriage to Asa Bailey. They begin with her wedding in 1767. They end with her divorce in 1792.[32]

We might divide the narrative of what happened into the following six stages.

Premonitions

Although she did not expect her husband to be a religious man, she had hoped when she wed that "He would wish for good regulations in his family, and would have its external order accord with the word of God." But, she soon found that he was rash and frequently unreasonable, capable of hard and cruel treatment. Still, she worked at loving him and "confided in him, as my real friend" (57–58).

Three years into their marriage he had an affair with a serving girl working in their house in Landaff, New Hampshire. The girl was eventually sent away, but Abigail felt as if her "earthly joys were fled," and she "mourned the loss" of her husband (58). Yet, she kept her troubles to herself and, in effect, "condoned" the affair by staying with him.[33]

---

32. She covers her childhood in one paragraph, the first twenty-one years of her marriage in 13 pages, the next four years in 110 pages.

33. Condonation remained until the recent past a standard part of divorce and separation law and practice. It is defined as "[t]he conditional remission or forgiveness, by means of continuance or resumption of marital cohabitation, by one of the married parties, of a known matrimonial offense committed by the other, that would constitute a cause of divorce [or separation]; the condition being that the offense shall not be repeated" (Black's Law Dictionary).

She did, however, begin to "vent" her grief and "broken heart" by writing about her spiritual situation (58). In these writings she focused on man's depravity, on how those who should be friends often become the worst of enemies, and on how it was wrong to put one's trust in mankind.

Three years later, in 1773, her husband sexually assaulted another serving girl, who would eventually go before the local grand jury to charge him. When Abigail confronted him with what had happened, "Mr. B. . . . fell into a passion" with her. He was overcome with anger and took to his bed. She went out milking and while there tried in prayer to intercede on his behalf. She still believed he could be brought to repentance. She then returned to the house, where she was met by her husband, who told her that he had thought about killing her. But suddenly:

> [H]e had a most frightful view of himself. All his sins stared him in the face. All his wickedness, from his childhood to that hour, was presented to his mind, and appeared inexpressibly dreadful. All the terrors of the law, he said, pressed upon his soul.

He had cried out to God for mercy. And then, he said, he had experienced a sudden revelation of grace. She knew better than to believe that. But she continued to live in "peace and comfort" with her husband, "willing to forgive all that was past, if he might but behave well in future" (60–61).

Over the next fifteen years, they grew prosperous, and he became a leading citizen of the town, holding a variety of local offices.

Incest

In 1788, Asa Bailey took a trip to the West, through New York and perhaps to Ohio. He was gone for several weeks, and while he was gone, Abigail had several frightening dreams. He returned and proposed that they all should move west.

In December, he began to behave strangely. He told her again of his plan to move to Ohio, and he asked for her consent and the consent of the children. None of them were pleased with the idea, but all "wished to be obedient"; all agreed "to follow our head and guide, wherever he should think best, for our family had ever been in the habit of obedience" (68–69). He proposed to take one son and one daughter with him to help him and serve him while he looked for a place for them all to live, a plan quickly changed to one where he would only take the one daughter. Abigail later realized that all this had been just a ruse to get the daughter, Phoebe, alone with him. But at the time, none of this was apparent.

He began spending extra time with Phoebe, while avoiding his wife and other children. He would tell her stories and riddles and sing songs to her.

> He thus pursued a course of conduct, which had the most direct tendency to corrupt young and tender minds, and lead them the greatest distance from every serious subject. He would try to make his daughter tell stories with him; wishing to make her free and social, and to erase from her mind all that fear and reserve, which he had ever taught his children to feel toward him. (70)

Phoebe found all this uncomfortable and disagreeable. She tried to stay out of his way, to avoid him. "But as his will had ever been the law of the family, she saw no way to deliver herself from her cruel father" (71). She also did not dare talk to her mother, or to any other person, about her situation, for she knew that her father watched her constantly.

Soon, his conduct toward this daughter changed again. Instead of "idle songs, fawning and flattery," he would be angry with her, would punish her and beat her for imaginary infractions, would forbid her from doing anything with her mother or any of the other children. He would keep her confined in the house. His conduct became more and more violent. Sometimes he beat Phoebe with a "rod," sometimes with a "beach [sic] stick, large enough for the driving of a team"; sometimes he threatened to whip her to death, if she tried to run from him again. The daughter, who had always been "obedient to him in all lawful commands," was ashamed, would not look anyone in the face (72, 75–76).

Meanwhile, Abigail slowly had to admit to herself what she saw before her. This was, as she said, "so different" from anything that had happened before or that she might have expected. And she almost abandoned herself to grief. She did not, at first, see any way to stop the evil. Even when convinced of what was going on, she did not believe that she could testify in court against her own husband. She had no way of getting her daughter to confide in her, let alone testify against her father: "Fear, shame, youthful inexperience, and the terrible peculiarities of her case, all conspired to close her mouth against affording me, or any one, proper information" (75–76).

It is important to note that her grief was only to a limited extent for her daughter. Toward her daughter, she felt a mixture of resentment and pity: resentment that her daughter would not or could not speak up against her father, pity for someone who was, like herself, basically powerless. "How pitiful must be the case of a poor young female, to be subjected to such barbarous treatment by her own father; so that she knew of no way of redress!" Her husband's actions were, more importantly, an affliction that she, Abigail, had to withstand or survive. The nature of the affliction remains unclear. To some extent, the affliction was the pain and cruelty inflicted on Phoebe. But to a much greater extent, it was, I think, the revelation that she was the wife of such an evil and uncontrolled man, that she was part of his household and under his government. "It was not an enemy; then I could have borne it. Neither was it he that hated me in days past; for then I would have hid myself from him. But it was the man mine equal, my guide, my friend, my husband!" (73).

First Separation

While the assault on her daughter continued, Abigail Bailey was also pregnant (for at least the fifteenth time), and in September 1789 she gave birth to twins, one of whom died after seventeen days. Once her health returned, she decided to "adopt a new mode of treatment with Mr. B." She introduced the subject of incest and told him what she thought of his wicked conduct. She had waited until God would tell her that the right moment had come. Now it had, and she would do what she could to stop his "abominable wickedness and cruelties," for, if she didn't, she would be condoning his sins (77).

His response was to assert his legal power over her. "He wished to know whether I had considered how difficult it would be for me to do any such thing against him? as I was under his legal control; and he could overrule all my plans as I pleased." She answered that while she would gladly have remained his faithful and obedient wife for her life, he knew he had violated the covenant of their marriage and "hence had forfeited all legal and just right and authority over me" (77–78).

He quickly realized how bold and determined she was, and he became panic-stricken. He tried to flatter her into abandoning any plans she might have to begin a legal process. He took an oath of innocence, which disgusted her.

He asked her forgiveness, which she said she might grant if she had real evidence of reformation, but at the same time she insisted that she could never more live with him "in the most endearing relation" (79). He grew terrified at the idea of her seeking a separation. She told him that he had brought it on himself by his actions and that she regarded it as her duty to save her family from further moral destruction.

Then she thought again of the difficulties of proving the crimes she alleged against him, since Phoebe had not yet consented to testify. She gave him one last chance to reform.

But a few weeks later she received evidence that he had again assaulted his daughter. She confronted him and told him she would never believe him again. He offered to leave; he would move "to some distant country, where I should be troubled with him no more" (82). They did not need, he said, a formal legal separation. He would simply go.

Meanwhile, Phoebe turned eighteen and moved out of the house. She remained for a time unwilling to testify agianst her father. But Abigail would eventually hear more evidence of his conduct toward Phoebe from another daughter, and soon thereafter Phoebe agreed to talk to her.

Abigail fasted and prayed. Gradually, she came to the settled conviction that she should seek a separation from her husband. But should he also be turned over to criminal justice? Doing the latter looked to her to be "inexpressibly painful" (87). She convinced herself that if he would do the right thing by her and their children, relative to their property, and if he would go far away, she should not have to prosecute him.

She told him her resolution. "I informed him, I now could see no better way for him than this; that I had rather see him gone forever, than to see him brought to trial, and have the law executed upon him, to the torture of myself and family; as it would be, unless

he prevented it by flight" (88). She proposed that he should sell a
one-hundred-acre farm he owned and that he should take the proceeds
of that sale for himself, leaving the rest for her and the children. She
then packed his belongings, including in his saddlebags some letters—
exhortations directed to his spiritual salvation—to read on his way.
One of these described how his conduct had probably brought on
an eternal separation between them. She closed the letter describing
herself as his "afflicted and forever deserted wife" (92).

He then left on 8 September 1790.

Second and Third Separations

After he left, she tried to keep the cause of his going a secret, but
she soon learned that others in the community already knew of his
conduct. She told the children "that they must no longer expect to
derive the least advantage from being known as the children of Major
Bailey" (95).

Five weeks later, he returned. He worked hard to convince her
to take him back, to convince her of his moral reformation. He had
had no peace of mind while on the road. He was constantly tormented
by the sight of other men with their wives and children. She was
hurt at seeing him so broken, felt compassion for his situation, and
began to weaken. He played on her fear of taking full responsibility
over their family.

In the end, though, she did not believe in his penitence. His
situation must, she said to him, be distressing. "For a man of such
a temper, such a disposition, who had ever felt so important, so
wilful, and haughty, and so unwilling to acknowledge any wrong;—
for him now to be upon his knees, upon his face, and begging of
me to put my feet upon his neck; appeared like a strange turn of
things." She agreed with him that the family needed "a head, a kind
friend, a comforter, a guide, to protect us from the thousand evils,
to which we were exposed." Yet she still insisted on a separation and
a property division. Without the latter, she worried that he would
retain the power "to injure and distress us" (97–99).

He again prepared to leave. But before he did, the selectmen of
Landaff came one day to talk with him. He tried to avoid them and
escape the shame of talking with them about his situation. But they

found him, and he confessed to them that his conduct had been bad,
and he promised them that he would leave his family well provided.

He left again.

When he returned several months later, he was no longer humble
or penitent. His attention was focused on their property and on the
property division. Although he said he would stay only for a few
days, he stayed longer. He proposed one plan of division after another.
Sometimes he would tell Abigail to forget the past. Sometimes he
would call her "stubborn and rebellious" (103). He warned that if
she ever went to complain to the selectmen, he would kill everybody.
He worried that she prayed for his damnation, clearly frightened of
her religious authority.

In fact, she was still unwilling to begin a legal process against
him. (She was also pregnant again.)[34] And finally, he agreed to a
fifty-fifty split of his property. They would sell all the land and divide
the proceeds.

His property was put into the hands of his brother, who, she
thought, was ordered to sell it. Asa departed, taking two of their
sons with him to work for him. One of the sons was later left to
work as a hired man on a farm nearby in Hartford, Vermont. The
other went with his father to New York, where he too was hired out
to a farmer.

She heard nothing from her husband or son for eight months,
until one day a man named Ludlow, a lawyer, appeared to tell her
that Asa was living in Whitestown, New York. Ludlow was sent by
her husband to buy his property, to exchange it for "wild land" in
New York. She refused to consent to the transaction.[35] Ludlow tried
to convince her to reconcile with her husband. He had evidently been
told something of their situation by her husband, but not enough.
He told her that if she did not reconcile she was in danger of losing
her interest in the family property. She replied: "I told him, he could
talk very fast, and make things seem smooth, and fair:—But his talk
was in vain" (112–13). And, after talking to some of her neighbors,
Ludlow relinquished his goal of bringing about a reconciliation.

---

34. Nancy Hartog thinks I should be able to explain why she let herself become
pregnant again at this late date in their negotiations. I can't.

35. Assuming that the land was in fact land owned by Asa, its sale would still
require the consent of Abigail to release her dower rights in the property.

Journey to New York

Soon thereafter, in the winter of 1792, her husband came to Newbury, Vermont, across the Connecticut River from Landaff. He was unwilling to come to Landaff (perhaps for fear of legal process). She went over to meet with him to settle their affairs. They talked for several days, trading the Landaff farm for one in Bradford, Vermont, which would be easier to sell.

He then told her that a Captain Gould in Granville, New York, would give them five hundred pounds for the Bradford farm, but they needed to reach him before spring in order to close the transaction. She must come along, because her signature would be necessary, presumably in order to release her dower rights. She did not wish to go, since she would have to leave eight young children behind, but she saw no other way to conclude the business between them.

The trip to New York, alone with her husband, was a terrifying experience. As they went along, she became more and more convinced that the trip was all a trick. Yet, according to the memoirs, she remained passive and obedient. He continued to deny any bad motive, but on the fifth day of their trip, he stated "that if he had been so crafty as to lead me from home, as he had done, to answer his own worldly purposes, he could not be to blame for so doing" (123). The next day, after they had crossed into New York, he admitted that he was not selling his property to any Captain Gould. His sole purpose was to get her into that state, whose laws are "more suitable to govern such women as you," away from her relatives and friends, where he could bring her to more advantageous terms. "And now, if I would drop all that was past, and concerning which I had made so much noise, and would promise never to make any more rout about any of those things; and to be a kind and obedient wife to him, without any more ado; it was well!" (124). If not, he might carry her on to the Ohio, or take her among the Dutch, where she would not understand the language, or to Albany, where he might sell her on board of a ship. She would never go home again, he assured her. But if she should escape and get home, he would empower his brother to keep all property out of her hands and to advertise in his name that she should not be trusted with the purchase of any necessaries on his credit. No one could harbor or trust her.

Later, when she pleaded to be allowed to return to her children, he told her that she too was tarred by the same brush as he. What crime had she committed, she asked. "He replied that he understood my fault was, in being too favorable to him, after it was believed he had committed such abominable crimes" (136). She replied that even if it were true that that was how people felt, she would never run from them.

They traveled on, she now thinking of herself as his captive and of him as her enemy. They reached Whitestown, where there was smallpox. She decided that she had better have herself inoculated. They lived in a dirt hovel, where she became quite ill and weak.

The Return

He had told her that he would leave her in Whitestown, return to New Hampshire, settle their property relations, and pack up the children who would be brought to New York. She was convinced that he meant to disperse the children into other households, not to bring them to her. She was also desperately worried about their condition, as they had been left basically on their own. She began to plan her escape. She had never before ridden anywhere unaccompanied. Now, she would have to travel 270 miles alone.

Her husband left Whitestown on 9 May 1792, about two months after they had first left Landaff. A few days later, she left, even though she was still quite weak. Everything was new and hard for her. She had, for example, to stay in a tavern by herself. But every day she got stronger. On 30 May, she crossed the North River (the Hudson), "not as a captive, or in fear of falling through the ice, as when I came over it before. I well remembered the wormwood and the gall, when I was dragged over it by the man who vaunted over me, and seemed to rejoice in the imagination, that no power could take me out of his hands." As she traveled, she was struck by how different everything appeared when she had been dragged along with her husband four months earlier. "Now God smiled upon me. His providence smiled. And all his works and creatures seemed to smile" (166).

She reached the Connecticut River, only a few days behind her husband. She crossed over on a Saturday with her brothers and found her children well and still together, as well as her husband. He was, needless to say, shaken and tried to talk with her alone. She turned to return across the river. He asked if she did not mean to stay with her children. She said she could not. He tried to forbid her brothers from harboring her without his permission, but they all ignored him.

In Newbury, she swore the peace against her husband before a justice of the peace, who issued a writ to have Asa Bailey arrested on Monday.[36]

Over the weekend, Asa made plans to pack the children off to New York. On Monday he was arrested (a "solemn sight," to see "the husband of my youth, whom I had tenderly loved, as my companion, in years past, now a prisoner of civil justice" [173]), but before he was taken into custody, he told a confederate to put the children in a cart and to drive on as fast as he could. She and her brothers went immediately to an attorney, who told them that he knew of no authority by which she could take the children back. "The law had given a man a right to move his children where he should think best and the wife had no right by law to take them from him" (174). But, he added, no law kept her from trying to frighten her husband's confederate.

Abigail wrote a note to the man, telling him that he might expect serious trouble, if he did not return the children. Her brother rode after the cart, gave the confederate the note, and told him that no one would wish to harm him if he would comply with the note immediately. And the children were "released from captivity" (174–75).

The final negotiations between Asa and Abigail Bailey were prolonged. He sat in the local jail. She and her brothers had decided that if he would come to an honorable settlement, they would rather he would simply go. And so they put off the court hearing, while trying to get him to come to terms.

Still, he procrastinated and resisted. He still did not want a formal legal separation, insisting that it was "costly to settle in law" and trying to get her to agree to an informal separation. He still relied on her "tender feelings," believing that they would "set him at liberty" (176).

---

36. Typically, such writs required the defendant to post a bond as security to require him to maintain the "peace," and to protect the complainant from any further violence or abuse. See generally, Hendrik Hartog, "The Public Law of a County Court: Judicial Government in Eighteenth Century Massachusetts," *American Journal of Legal History* 20 (1976): 282–329.

Finally, she and her brothers decided to take him to New Hampshire, across the river, and have him indicted for incest, a capital crime. He broke down, and he quickly came to terms. They divided the property. He relinquished his rights over all the children, except for the three oldest sons. He first insisted on retaining custody over all the sons but relented when the younger ones cried for their mother. He left with the three sons.

Abigail petitioned for a divorce, which was quickly granted.

The Uses of Law

The Law of Separation

Reduced to its barest legal essentials, Abigail Bailey's memoirs appear to tell a very modern story. Mr. and Mrs. Bailey married; they divorced. As it is for many modern couples, periods of separation provided a necessary, but nearly inevitable, transition toward the divorce, which was the final (and relatively complete) conclusion of the marriage.

And yet, that rendition is, of course, not the legal story of Abigail and Asa Bailey, for it misses entirely the contextual significance of the legal choices they made and unmade. In particular, it misunderstands the struggle over separation that lay at the heart of the narrative of their marriage. Abigail Bailey worked to separate herself from her husband. That the story ends with her divorce is an unexplained and perhaps accidental conclusion to the narrative.[37]

---

37. Her divorce petition is transcribed in Taves's footnotes (197). In 1791, the New Hampshire legislature passed a statute granting both husbands and wives the right to seek divorces from the Superior Court of Judicature for incest, bigamy, adultery, abandonment for three years, and/or extreme cruelty. *Laws of New Hampshire*, chap. 94, 732–33. Abigail's petition, recorded in May 1793, alleged that Asa had repeatedly committed adultery, had abused her, and had abandoned her for more than two years ("and hath utterly forsaken her and neglected and refused in any wise to perform the duties of a husband unto her"). It is odd and unclear why she raised the issue of abandonment. First of all, only a three-year abandonment would do under the statute. Secondly, it is hard to see that he had utterly forsaken her even for two years, given that he had left her only in June of 1792. Thirdly, before he left he had made a property settlement with her, leaving her hardly in the position of the neglected or forsaken woman. Perhaps the allegation was meant simply to indicate the aggravated quality of the adultery and the abuse. More likely, the language was largely formulaic.

To us, separation is a transition between marriage and divorce. It comes into being in order to be resolved by divorce, although occasionally couples return to each other instead of divorcing. But basically a man and woman once married (and both living) are either still married or are divorced from each other.

In the legal world of Abigail Bailey, by contrast, separation would have been understood as a more or less permanent condition,[38] and a permanent separation was what she aspired to. In the absence of her husband's extraordinary conduct in kidnapping her, nothing would have driven her toward divorce. Yet English and American judges rhetorically despised separation. To them, this condition appeared anomalous, creating the "undefined and dangerous position of a wife without a husband and a husband without a wife."[39] But it was also a condition that described the marital situation of an extraordinarily large number of Americans in the eighteenth and nineteenth centuries. Some few Americans obtained divorces in eighteenth-century America.[40] A far larger number would live lives separated from their spouses.

---

38. An exception to the notion of its permanence: in colonial Connecticut and Massachusetts, if one's spouse had disappeared long enough to be declared legally dead—usually seven years—one could get a full divorce and marry again. After 1791, it was theoretically possible to seek a divorce for abandonment after three years in New Hampshire. But see Mary F—— v. Samuel F——, 1 N.H.298 (1818), where the New Hampshire court denied a divorce sought by a woman whose husband had "absented himself from her for the space of three years together, without making suitable provision for her support and maintenance," since it did not appear that he had the financial ability to make any provision for her because he was a poor man. See generally, Salmon, *Women and the Law of Property*, 58–80; and Cott, "Divorce and the Changing Status of Women," 586–614. In New York, by contrast, bigamy was the only choice, since only proof of adultery would give the court discretion to order a divorce. Abandonment was never enough. See Williamson v. Williamson, 1 Johns. Ch. 488 (1815).

39. This sentence was repeated by judge after judge and in numerous treatises in England and in America. It is usually ascribed to Lord Kenyon. See Hendrik Hartog, "Marital Exits and Marital Expectations in Nineteenth Century America," *Georgetown Law Journal* 80 (October 1991): 95–129.

40. There is a robust historical literature on divorce in early America, a literature that is largely an artifact of the relative availability of records. See sources collected in Salmon, *Women and the Law of Property*, 209. By contrast, little attention has been paid to separation. According to Taves, only eleven petitions for divorce were granted by the Grafton County Superior Court (the county court of Landaff, New Hampshire) between 1786 and 1800 (43–44). Between 1766 and 1784, divorces were the responsibility of the General Court, the legislature of the province. Over that eighteen-year period, eighteen divorces were granted for the whole province. If today

What was separation? Let me try to give a very preliminary sketch.[41] It was, in the first place, a condition of daily life, a situation. One lived life in the awkward condition of a wife without a husband or a husband without a wife. This situation of daily life carried with it legal consequences, in terms of the capacities of both husband and wife to carry on a variety of legal transactions—buying, selling, borrowing, inheriting, remarrying, fornicating, disciplining children, among others. But this situation of daily life also carried with it the core consequence that one was still a husband or a wife, even though separated from one's mate. Separations occurred within, although at the boundaries of, marriage and coverture.

The quasi-legal category of separation incorporated three linked legal categories: a divorce à mensa et thoro (otherwise known as a judicially ordered limited divorce), a separation shaped by an equitably enforceable separate maintenance agreement, and a variety of "informal" separations—including abandonment and bigamy—some framed by an unenforceable written agreement, some not.[42]

---

we typically make separation a function of divorce, in the eighteenth century it may be that divorce was a subset of separation. Many separated; some few of those who did would eventually get a divorce. Of the eighteen successful divorces in New Hampshire between 1766 and 1784, ten involved separations of more than seven years duration. See *Laws of New Hampshire*, vol. 3, 376, 554–55, 584, and *Laws of New Hampshire*, vol. 4, 145, 220–21, 225, 245, 297, 352, 361, 366, 425, 426, 462, 463, 490, 511, 531–32.

41. I am writing here in summary terms about conditions and categories that appear to me to have been continuous from roughly the mid–eighteenth century to the 1840s in both England and in the northern colonies (states) of America. See generally, Salmon, *Women and the Law of Property*, who properly emphasizes the differences between the various American jurisdictions.

42. A limited divorce would allow the wife to live alone. Where the husband was named as the guilty party, as was usually the case, the court order would also order an alimony and maintenance award, would allow the wife to regain control of property she had brought to the marriage, might free the husband from his obligation to provide for her necessaries, might, occasionally, give her custody over her children, but would not give either party the right to remarry. Such a court order required proof of conduct—of adultery or of abuse or, in New England at least, of abandonment—as would make it (morally or physically) unsafe for the wife to remain "within" the husband's household. The trial that preceded such a court order had much of the flavor of a criminal proceeding, requiring a proof of guilt. It was, in this regard, indistinguishable from an action for a full divorce. See Van Veghten v. Van Veghten, 4 Johns. Ch. 501 (1820); Haviland v. Myers, 6 Johns. Ch. 25, 178 (1822); Codd v. Codd, 2 Johns. Ch. 141 (1816); Barrere v. Barrere, 4 Johns. Ch. 187 (1819).

The terms of a separate maintenance agreement between husband and wife could incorporate any or all of the terms of a judicially ordered limited divorce, but it was

The boundaries between these legal categories were fuzzy. Indeed, it may be that they are better seen as a continuum of remedies ranging from limited divorce at the formal side, through a variety of enforceable voluntary separations in the middle, to simple and unremedied abandonment on the informal side. An informal separation was often simply an unenforceable formal separation. The covenants contained within a formal separate maintenance agreement—covenants granting a wife control of her separate property under the supervision of trustees, or ones allowing her custody of her children, or ones freeing the husband from any liability for her future support, for example—might be enforceable in equity, if they did not violate some moral norm. But nearly all formal separate maintenance agreements were unenforceable as separation agreements, as agreements to live apart, for courts would not enforce an immoral agreement to live outside of the bonds of matrimony, except in those limited circumstances when one of the parties might have been anyway entitled to a divorce (limited or full).

In one sense, there were as many forms of separation as there were separations by husbands and wives. Unlike divorce, whose form was determined by legislative enactment, couples created their own separations. But they did so using a conceptual and a moral vocabulary shaped and limited by legal practices and expectations.

---

never certain which, if any, of those terms would actually be enforceable in court. These agreements, both in England and in the various American jurisdictions, were the stuff of continuing doctrinal conflict throughout the eighteenth century (and continuing on into the nineteenth century). Courts—both in equity and at common law—rejected the notion that a married couple should be free to construct their own "private" marital arrangements. Yet those same courts found ways of enforcing some of those private arrangements. See Joseph Story, *Commentaries on Equity Jurisprudence, as Administered in England and America* (Boston, 1836), vol. 2; James Kent, *Commentaries on American Law* (New York, 1827), vol. 2, lectures 26, 27, 28; John Joseph Powell, *Essay upon the Law of Contracts and Agreements* (Dublin, 1790); and James Clancy, *A Treatise of the Rights, Duties and Liabilities of Husband and Wife, at Law and in Equity*, 2d American ed., from the last London edition (New York, 1837). See also Salmon, *Women and the Law of Property*.

Informal separations occurred by definition outside of the law. Couples parted, sometimes with an (unenforceable) agreement; husbands abandoned wives; wives deserted husbands. These partings could not be ratified by the law. Yet, courts dealt constantly with the consequences of desertions, as well as with those resulting from more consensual separations. They dealt with those consequences in actions for necessaries against husbands by merchants who sold goods to separated wives, in actions by town selectmen against husbands to remove ("warn out") abandoned wives from their towns before they became public charges, and in conflicts over marital property—including dower rights—between separated spouses.

More importantly, the categories and the situation of separation stood in an unstable relation with the categories and the situation of marriage (and of divorce). Separation, as a general category, often shared features of divorce. A separation might have been founded variously on the agreement of the parties to live apart, or the abandonment of one of the parties, or the decision of a court to allow one to live apart from the other. But an enforceable agreement to separate, as well as a court-ordered separation, required proof that one of the two spouses had breached a fundamental marital obligation. "Guilt" was central to legal separation. Adultery was, of course, the paradigm case for separations as well as for divorce. Both situations required a demonstration of guilt.[43] It probably did not matter very much, therefore, whether Abigail Bailey "ended" her marriage with a formal separation or with a divorce. Either way, Asa would be identified as the guilty party, and the nature of his guilt would be publicly revealed.

On the other side, how to distinguish separations founded on economic necessity or economic opportunity or military service from separations founded on marital breach? How to distinguish the man who went to sea for two years and more in order to earn a living from the man who abandoned his wife and children in the wake of his (or her) adultery? All separations remained legal marriages; some separations were not "separations" at all in any legal sense. Asa Bailey went west in 1788, leaving his family for several months. Two years later he went west because his wife no longer would live with him. He and she knew that the two separations were different, but one can well imagine Asa's desire to maintain the public illusion of an "informal" separation.

A marriage was, of course, more than merely a relationship for life. Although both Puritan religious thought and legal theory declared that marriage was a civil contract, there was another aspirational vision that competed with the formal contractual understanding. Marriage promised the permanent union of two souls. Through eternity. Did a separation that ratified a temporal breach in the unity of husband and wife also breach their eternal unity? Perhaps, but perhaps not. They were, after all, still married. When Abigail Bailey described Asa's conduct as having possibly brought on an "eternal

---

43. See Mary F——— v. Samuel F———, 1 N.H.298 (1818)

separation" and described herself as "forever deserted," we should understand these as literal images, ones that suggest the serious consequences of separation. But these images also tell us something of the uncertain relationship between marriage and separation. On the one hand, their separation did not end their eternal relationship; on the other hand, his conduct might have (presumably because he was going to hell, while she had hopes of a better future). Because of their presumptively eternal relationship, moreover, she had to separate from him or risk being implicated in his own sinful conduct, which would result in her own eternal damnation (90–91).

Separation did not mean legally that husband and wife were generally released from the bonds of matrimony. Particular agreements that allowed a wife, for example, to live apart and keep her own wages or income, or that substituted a property settlement, as in the Bailey's case, for the husband's general obligation to support his wife, might be enforceable by a court of equity. But in the absence of such agreements all marital obligations continued.

At the same time, all marital obligations were framed by images of reciprocity. If a wife disobediently left the care of her husband, separated without cause, all he had to do was advertise that fact in local newspapers and he would be absolved of any obligation to provide for her support. Merchants would be placed on notice that if they "trusted" her and allowed her to purchase her necessaries on his credit, they would not be able to recover from him. This is, of course, what Asa threatened Abigail with when she protested her captivity with him in New York. Conversely, if Abigail had good cause for her separation (as she had), or if he was responsible for the separation (or, in other cases, for the failure of efforts to reconcile), his duty of support, his responsibility for her necessaries, would have continued (or revived), whether or not he advertised. Abigail might not have known it at the time that he threatened her, but in fact he had no legal grounds to threaten her with. She could probably have continued to rely on her husband's credit, even if they were not living together.

A wife's duty to obey and to accept her husband's continuing authority over her life was conditioned on his good conduct as a ruler.[44] In that sense, Asa's misconduct gave Abigail an immediate

---

44. This is, of course, the subtext of Kate's famous last speech in the *Taming*

right to live apart from him. Indeed, she had a legal, as well as a moral, obligation to act immediately on that right. Otherwise, she would be condoning his conduct, as she had with his earlier infidelities. Condonation would deprive her of the right to separate, since she would be legally implicated in his conduct.[45] On the other hand, an immediate legal separation would provide a public notice of his misconduct, and of her moral separation from his sin.

And yet, to raise the obvious tension lurking in the early American law of separation, misconduct by one spouse did not necessarily free the other from the moral or legal bonds of matrimony. The indissolubility of marriage was a serious commitment and an organizing understanding for marriages in early America. Marital unity meant that one's moral identity was intertwined with that of the other. One took the spouse as he or she was, for better and worse. Conflict was an expected and accepted part of the relationship, not an opportunity for termination of the relationship. Of course the law did not require you to commit physical or moral suicide—to accept abuse or treatment that endangered you or your children or that put you in a position of public disgrace. But knowing when separation was proper and called for remained a tricky business.

The Law in Separation

From a slightly anachronistic perspective, we can imagine Abigail Bailey's narrative as incorporating six negotiating sessions over the

---

of the Shrew:

> Thy husband is thy lord, thy life, thy keeper,
> Thy head, thy sovereign; one that cares for thee,
> And for thy maintenance commits his body
> To painful labour both by sea and land,
> To watch the night in storms, the day in cold,
> Whilst thou liest warm at home, secure and safe
> And craves no other tribute at thy hands
> But love, fair looks and true obedience
> Too little payment for so great a debt.
> Such duty as the subject owes the prince
> Even such a woman oweth to her husband;
> And when she is froward, peevish, sullen, sour,
> And not obedient to his honest will,
> What is she but a foul contending rebel,
> And graceless traitor to her loving lord?

(act 5, scene 2)

45. Thus, Asa's statement to her, while they were on their way to Whitestown, New York, that she was believed to be at fault "in being too favorable to him," suggests the close links between community sentiments and the legal rules of coverture and separation (136).

necessity for and the terms of separation with Asa. The first two sessions occurred in the approximately nine months between September 1789 and late spring 1790, when he was first confronted with her knowledge of his conduct. The third occurred when he returned from his first separation, the fourth when he returned after his second separation, the fifth when she crossed the Connecticut River to talk with him in Newbury, and the sixth while he sat in jail after their separate returns from New York. In these sessions, what was the law that they bargained in the shadow of, to use the modern image?[46] How did the complex and contradictory "law" of separation sketched in the last few pages shape the negotiating strategies of Asa and Abigail Bailey? How much did they know of this law?

To begin with an answer to the last question, they knew some things, certainly, about the law of separation.[47] Both clearly understood that Abigail had a "right" to a separation based on Asa's conduct. When, after the birth of her twins, Abigail first told Asa that she would no longer tolerate his conduct within the family, he tried, as we have seen, to assert his legal power over her—arguing that she was "under his legal control," and that he could overrule her plans "as he pleased." Her response was that because of his violation of the marriage covenant he had "forfeited all legal and just right and authority" over her. "You," she said to her husband, "have done all in your power to bring about such a separation, and to ruin and destroy our family. And I meet it as my duty now to do all in my power to save them from further destruction." Thus, her actions were founded on "principle" (77–79). He apparently must have agreed with her, for from then on, he never challenged her legal right to separate. He intimidated her; he played to her fears of managing a family alone and her longstanding identity as a married woman; he tried to convince her of the high cost of seeking a formal separation; he worked to make her feel implicated in his conduct; he worried her about difficulties of proof; he threatened her with the loss of her children; he asserted his repentance. He knew, however, that she had

---

46. See Robert Mnookin and Robert Kornhauser, "Bargaining in the Shadow of the Law: The Case of Divorce," *Yale Law Journal* 88 (1979): 950–97; for use by a historian of the image, see Michael Grossberg, "Drawing Lines: The d'Hautville Case and the Creation of a Feminine Sphere in Nineteenth-Century American Law" (manuscript, 1988).

47. How specifically they came by that knowledge I cannot say. I am assuming that their knowledge represented common sense or conventional wisdom that would have been available (and part of the normative universe) of many rural Americans living in the late eighteenth century.

a legal right to live outside of his control and authority, in the wake of his immoral and illegal conduct.

More than just the possessor of a right, Abigail grew to understand she had a duty to make a final separation from Asa in the months that followed the conversation described in the last paragraph. In that early conversation, she had declared that she could no longer live with him "in the most endearing relation," that she no longer "*could, or ought* to do it!" (79). But in the end, she gave him one more chance. When, however, she received renewed evidence of incest a few months later, she made it clear to him that they should never live together again. And then, following a period of prayer and reflection, she came to the "settled conviction" that she "ought to seek a separation" from her "wicked husband." After talking to Phoebe, she told Asa of her resolution: "He asked me, what I intended to do? I replied, that one thing was settled: I would *never live with him any more!*" His anguish in response to this statement moved her, but she realized the need for "christian fortitude" and for being "firm in pursuing my duty." She was "determined to put on firmness, and go through with the most interesting and undesirable business, to which God, in his providence, had called me, and which I had undertaken" (86–89). Until now, her husband had rejected all her religious and moral counsel, but now he would have to listen.

And so, she told him, she would rather that he left immediately, without any public trial or proceedings, so long as he no longer afflicted any in the family. He should take a horse and enough property "to make him comfortable." (At this point, she had obviously not thought about the fact that an informal separation would leave her without any control over the property remaining.) She hoped he would repent and reform, and she wished him well "and so much peace as was consistent with the holy and wise purposes of God." But it is clear that under no circumstances was she willing to live with him again (86–89).

From this moment on in the late spring of 1790 until the end of the narrative, 2½ years later, when Asa had left, and she was about to get a divorce, her settled conviction never wavered. She did not change. It was, rather, Asa's increasingly desperate and erratic responses to that conviction, his unsuccessful efforts to regain control over his wife, that shaped the story of the end of their marriage.

The question, then, of when she became autonomous, a separate individual, no longer "covered" by her husband, is quite complicated and difficult. Many of us retain a Protestant vision of how change occurs, that there must be a moment when the earth shook, when truth filled the soul, when an inner light glowed. And all was suddenly changed. Abigail Bailey's memoirs make it apparent that there was no such moment in her life with her husband. There were no radical discontinuities, no sudden moments of transformation. She did not, all of a sudden, come to a realization of her rights as a married woman, that she did not have to put up with his sexual abuse of her daughter, or with the other actions of this violent man. She always knew she had those rights, although her husband often tried to threaten her with visions of his unilateral authority. She understood that it was "no small thing for a husband and wife to part, and their family of children to be broken up; that such a separation could not be rendered expedient or lawful, without great sin indeed: and that I would not be the cause of it, and of breaking up our family, for *all the world*" (79). But that cost was one she was willing to assume, given what he had done.

On the other hand, she did not realize how resistant her husband would be. For too long, she assumed that he would eventually come to an appreciation of his own sinfulness, his own evil, and withdraw. She implicitly believed (fantasized?) that the decision to separate would be a decision they could come to together, a shared understanding, based on what he would learn from her that he needed to do. In a sense, the decision to separate would be a decision to live (apart, not together) in a different marital relationship. She assumed— in common with much legal doctrine—that separation was intertwined with their marriage, not an end to their marriage. And that was her great mistake.

For Abigail Bailey, knowing when one had a right or even a duty to separate from one's husband was not the same thing as knowing when one ought to invoke legal power as support for the former decision. The first came easily; the latter awaited her discovery of her husband as her unambiguous enemy.

In their negotiations, Abigail and Asa made a variety of assumptions about separation law. Some of them conformed to doctrinal statements of that law; some did not. My goal is not, however, to line up their understanding of separation with the law of separation as expounded in case law and treatises. It is, rather, to explore their commonsense understanding of law both as constraint and as tactical weapon. They constantly referred to law as an external force shaping their conduct. Yet the legal shadow within which they bargained was in large part the product of their own interpretations, interpretations constructed out of mixed images of legal and religious and local authority, as well as of structures of formal law.[48]

Neither of them, for example, knew or cared much about the differing legal categories of separation. Both, by contrast, saw a sharp and important practical distinction between a formal and an informal separation, between one involving a public statement of grounds and legally enforceable remedies and one in which the two of them simply parted, perhaps with a property settlement. Asa continually pressed her to accept an informal separation. When she first told him that she would no longer live with him, he replied that she "need not be at any trouble to obtain a legal separation. For he would depart to some distant country, where I should be troubled with him no more" (82). At the very end of the story, while he sat in the jail, he again worked on her "tender feelings," to convince her to come to an informal agreement:

> He said it was costly settling differences in the law. That our interest was now wasting as dew before the sun; and our poor little innocent children must suffer for our folly. That if I would be persuaded to take this matter out of the law, he would do what was fully right; and our friends might assist in the settlement, as well as the court. That it would hence be much better for our family to have it taken out of the law. (176)

We can imagine that for Asa an informal separation represented a way of blurring the line between a parting caused by his immoral conduct and the sorts of separations that occurred regularly—and more or less innocently—between couples, when jobs or military service or lack of love drove them apart.[49] The meaning of the sep-

---

48. In a recent study of divorce cases in Madison, Wisconsin, Howard Erlanger, Elizabeth Chambliss, and Marigold Melli describe the image of what they found as being "law in the shadow of bargaining." See "Participation and Flexibility in Informal Processes: Cautions from the Divorce Context," *Law and Society Review* 23 (1987): 585–604.

49. This statement, while accurate as an image, is formally anachronistic, because lack of love would never have been a proper explanation for separation in early America.

aration—the reasons that he and Abigail would find themselves in the awkward position of separated spouses—could remain ambiguous and private. Such a separation would, moreover, leave him with the option of publicly regarding himself as a husband and also with the possibility of later reinserting himself back into the family.

Abigail had her own reasons for preferring an informal separation, for not invoking a process that would have brought Asa's domestic conduct into public view. She wished only "for an equitable adjustment of our affairs of interest; and then for Mr. B. to be gone." She worried that she lacked sufficient evidence to bring legal charges against him. More importantly, she felt that suing him—making him "a monument of civil justice"—would be "inexpressibly painful," and she wanted to spare herself "the dreadful scene of prosecuting my husband" (87). Reading slightly between the lines, one senses her own feelings of being implicated in the failure of the marriage. She too would be shamed in a public process.

She assumed wrongly that the unexercised but continuing threat of public exposure would force him to make an adequate property settlement, so that she and their children would be supported. And that would be enough. She believed that with such a settlement, he would lose the power "to injure and distress" her and her children (103, 86–88, 100). She must have assumed that a property division between husband and wife would be legal and enforceable if the two agreed. In fact (meaning, in formal law), absent a transfer to trustees, such a division—even one voluntarily arrived at—was patently unlawful. Given the unity of husband and wife under coverture, a husband would only be giving property to himself, an act he could undo at will. Moreover, she evidently did not understand until the very end that a simple parting, even with a property division, would not change any of the terms of the marital relation. For too long she did not worry about the fact that she would still be formally under his legal control and power, even if they lived 270 miles apart. Perhaps she believed that shame on his part, combined with the support of her friends and relatives in the local community, would prevent him from daring to exercise any of his continuing legal rights.

One senses that for Abigail Bailey the best resolution of their marital situation would have been one that left her unchanged in her social position as a married woman, even as she rid herself of the presence of her husband. She was a wife, and she wished to retain her identity as one, even as she demanded a separation.[50] Thus it makes sense that she, like her husband, at first hoped for an informal separation. What she learned from her trip to New York was how degraded her position as a married woman had become, how little social value that identity provided. Thus, on her return she had grown willing to sue out articles of the peace against her husband, to make him the subject of a public process, and she had become insistent on the need for a more formal separation.

Legal concepts and ideas played three different but overlapping roles in their negotiations: as organizing assumptions, as background threats, and as overt tactical tools. We have already seen instances of the first two roles. The distinction between formal and informal separations was an organizing assumption of their discussions. The usually unstated but always present possibility that Abigail would charge him publicly, either by suing for a formal separation, or by taking out articles of the peace against him, or by charging him with the crime of incest, exemplified the use of law as a background threat, as did Asa's implicit threat that he would disperse all of their children if she was anything but compliant in New York.

The overt tactical uses of legal images litter the narrative. Asa was clearly much more legally sophisticated than Abigail and continually used his knowledge tactically. Thus, the trip to New York; thus, also, his attempt in New York to convince her that she had waited too long to act, that she had implicitly condoned his conduct and had therefore lost her right to act alone. Asa's tactics were designed to make her believe that he knew the law and that the law gave him full and continuing power over her: that New York's laws gave him the right to make her live anywhere he chose, even to sell her to a ship if that were his pleasure, that he could advertise her as a runaway if she escaped him. When she confronted him after their separate returns to Landaff, he tried to reassert his control over his marriage by trying to keep her brothers from "harboring" her. Sometimes, as in the latter example, these tactical uses of legal power failed. Often, these tactical invocations of legal rights were fraudulent. No husband had the right to sell his wife onto a ship. Asa, in particular, did not have the right to advertise Abigail as a runaway and to refuse to pay for her necessaries if she escaped from his control.

---

50. See Hendrik Hartog, "Mrs. Packard on Dependency," *Yale Journal of Law and the Humanities*, 1 (1988): 79–103, for a description of a nineteenth-century version of the right to be a married woman.

But, given her relative ignorance, these invocations could be used to terrify her, whether or not they were accurate.

By the end of the story, on the other hand, Abigail too had learned to use legal knowledge tactically. When Asa attempted to have their children driven away, after his arrest, she had the autonomy and the character to ignore the attorney's statement of the legal rule that her husband had the right to move his children where he chose and to focus, instead, on the attorney's advice that no law would stop her from trying to scare Asa's confederate. When Asa continued obdurate even after his arrest, she used the explicit threat of criminal charges, of the shadow of the criminal law, to force him to terms.

These tactical moves and countermoves are of enormous significance in shaping the narrative of change, as are the roles of legal concepts as organizing assumptions and background threats. Still, we are left with the question of what role, if any, the law played in helping her break the habit of submission mandated both by coverture and by the religious norms of marital unity.

We can tell her story in a way that makes law crucial. That is, Asa violated a series of legal expectations implicit in legal marriage: he committed adultery, he was violent and abusive, he committed incest. Abigail responded by declaring that she had both a legal right and a duty to separate from him, that his legal authority over her should be at an end. That statement led him, in terror at the shame and the loss of control over his domestic situation, to increasingly desperate acts, notably dragging her to New York. These acts brought her to the realization that she shared nothing with him, that he was merely her enemy. And thus she became free from him, willing to invoke legal processes against him, no longer just a feme covert.

But, of course, that story is only a distinctively "legal" story if we choose to characterize it as such. We could, as easily and more convincingly, emphasize Asa's violation of moral and religious norms and Abigail's assertion of religious authority as the causes of change. Such a religious characterization would also be limited by its terms, just as the legal story is limited and partial, for, in part hers was a story of legal change. Neither variation, legal or religious, is complete without the other. But an emphasis on religious motive would better capture her understanding of what went on in the last days of their marriage than one focused exclusively or largely on legal identities and legal tactics.[51]

---

51. Or, there might be a third variation. We could tell her story as fundamentally

This paper is about the roles law played in her story. But it is

"about" honor. Buried in her memoir is another story—Asa Bailey's story—that is also about the evolution of a self. In his case, rather than a story about the exploration of the self by a person locked within a hierarchical and patriarchal order, it is about the loss of a privileged self, about the destruction of an autonomous identity. It is a story about honor, and focusing on it for a moment may remind us of the intimate links between conceptions of honor and coverture.

Men could pretend that they were not changed by marriage. Women became wives, feme coverts; men remained men, albeit with increased responsibilities. But, in fact, early American male identity was bound up with notions of the care of dependents. Indeed, in legal theory, the husband's personhood was extended to incorporate his dependents. Notions of marital unity, of the "one flesh" of the married couple, were taken quite seriously. If his wife were seduced, a husband would sue the seducer for the tort of criminal conversation, under a theory of trespass. The seducer had robbed him of his exclusive right in his wife's sexuality. If his wife or his children were taken from him, or, indeed, if they left of their own accord, he would sue out a writ of habeas corpus, alleging that they were being held under unlawful restraint, that is, not under his control. There was, in fact, little difference between the writ he would take out if he were deprived of his own liberty and the writ he would take out to regain control of his dependents. Although it is not true that the law confirmed a husband's right to use physical force against his wife, it is true that legal discussions of domestic violence were laced with quips about the legal significance of a man striking himself. See Elizabeth Pleck, *Domestic Tyranny* (New York: Oxford University Press, 1987), *The Laws Respecting Women, As They Regard Their Natural Rights, Or Their Connections and Conduct* (London, 1777); Codd v. Codd, 2 Johns. Ch. 141 (1816); *A Faithful Report of the Trial of Doctor William Little, on an Indictment for an Assault and Battery, Committed upon the Body of his Lawful Wife, Mrs. Jane Little, a Black Lady* (New York, 1808); *William Jeffers vs. John Tyson, being an Action for Crim. Con.* [Common Pleas, October 28, 1808] (New York, 1808); and *George Parker vs. Alexander M'Dougall, being an action for Crim. Con. tried at the present sitting of the Mayor's Court, before the Recorder of the City of New-York, on Wednesday, the 19th of October, 1808* (New York, 1808).

Being a householder, being someone who cared for and controlled a family, gave a man political significance. It was a foundation for republican virtue. As the possessor of women, children, and servants, a man became the sovereign of a domain, able to meet with other rulers and to participate with them in government. Indeed, it is hard to imagine any other way for a man to develop a political identity, except through the possession of dependents. See Ruth Bloch, "The Gendered Meanings of Virtue in Revolutionary America," *Signs* 13 (1987): 37–58; Kerber, et al., "Beyond Roles"; and Hendrik Hartog, "Imposing Constitutional Traditions," *William and Mary Law Review* 29 (1987): 78–82.

Conversely, loss of a household identity, loss of control over one's dependents, could only have been seen as a disaster, a source of overwhelming shame. It is easy for us to rush past Asa Bailey's situation, to blame him for his conduct and his lack of self-control. But as we do so, we should not forget the extent to which Abigail's tentative, although unambiguous, assertions of a right to separate, to break up the family, and to hold him to public shame, endangered what we might imagine was an already somewhat embattled sense of self. As she noted in one of their conversations, he was the first victim of his actions. The result was that he "degrade[d] and ruin[ed] himself, soul and body." He seemed "to be too willing to throw himself

important not to engage in a spurious drawing of lines; I see no point in trying to identify the distinctively legal in her worldview, in contradistinction to the distinctively religious (or the distinctively timocratic, for that matter). As I have argued, I believe that religious understandings took primacy, shaping her understanding of her legal rights and duties. But I am not particularly concerned to prove religion's hierarchical significance in her normative order. My goal is not to draw boundaries between legal and religious understandings but to recognize that in Abigail Bailey's complex normative world both mixed freely. At times, they appeared to contradict each other; more often, they served to reinforce each other. Both religious and legal understandings, in so far as they can be distinguished at all, provided a symbolic universe of justifications for domestic submission, as did the vocabulary of honor. Both also provided a vocabulary of aspirations, of restraints and constraints on the exercise of power, and of justifications for resisting arbitrary power, all of which served as tools in her narrative of separation.

---

away, as though he were of no worth." But her actions, in insisting on making him leave and in demanding a property settlement, made him into a different kind of victim, for they threatened to hold him up to public scorn. "I asked, if any sum of money would induce him to be willing that those gentlemen should know that of him, which I knew?" (82).

During his first separation from her, wherever he went he found himself tormented by the sight of "men at home, with their wives and children. . . . [H]e could not endure the sight, but was obliged to get away to bed as soon as possible, that he might hide from the face of mortals, and gnaw his own tongue for anguish of soul." When he returned and tried to persuade her of his reformation and contrition, she could only note "how distressing" his situation must be, that "a man of such a temper, such a disposition, who had ever felt so important, so wilful, and haughty, and so unwilling to acknowledge any wrong," should now be begging for forgiveness from his wife. When he left the second time, he announced that he would have to leave by cover of night. "He could not endure to be seen in this town, or in these parts, where he was known. . . . He once was not afraid to be seen; was fond of home, and of quiet nights. But now the scene was changed. His iniquities had found him out, and were hateful." Worst of all, the selectmen of Landaff came to see him before he could get away (197, 101, 102). Once he himself had been one of them, a selectman himself. See Stanley P. Currier and Edgar T. Clement, *History of Landaff, New Hampshire* (Littleton, N.H.: Courier Print Co., 1966). Now, he was being treated as the object of town concern and scrutiny, as the kind of man who might not be able to care for his family, as someone who might leave them dependent on local charity.

We can well imagine how terrified he would have been of his wife's tentative moves toward separation. We can well imagine that tricking her into coming with him to New York appeared as an attractive solution to his situation, a way of recreating honor in a new location.

Is honor a legal category?

A Note on What Did Not Change

At the end of the story, at least as Abigail Bailey told it, Asa Bailey was a broken man, who appeared "as though he sensibly felt himself to be beaten and defeated." He gave her half of "his" property; they divided their furnishing; and he "relinquished" to Abigail all but their three oldest sons. He had wanted to take "several more of the young sons" and made plans to do so, but these young children had cried so plaintively at the thought of being separated from their mother that he had given in on this as well. She noted that in this final concession, "His self-interest here wrought in my favor. He knew not what to do with them" (177–78).

In the disposition of their children, Abigail assumed she was without legal power. Even after all that had happened in the family, even after what he had done to his daughter, nothing would change the legal fact of his patriarchal authority. She might receive custody of the youngest children, because he alienated his custody rights over them, but if he wished to retain control over the three oldest boys until they reached their majority, nothing in his past conduct prevented that. He was and remained their father, the only relevant parent in terms of legal authority.

In thinking about Abigail Bailey's narrative of change, it is important to note that the change described in the memoirs is only in the relation of husband and wife. Nothing in her legal world told her that separation necessarily gave her any increased rights over her children. Nothing about his more or less public guilt as an incestuous and abusive parent apparently required him to give up parental authority.[52]

Much of Abigail Bailey's narrative is taken up with reflections over her love and concern for her children. As they moved through New York, every child she saw reminded her of her lost and abandoned children. She used her fears for her children, her belief that they needed her, as justifications for her return from the desolate land Asa had dragged her to. Yet, in taking action to complete her separation from her husband, nothing changed in her legal relationship

---

52. In fact, courts did sometimes give mothers custody rights in the wake of a divorce à mensa et thoro. See Codd v. Codd, 2 Johns. Ch. 141 (1816), and Barrere v. Barrere, 4 Johns. Ch. 187 (1819).

to her children. Until he voluntarily transferred custody of some children to her, she remained, in Blackstone's famous (or infamous) phrase, "entitled to no power, but only to reverence and respect."[53] While his actions had taught her that she had to act (and had the right to act) as an "uncovered" person, nothing in his actions gave her a sense that she ought to have legal rights over her children.

Taking seriously her sense of legal powerlessness over her children may help us to understand a mystery lurking in her narrative: her relative insensitivity towards her daughter, Phoebe. Abigail claimed that no one could "describe the anguish of my heart" in witnessing her husband's abusive behavior. Yet she sketched the abuse quickly and in relatively distant and abstract tones. She constantly reminded the reader of her own powerlessness in the situation:

> It may appear surprising that such wickedness was not checked by legal restraints. But great difficulties attend in such a case. While I was fully convinced of the wickedness, yet I knew not that I could make legal proof. I could not prevail upon this daughter to make known to me her troubles; or to testify against the author of them.

"My soul," Abigail continued, "was moved with pity for her wretched case." Yet she also admitted feeling resentful that Phoebe would not act to "expose the wickedness of her father, that she might be relieved from him" (76).[54]

We, along with the editors of her memoirs, might expect more from her. But in expecting more from Abigail, we may be committing an anachronism, and not only because we underestimate the significance of her religious faith. Today, it is conventional to blame mothers for passivity in the face of their husbands' abuse of their children. In apportioning such blame we assume that mothers are responsible for their children's well-being, that they have moral and legal responsibility, the legal capacity as well as the legal duty to act. But what should we expect of a mother in a world where parental

---

53. *Commentaries*, 1:453. As with other Blackstonian aphorisms, this one was at least sometimes wrong.

54. Having admitted to resentment, Abigail quickly recalled that his power—"his intrigues, insinuations, commands, threats, and parental influence"—undoubtedly led Phoebe to feel that it was in vain to seek redress (76).

rights are exclusive, a male monopoly? How should we expect her to have acted?

Indeed, within the terms of Abigail Bailey's narrative, Phoebe's incest was an opportunity, as well as a disaster. In "allowing" her father to succumb to his passion, Phoebe ironically gave her mother the legal and moral right to seek a separation. Phoebe was their daughter, but she was also the passive object of her father's adulterous lust. Because Phoebe was nearly destroyed as a result of her "habit of obedience," Abigail could imagine breaking up her marriage. Asa had destroyed domestic peace, had violated his responsibilities as the head of the household and a parent. He had also committed a form of adultery that she would not condone. She, Abigail, was not responsible for the event, because she was only a wife and mother, a victim herself.

In a sense, Asa's assault on Phoebe was simply a particularly aggravated form of adultery, different only in degree from his earlier adulteries. It gave Abigail the right to act to separate herself from him. And because of her legal powerlessness over her children, she could act without feeling complicit in her husband's conduct.

Thus, to some extent the marital change detailed in the narrative rested on what Abigail Bailey implicitly took to be an unchanging structure of parental power.

Conclusion

In this chapter, I have tried to show how legal concepts and understandings played in and out of the negotiations of Asa and Abigail Bailey and how those concepts and understandings rested on and were intertwined with religious understandings. My goal throughout has been to paint a picture of a legal culture that both reinforced submission and, at the same time, provided justifications and support for acts of resistance and reconstruction.

More theoretically, I have used the dialogues and monologues of Abigail Bailey's memoirs to illustrate a view of legal consciousness that is, I think, of broad relevance. Abigail Bailey's thoughts, prayers, and arguments were filled with law; legal facts, remedies, strategies, and institutions were constantly present. Yet the nature of her consciousness was not determined by law. She bargained in the shadow of law. Yet the law in whose shadow she bargained was a complex and contradictory structure: experienced as an external control and constraint, reconstructed regularly in conversations and arguments, intertwined in significant tension with religious beliefs and norms. Law made a difference, gave her significant remedies. In that sense, her situation is distinguishable from that of the sixteenth-century women studied by Natalie Davis who probably lacked the legal remedies she had. Yet, one would be hard-pressed to turn her into the legally constituted individual posited in modern legal theory, who is imagined as (almost necessarily) exercising rights and remedies because of their availability. For Abigail Bailey, as for many others throughout American history, law was inescapably, at times overwhelmingly, present yet at the same time not the most important determinant of her moral situation.

Abigail Bailey's memoirs provide a case study in the evolution of relative autonomy and relative individualism, along lines suggested by Natalie Davis. In emphasizing the story of change, I have told the story in ways that Abigail Bailey might have wanted me to: highlighting her religious motivations and her moral autonomy, even as I have also insisted on the constraining power of the constellation of commitments identified with coverture. The end of the story is the discovery of a less encumbered self, one capable of relatively greater agency.

And yet it may be a mistake to tell this story in terms of its apparent conclusion. The point is not that Abigail yearned for and achieved separation from her husband, that she changed, but that she found in her commonsensical understanding of law and morality support for the claim that she had a right to a separation. From Abigail Bailey's own perspective, her story is less about change than it is about sustaining a moral identity in the face of moral danger. The right to separate existed not to permit its possessor to reconstruct a new life, as happy divorce manuals today proclaim, but rather because without it she would be publicly (and legally and morally) joined with her husband in sin and dissolution. Marital unity was serious business in early America, meaning that a wife risked assuming the moral colors of her husband. The right to separate offered an escape from that disaster. Separation offered the possibility of continuity and protection from the cruelty and the chaos of a disordered life.

Thus, to conclude with a familiar paradox of historical studies of rights consciousness, Abigail Bailey claimed rights in order to undo the power and the legal rights of her husband.[55] Her claim offered no challenge to his ordinary legal authority over her; indeed, it rested on the same normative assumptions that underlay his conventional assertions of authority. He had changed, had abused his legal rights; thus, she had to claim her right to separate, else she would be complicit in his abuse. She would separate, not in order to end her marriage, but so that she could remain a good wife.[56]

55. See Hendrik Hartog, "The Constitution of Aspiration and 'The Rights That Belong To Us All,'" *Journal of American History*, 74 (1987): 1013–34. Did Abigáil Bailey have a rights consciousness? Not as it would be understood and theorized in recent legal histories. Rather, it might be better to pose her consciousness as being, in the first instance, a duty consciousness. She used (and was used by) the legal system. She asserted rights. But before asserting rights, she had to mediate her sense of rights through a whole range of other understandings and desires. Her aspirations were never tightly identified with her rights.

56. Throughout her narrative, the political context of American independence and new nationhood is never mentioned, a fact social historians might cherish as revealing both the marginality of those events in the lives of many Americans and, more tellingly, the vast gulf that separated the male world of politics from the normative universe of even a relatively knowing woman like Abigail Bailey. And yet, it is important to note that Abigail Bailey's way of constructing herself as a rights bearer bears important similarities in structure and form to the way of the American [male] revolutionary. As historians have learned, in particular from the recent writings of John Reid, to the Americans of 1776, independence was forced on them by the corruptions of the English. Americans, in separating, knew themselves to be true to the English constitution. And independence became a necessity so that they could remain, in all the important ways, good Englishmen. See generally, John P. Reid, *Constitutional History of the American Revolution*, vol. 3 (Madison: University of Wisconsin Press, 1986–92). Likewise, Abigail Bailey's rebellion was forced on her by her husband's corruption. In rebelling she remained true to the strictures of Christian marriage. And rebellion became a necessity so that she could still be a good wife.

Reflections on Law in the Everyday Life of Women

Catharine A. MacKinnon

For most women, life is little but everyday, a constant cycle of minutiae with few landmarks or dramatic demarcations of time, a litany of needs served but never satisfied, time spent but seldom occupied, lines drawn that, like the horizon, recede on approach. Across time and culture, and in individual biographies, the sameness in women's lives is as striking as the diversity of conditions under which it is lived. Men rise and fall. Their dynasties and revolutions and intellectual fashions come and go. Things happen. In the lives of women, men are served, children are cared for, home is made, work is done, the sun goes down.

Most women will tell you that law has little to do with their everyday lives. They seldom hit walls that look legal—they do not get that far. The lives of women in poverty are circumscribed by rules and regulations that they know are stacked and enforced against them and could be different, but nothing so majestic as "the law" is accessible to them. Many women encounter official obstacles, but few have the law in their hands. If a woman complains to the police of a crime against her, the law is in the hands of the prosecutor. On the civil side, it usually takes money to get the law to work for you in the United States. Even when a woman's injury is recognized by law, which is seldom, most women lack the resources to use it.

To most women, the law is a foreign country with an unintelligible tongue, alien mores, secret traps, uncontrollable and unresponsive dynamics, obscure but rigid dogmas, barbaric and draconian rituals, and consequences as scary as they are incomprehensible. Actually, this is true for most men as well.[1] The difference is that those who can and do make law work for them, those who designed it so it would work for them, as if they were the whole world, are men—specifically, white upper-class men. Women reflect this reality in their view that if you try to use the law, it is as likely to blow up in your face as to help. Law is Kafka's trial, Dickens's *Bleak House*. Mostly women feel that the law is not about them, has no idea who they are or what they face or how they think or feel, has nothing to say to them and can do nothing for them. When the law and their life collide, it is their life that gets the worst of it.

Women in conflict with the law show this relation in highest relief. Most become criminals for responding in kind to male violence against them, for crimes of poverty, for being involved with a man who committed a crime (what the legal system treats as first-degree bad choice of boyfriend), or for prostitution—being sold by men to men for what men value women for, and then being devalued and considered a criminal for it. On my observation, most imprisoned women who are not inside for crimes of self-defense *against* men who batter them are in for crimes committed *with* men who batter them.[2] The law does little to nothing about the crimes against women that position them to commit the crimes that do matter officially. For instance, women's imprisonment by violent men who batter them is not thought official, even though it is widely officially condoned.

The law operates most visibly in the lives of women in such official captivity. They are surrounded, defined, debased, and confined by the law. Their everyday lives are taken over by it. It swallows them up: their liberties, their children, their bodies, their community ties, what initiative and self-respect they had managed to salvage, and sometimes their lives. To be in prison is what it is for women to live their everyday lives entirely inside the law. Even when women criminals do the same things and get the same sentences as men, which is not the norm,[3] their crimes are the crimes of women. They commit them as women, are punished as women, and, when the law

---

1. See the evocative treatment by Austin Sarat, "'The Law Is All Over': Power, Resistance, and the Legal Ideology of the Welfare Poor," *Yale Journal of Law and the Humanities* 2 (1990): 343–80.

2. I learned this from working with women in prison in the United States and Canada, specifically at Niantic, Conn., and Kingston, Ont.

3. Rita J. Simon and Jean Landis, *The Crimes Women Commit, the Punishments They Receive* (Lexington, Mass.: Lexington Books, 1991).

is finished with them, they are thrown back onto society's trash heap for women.

The law that is applied to them and to all women has not been written by women, white or Black, rich or poor. It has not been based on women's experiences of life, everyday or otherwise. No one represented women's interests as women in creating it, and few have considered women's interests as women in applying it.[4] Unlike men, many of whom are also estranged from the law—especially unlike white upper-class men—no women had voice or representation in constituting this state or its laws, yet we are presumed to consent to its rule. It was not written for our benefit, and it shows.

The exclusion of women from a formative role in the law has meant that much legal intervention in women's lives is unconstructive, to say the least, while most of women's lives is carried out beneath explicit legal notice. Crimes and civil injuries do not imagine most harms distinctive to women, such as the stigma of female sexuality, which pervasively imposes inferiority on women in everyday life. Canons of legal interpretation in laws that might apply to real events in women's lives are shaped to assume the validity of the male point of view. An example in the law of sex discrimination is the "intent" requirement, which bases a finding of discrimination on the perspective of the alleged discriminator rather than on the consequences of his actions for the discriminated against. Burdens of proof and evidentiary standards as well as substantive law tacitly presuppose the male experience as normative and credible and relevant. An example is the mens rea requirement in the law of rape, which bases its determination of rape on the perspective of the accused rapist as opposed to that of the victim. Proceeding by analogy, as the law does, means that new crimes and injuries must be like old ones (read, men's) before they can be recognized as crimes and injuries at all. When a woman tries to raise her voice, precedent often requires decisive deference to a law built on the silence of women, a law that originated when we were not even permitted to vote or to learn to read, in a society premised on our subjection.

No law addresses the deepest, simplest, quietest, and most widespread atrocities of women's everyday lives. The law that purports to address them, like the law of sexual assault, does not reflect their

---

4. There are striking exceptions like Wanrow v. State of Washington, 88 Wash. 2d 221, 559 P.2d 548 (1977).

realities or is not enforced, like the law of domestic violence. Either the law does not apply, is applied to women's detriment, or is not applied at all. The deepest rules of women's lives are written between the lines, and elsewhere.

Yet the actions and inactions of law construct and constrict women's lives, its consequences no less powerful for being offstage. Focusing on the areas the law abdicates, its gaps and silences and absences, one finds that women's everyday life has real rules, but they are not the formal ones. They have never been legislated or adjudicated. They have not had to be. They effectively prescribe what girls can be, what the community encourages and permits in a woman, what opportunities are available and hence what aspirations are developed, what shape of life is so expected that it is virtually never articulated. These rules go under the heading of socialization, pressure, religion, popular culture, masculinity and femininity, everyday life. The rules of everyday life, in this sense, are that law which is not one, the law for women where there is no law.

The content of the formal legal system, the output of legislatures and courts, has a real effect on these processes, but, from the vantage point of life being lived, it is a distant one. Whether sex discrimination in athletics is illegal, whether women's supposed "interests" make occupational segregation nondiscriminatory,[5] whether pornography is protected by the state,[6] whether legal abortion is available[7]—all deeply shape women's realities, but from high up and a long way off. Women seldom have much say in these matters yet live their consequences every day in factories, behind counters, in beds, in gyms, on streets, in their heads, and in the eyes and at the hands of men, where the everyday lives of most women is largely lived out. Women's exclusion from law and marginality within it does not make the law inactive in women's subordination day to day. The fact that women have nothing to say about a sphere of life does not mean that it does not affect us—to the contrary. Especially if one thinks

---

5. EEOC v. Sears, 839 F.2d 302 (7th Cir. 1988).

6. Rabidue v. Osceola Refining, 548 F. Supp. 419 (E.D. Mich. 1984); but cf. Robinson v. Jacksonville Shipyards, 760 F. Supp. 1486 (D. Fla. 1991).

7. Roe v. Wade, 410 U.S. 113 (1973) (abortion decriminalized); Webster v. Reproductive Health Services, 492 U.S. 490, 518, 529 (1989) (*Roe's* decriminalization of abortion questioned). See also Planned Parenthood v. Casey, 112 S. Ct. 2791 (1992) (*Roe's* fundamental holding affirmed).

of everyday life as not having to be the way it is, the role of law in keeping it the way it is becomes visible, compelling.

Of all of everyday life, sexual relations between women and men may seem the farthest from the reach of law. Sex occurs in private, in presumed consent, in everyday intimacy. Sex is thought of as a sphere to itself with its own rules, written by desire or individual taste or mutual negotiation or tolerance, not by law. Yet the law of sexual assault has a very real everyday impact on sexual life. Rape is supposedly illegal. Yet the rape that the law actually recognizes as illegal is a far cry from the sex forced on women in everyday life. The law's rape is by a stranger, Black, in a strange location, with a weapon, which the woman resisted within an inch of her life. Preferably the woman is white. Most rapes that actually happen are by someone the woman knows, of the same race, often to women of color. Rape happens at home or on a date, without weapons other than hands and a penis, and the woman is too surprised or too terrified or too learned in passivity or wants to get it over with too badly or has heard too much about men who kill women who resist to fight back. Or she does fight back and is not believed, either by the rapist or in court, because sex is what a woman is for.

To the extent your reality does not fit the law's picture, your rape is not illegal. The implications of this for everyday sex life are that any man who knows a woman of the same race can probably get away with raping her. The better he knows her, the more likely he is to get away with it. Married women in states that do not have a law against marital rape are the ultimate example. Until the early seventies, a woman was not considered a reliable witness about her own rape, but the defendant was.[8] Unless someone besides the woman saw it, it was not legally real. Many jurisdictions, like California and Canada and England, still require that the state prove that the accused rapist honestly believed that the woman did not consent, no matter how much force was used.[9]

What does all this mean for having no mean no? When no can legally mean yes, what does yes mean in everyday life? When rape passes legally as intercourse, what is sexual intimacy? The law of

---

8. Of course, this would only be effective for the defendant permitted to testify in his own defense, a relatively recent development.

9. People v. Mayberry, 15 Cal. 3d 143, 542 P. 2s 1337 (1975); Pappajohn v. The Queen, 11 D.L.R. 3d 1 (1980); DPP v. Morgan, 2411 E.R. 347 (1975).

rape deeply affects sexual intimacy by making forced sex legally sex, not rape, every night. Every day, because women know this, they do not report rapes nine times out of ten.[10] When a woman does report, the media has the legal right to print her name and picture, making her into everyday pornography.[11] The racism of the criminal justice system is an everyday reality for women of color, who do not report their rapes by men of color because of it. In reality, there are no laws against what can be done to them. Many women, no matter how violated they were, do not call what happened to them rape if they do not think a court would agree with them. In this ultimate triumph of law over life, law tells women what happened to them and many of us believe it. When asked, "Have you ever been raped?" many women answer "I don't know."[12]

A similar combination of utter neglect with malignant concern animates the law of reproduction. Women get pregnant every day without wanting to be and at the same time are prevented from having children they want to have. The question here is who controls the reproductive uses of women, a process to which controlling the fetus is instrumental. When a woman is sterilized against her will and even without her knowledge, as has most often been done to women of color and to "mentally disabled" women, no law prohibits it or even compensates it after the fact.[13] Does law then have no relation to each day of the rest of their lives, on which they now cannot have children? If a woman dies from a desperation-induced self-abortion because a funded, safe one is not available by law—and most such women have been Black or Hispanic[14]—did law not end her everyday life?

Pornography suffuses women's everyday life, crisp at child's eye level in the 7-11, hidden at the back of the boss's drawer at work, smack in your face on the wall of the repair shop or the Film Society's

---

10. Diana Russell, *Sexual Exploitation* (Beverly Hills: Sage Library of Social Research, 1984), 36. ("[O]nly about 1 in 10 nonmarital rapes in the Russell sample were ever reported to the police.")

11. The Florida Star v. B.J.F., 491 U.S. 524 (1989).

12. See, generally, *Senate Judiciary Committee, The Response to Rape: Detours on the Road to Equal Justice*, May 1993.

13. This is documented in Catharine MacKinnon, "Reflections on Sex Equality Under Law," *Yale Law Journal* 100 (1991): 1301 n. 94.

14. See Laurie Nsiah-Jefferson, "Reproductive Laws, Women of Color and Low-Income Women," *Women's Rights Law Reporter* 11 (1989): 15-38.

spring roster at school, soggy under your son's mattress. Under the law of obscenity, pornography is supposed to be against the law. In the real world of everyday life, it is effectively legal because it is pervasively there, available without fear of sanction. This is what a dead-letter law looks like. The combination of pornography being putatively forbidden but totally available, decried in public but permitted and used in private, intrudes the law deeply into women's everyday lives. The allegedly forbidden quality of pornography sexualizes it by surrounding it with power and taboo and makes defending and using it appear to be an act of daring and danger, a blow for freedom against repression. Its actual availability belies the taboo and promotes the power, spreading it and supporting it as a model for women's everyday lives.

The everyday reality of pornography supersedes the formal law against pornography and becomes the real rules for women's lives, the sacred secret codebook with directions about what to do with a woman, what everything she says and does means, what a woman is. All the sexual abuses of women's everyday lives that are not recognized by the law are there in the pornography: the humiliation, the objectification, the forced access, the torture, the use of children, the sexualized racial hatred, the misogyny. As Andrea Dworkin has said, "Pornography is the law for women." Open your mouth this far. Spread your legs this wide. Put your arms like this. Talk dirty to me. Now smile.[15]

In this way, visual and physical intrusion on women—a normative experience of objectification and dehumanization made to seem deviant and marginal when medicalized as voyeurism and other exotic paraphilias—becomes the paradigm for sex. Sex in this sense is not just an activity at a time and place but a pervasive dimension of social life as lived every day. A woman's physical condition (Knocked-Up Mamas, Milky Tits), occupation (lady lawyer, hot housewife), racial or ethnic or religious heritage (Geisha Gashes, Black Bondage, I was a Gestapo Sex Slave), age (Cherry Tarts, Ten), family status (Daddy's Girl), pets (Doggie Girls), facts of everyday life to her, become sex to the consumer in the world pornography creates, along with everyday objects like telephones, cucumbers, beer cans, ropes,

15. Andrea Dworkin said this in many public speeches in 1983 and 1984. The analysis behind it was originally developed in her *Pornography: Men Possessing Women* (New York: G. P. Putnam's Sons, 1979), 70–100.

paper clips, razors, candle wax, police uniforms, plumber's helpers, lollipops, and teddy bears. In this process, the law helps constitute what is called desire by defining what amounts to sexual use and abuse of women and children as illegal and out of bounds and then doing nothing about it. Women realize that reporting sexual assaults is futile because this is a society that considers them freedom. When the state goes a step further and declares that pornography is affirmatively protected after all, and its harm to women is real but does not matter as much as the pornography of us matters,[16] women's despairing relation to the state and its laws—our belief that they will never see us as real—becomes total.

Even in the world pornography has made, it never occurs to most women, living their lives day to day, that having sex with a man to whom one is married is part of being a good mother. The law of child custody in general, of lesbian custody in particular, reveals that there are sexual requirements for the legal adequacy of women's parenting. If a woman has a sexual relationship with a woman, she can lose her children,[17] lesbian being pornography for men, to which they do not think children should be exposed. The everyday sexuality of many women is thus controlled every day through fear due to the recently strengthened possibility of men seeking custody of children.[18] This is not to say that the men actually want the children, although sometimes they do. More commonly, they want to use the threat of challenging custody as a financial lever to reduce support payments, and as control generally. The new norm of joint custody has a similar effect. Day to day, the mother has the major responsibility and does most of the work, but because of joint custody, the father can still control the big decisions. In other words, now not even divorce disturbs the power relation of marriage. And women who were raped in their marriages face sharing custody of their children with their rapist.

Family law keeps a lot of women in place and in line, fearful of

16. Hudnut v. American Booksellers Ass'n., Inc., 771 F.2d 323 (7th Cir. 1985).

17. See Dailey v. Dailey, 635 S.W.2d 391 (Tenn. Ct. App. 1982); Jacobson v. Jacobson, 314 N.W.2d 78 (N.D. 1981); L. v. D., 630 S.W.2d 240 (Mo. Ct. App. 1982); Constant A. v. Paul C.A., 496 A.2d 1 (Pa. Super. Ct. 1985). But cf. S.N.E. v. R.L.B., 699 P.2d 875 (Alaska 1985); Stroman v. Williams, 353 S.E.2d 704 (S.C. App. Ct. 1987). See also Roe v. Roe, 324 S.E.2d 691 (Va. 1985).

18. See Comment, "The Emerging Constitutional Protection of the Putative Father's Parental Rights," *Michigan Law Review* 70 (1972): 1581; Phyllis Chesler, *Mothers on Trial* (New York: McGraw-Hill, 1989).

altering their lives because of how it could be made to look in court. Some do not go public with past abuse through pornography for this reason. Many stay with men who abuse them because they fear the man would try to take their children away, and he would look better under existing legal standards—high income, intact family, white picket fence—than they do. Most women feel they married an individual but find on considering divorce that he represents the law and the law represents him. He is the law of the state in the home.

The realm in which women's everyday life is lived, the setting for many of these daily atrocities, is termed the private. Law defines the private as where law is not, that into which law does not intrude, where no harm is done other than by law's presence. In everyday life, the privacy is his. Obscenity is affirmatively protected in private. Wives are raped in private. Women's labor is exploited in private. Equality is not guaranteed in private. Prostitution, when acts of sex occur out of public view, is often termed private. In private, women who can afford abortions can get them, but those who cannot afford them get no public support, because private choices are not public responsibilities.[19]

Women in everyday life have no privacy in private. In private, women are objects of male subjectivity and male power. The private is that place where men can do whatever they want because women reside there. The consent that supposedly demarcates this private surrounds women and follows us wherever we go. Men reside in public, where laws against harm exist—real harm, harm to men and whoever has the privilege to be hurt like men—and follow them wherever they go. Having arranged the law against rape and battering and sexual abuse of children so virtually nothing is done about them, and having supported male power in the home as a virtual absolute, the law then proclaims its profoundest self-restraint, its guarantee of liberty where it matters most, in "the right to be let alone."[20] This home is the place Andrea Dworkin has described from battered women's perspective as "that open grave where so many women lie waiting to die."[21] As a legal doctrine, privacy has become the affirmative triumph of the state's

---

19. Harris v. McRae, 448 U.S. 297 (1980).

20. Roberson v. Rochester Folding Box Co., 171 N.Y. 538 (1902); Cooley, *Torts*, 4th ed. sect. 135 (1932). See also Warren and Brandeis, "The Right to Privacy," *Harvard Law Review* 4 (1890): 193; Samuel Hofstadter and George Horowitz, *The Right to Privacy* (New York: Central Book Co., 1964), 1–2.

21. Andrea Dworkin, "A Battered Wife Survives," *Letters from a War Zone* (New York: Dutton, 1988), 100.

abdication of women.[22] Sanctified by the absolution of law, the private is the everyday domain of women in captivity, abandoned to their isolation and told it is what freedom really means.

This is to say that the law is complicit in the impoverishment of the average woman who makes nowhere near the income of the average man,[23] in the everyday aggression against the forty-four percent of women who are victims of rape or attempted rape at least once in their lives,[24] in the assaults of the quarter to a third of women who are battered in their homes,[25] in the denial to women of the choice not to have children and the choice to have children and not to have them stolen, and in every act of violation or second-class citizenship that involves pornography. The law of rape collaborates with rapists to the extent it precludes recognition of the violations it purports to prohibit. The law of discrimination collaborates with perpetrators of discrimination to the extent its doctrines reproduce inequality rather than remedy it, requiring that equality already effectively exist before it can be guaranteed. The law of pornography collaborates with pornographers by protecting their right to abuse women behind the guarantee of freedom of speech, at the same time participating in their marketing strategy of sexualizing pornography by making it seem forbidden. The law of child custody collaborates with patriarchy in imposing male-dominant values on women in the family, and the law of privacy collaborates with whoever has power by guaranteeing spheres of impunity in which the law leaves men to their own devices. Even when the law does nothing—and it does nothing in so many ways—it is responsible for not working for women, whether law permits nothing when it pretends to do some-

---

22. On the structural level, see, e.g., Harris v. McRae, 448 U.S. 297 (1980); 30Deshaney v. Winnebago County Dep't of Social Services, 489 U.S. 189 (1989). For further discussion, see Catharine MacKinnon, *Toward a Feminist Theory of the State* (Cambridge: Harvard University Press, 1989), chap. 10. For an attempt to reconstruct the privacy right, see Anita Allen, *Uneasy Access: Privacy for Women in a Free Society* (Totowa, N.J.: Rowman & Littlefield, 1988).

23. U.S. Equal Employment Opportunity Commission, *Job Patterns for Minorities and Women in Private Industry 1986*, (1988, occupational segregation by race and sex); Kevin L. Phillips, *The Politics of Rich and Poor* (New York: Random House, 1990), 202–3.

24. Russell, *Sexual Exploitation*, 1984, 50.

25. Harold Lentzner and Marshall DeBerry, *Intimate Victims: A Study of Violence among Friends and Relatives* (Bureau of Justice Statistics, U.S. Dept. of Justice, 1980).

thing, is inadequate, is not enforced, or does not exist at all. If it does not work for women, it does not work.

Those who have power in life have had power in law, and the reverse. This relation is a process, though, not an inert or static fact, as one counterexample serves to reveal. Women have made one law: the law against sexual harassment. Before sexual harassment became actionable as a form of sex discrimination, it was just everyday life. The sex role norm that empowers men to initiate sex to women under conditions of inequality is intensified in sexual harassment. Women are pressured and intimidated into sexual compliance and raped as the price for economic survival. This has been done for centuries with complete impunity. When women's experience was made the basis for the law against sexual harassment, everyday life altered as well. Men kept doing it, but the experience had a name, an analysis that placed it within the collective reality of gender, a forum for confrontation with some dignity and the possibility of relief. Most important, women's own sense of violation changed because it had legal expression and legitimacy and public sanction. Law told them back what they knew was true. Sexual harassment was against the law against treating women as unequals, the law of sex discrimination. This law told the truth: sex inequality is the problem, this problem. In going from everyday life to law, sexual harassment went from a gripe to a grievance, from a shameful story about a woman to actionable testimony about a man. Changing what could be done by law changed the way it felt to live through it in life, and the status of women took a step from victim to citizen.

To wonder whether women will ever become full citizens is partly to ask whether law in women's hands can mean what law in men's hands has meant. For better and worse, probably not. Even when clothed in law, no woman escapes the female body when she is in court, not yet. This may be why sexual harassment complainants still do better on paper than they do on the witness stand. The extent to which law in women's hands could improve upon law in men's is suggested by the pornography example. Obscenity law is men's attempt to regulate pornography. It has been an abject and total failure. It is clear that men do not want to restrict pornography very much or they would treat it seriously, like they treat air traffic control, for instance. In ignoring abuse to women entirely, obscenity law is an invitation to the pornographers to violate women and run, sheltered by the First Amendment. The obscenity definition, which requires the materials be "taken as a whole,"[26] invites the surrounding of abuse with literature, making the abuse look more legitimate. The "community standards" rule invites flooding communities with pornography, so that their standards will come to conform to it. The "prurient interest" requirement invites juries to deny the sexual appeal of the most violent materials, supporting their protection. Even given these built-in difficulties for the successful application of obscenity law to anything, the vagueness of the obscenity definition invites prosecution of nearly anything with sexual content. From the fact that the pornography industry has nearly quadrupled in size since the promulgation of this definition, given the potential scope of the definition, one concludes that men do not want to do anything about pornography. If one assumes that the law can only work as it has worked in men's hands, the failure of obscenity law makes a good case for the limits of the law as such. If one has an alternative, that failure shows that the law is impotent in men's hands when it helps men be potent in everyday life. In other words, men's law has been constructed and applied to conform to a deeper logic, supportive of male power.

The civil rights law against pornography Andrea Dworkin and I proposed, by contrast, puts the legal power to oppose the pornographers in the hands of women. Based on the reality of women's everyday lives, this law gives women the power of law to act against pornography's real abuses. It names the harm: sexual subordination on the basis of gender. It permits women to act without prosecutor's permission or police discretion. It does not forbid pornography, which would keep it sexy; it makes it actionable as a sexualized practice of bigotry, which makes it detumescent. The limits on law encountered with the obscenity approach do not exist here. This is the case both because the law women wrote has a real relation to the lives women live and because, once women are empowered to expose it, there is no place for the abuse to hide, because it needs to use them to exist.

The only question is: will the law permit this? The fact that this law directly confronts male power where it lives means it will be slated for extinction. This does not mean it should not exist, it merely means

---

26. For further critique of the obscenity definition and detailed citations, see Catharine MacKinnon, *Feminism Unmodified: Discourses on Life and Law* (Cambridge: Harvard University Press, 1987), 152–54.

its existence will be opposed. Making it possible for women to stand against the pornographers in court would be a change in itself. Maybe the lesson here is that law is not monolithic, that what it is depends on *how* it is used, on its social substance and interface. Perhaps equality initiatives are unlike other laws and can confront social inequality more directly and constructively than other laws do.

Among left-leaning academic lawyers, there is a big controversy over whether law matters to life and whether those who care about everyday life should care about law at all. Does life make law or does law make life, they wonder. When men make both, and you are a woman, the distinction may not count for much, except that law purports to have rules other than force and pretends to be accountable, whereas life does not. At this point, the case for giving up on law is even stronger for giving up on life. Women giving up does seem to be the point.

There is a legitimate question, though, about the relation between law and the power that produces it, and the degree to which change in one produces change in the other. Whatever we know about how change is made, we do know that *no* change in one definitely produces no change in the other. Women's experience makes us suspicious of those who seek to make women's legal exclusion and marginalization and invisibility into a radical virtue, even as their antistate position usually stops short of opposing pornography, while the state is clearly for it. Our everyday lives make us suspicious of those who tell us rights do not matter, even as they have them while we do not.[27] Our lives make us suspicious of abdicating the state—in favor of what? those bastions of sensitivity and receptivity to women, the media and organized labor? Besides, what does it mean to abdicate a society you are excluded from but more exclusion? It does not stop affecting you when you stop trying to affect it.

Surely one of the most effective strategies for maintaining a system of dominance is to convince those who seek to end it that the tools of dominance must be left in the hands of the dominant. Women need institutional support for equality, both because of and in spite of the fact that power in women's hands is different from power in men's hands. Getting power is not the same as transforming it, but how are we supposed to transform it if we cannot get it? How

27. For a vivid analysis of this point, see Patricia Williams, "On Being the Object of Property," *Signs* 5 (1988): 5–24.

can it be changed if it is authoritatively defined in male terms and retained in male hands? I am tired of people who have power—whether they identify with it or not—telling women that we can only have power if we transform it. They might begin by insisting it be transformed in the hands of those who already have it. They might also explain how they plan to produce equality without institutional support, indeed while leaving in place present legal structures that enforce women's inequality. It's like telling women we should transform the state in the face of a law that deprives us of the right to vote. What are we supposed to do? Picket and hope they listen? Start a new state? Get the bomb? Why aren't any of these critics doing any of these things or their equivalent? I would also really like to hear their argument against the franchise. Not why it is limited; why its limits mean we should not fight for it and have it at all.

Those who say law cannot make change so we should not try should explain why the law should be exempt in the struggle for social transformation. Some of us suspect that women, in particular, are being told that not much can be done with law because a lot can be. If law were to be made to work for women, the relation of law to life, as well as its content, might have to change in the process. As more women become lawyers and maybe the law starts to listen to women, perhaps the legal profession will decline in prestige and power. Maybe women using law will delegitimize law, and male supremacy—in its endless adaptability and ingenuity—will have to find other guises for the dominance it currently exercises through law.

This is not to urge a top-down model of change or to advocate merely inverting or reshuffling the demographics of existing structures of power, or to say that law alone solves anything. It is to say that putting power in the hands of the powerless can change power as well as the powerless. It is also to urge a confrontational engagement with institutions, one that refuses to let power off the hook. It is a political demand, integral to a larger political movement on all levels, that law recognize that we live here, too. Every day of our lives.

Law in the Domains of Everyday Life: The Construction of Community and Difference

David M. Engel

The Construction of Social Domains

As I sit at my desk and write, workers are building a new room at the back of our house. In what was open and undefined outdoor space, they frame and enclose an area with wood, then shingles, brick, and drywall. The space within the walls and roof is shaped, warmed, lighted, colored, and committed to a specific purpose. The walls mark out boundaries that exclude squirrels, birds, insects, and stray cats who had formerly wandered through this space. The boundaries also invite others—the occupants of our house—to enter the space and use it in particular ways.

This small domain has been measured, marked, and defined according to the plan of the architect and the occasional improvisation of the contractor. In everyday life, social domains are continually created and bounded in an analogous—but far less stable—

For their helpful and insightful comments, I would like to thank Anthony G. Amsterdam, Alfred S. Konefsky, Frank W. Munger, Jr., and Austin Sarat. For their research assistance in the fieldwork or in the preparation of this chapter, I am grateful to a special group of current and former law students: Ann Chung Jahnke, Wendy Ricks, Kathryn Smolarek, and Susan Weber. The fieldwork portion of this study was supported by the Law and Social Sciences Program of the National Science Foundation (grant SES 87-0330), the American Council of Learned Societies, and the Baldy Center for Law and Social Policy.

fashion, determining who may enter, where they may go, and what
they may do once inside. In everyday life, it is not usually possible
to identify individual architects. Domains are shaped by people and
groups as they engage in their day-to-day activities. And there is
also the law.

It is odd that those of us who are trained in the law know and care
so little about its role in everyday life. Law in the second half of the
twentieth century has been used to an unprecedented extent to transform (and sometimes to preserve) the values, beliefs, experiences, and
behavior patterns of ordinary people in their day-to-day activities:
in schools, in work settings, and in the neighborhoods and communities in which they live. Yet such legal efforts are accompanied
by a casual indifference as to the role law actually plays in these
everyday contexts. Law academics generally prefer to pitch their tents
in the shadow of the Supreme Court rather than on Main Street or
in urban or suburban neighborhoods. Judges and legislators tend to
follow the policy Tom Lehrer ascribed to Werner von Braun: firing
off their legal missiles and assuming that where they come down is
"not their department."

It is, of course, far easier to study the ritualized dramas of
landmark litigation or the public debates over pathbreaking legislation
than the quotidian routines of everyday life. The specialized discourse
and rituals of lawyers and legislators invite study in a way that day-
to-day reliance on common sense by ordinary people does not. Perhaps because of its obviousness and its ready accessibility to the
ordinary person, the culture of "common sense" is paradoxically hard
to discern and even harder to analyze. As Geertz has observed, "There
is something . . . of the purloined letter effect in common sense; it lies
so artlessly before our eyes it is almost impossible to see."[1] Despite
the difficulty in seeing it, that which we consider obvious, everyday,
and commonsensical does possess its own distinctive logic, its own
regularities, and its own norms and categories concerning human
beings and social relationships. What seems to be no more than
common sense turns out to be part of a cultural system. What seems
to be obvious and immutable reality turns out to be an "authoritative

---

1. Clifford Geertz, "Common Sense as a Cultural System," in *Local Knowledge:*
Further Essays in Interpretive Anthropology (New York: Basic Books, 1983), 92.

story" that, like other stories, can be told quite differently from place to place and from time to time.[2] It is important to ask what role law plays in the telling of such stories and in their variation from one locale or time period to the next.

De Certeau, one of the most influential theoreticians of everyday life, suggests that we view everyday life as a form of cultural production by those who are without power and who are essentially "consumers" rather than producers of the cultural forms imposed upon them. Everyday life, in de Certeau's view, is constituted by the tactics of resistance through which ordinary people attempt to "reappropriate the space organized by techniques of sociocultural production." For him, everyday life is an "antidiscipline," a kind of guerrilla war waged by those who lack the power to create culture and who must "invent" everyday life "by *poaching* in countless ways on the property of others."[3]

The implications for law contained in de Certeau's theory of everyday life are not entirely satisfying. Law would appear to be among the instruments of "sociocultural production" that emanate from the center of power and, in this view, everyday life is essentially a form of resistance against legal domination. If this is indeed the relationship de Certeau would envision between law and everyday life, it is ultimately inadequate. Analyses that assume a clear boundary between law and everyday life inevitably confront problems of reification. Law, despite its apparent claim to "self-totalization,"[4] is dependent on everyday life to give meaning to its central concepts (what is "reasonable," "customary," "excessive," or "appropriate"?), to root its abstract rules and principles in human understanding, and to produce implementation, compliance, and judgment. It is misleading to regard law as capable of existence apart from or in opposition to everyday life.

It is also misleading to regard everyday life as essentially resistant to law. Law is not a distinctly bounded "thing" that belongs exlusively to the state. It is a continuum of normative orders ranging from the "law" of the supermarket check-out line[5] to the constitutional

---

2. Id., 84.

3. Michel de Certeau, *The Practice of Everyday Life* (Berkeley and Los Angeles: University of California Press, 1984), xiv, xii.

4. Carol J. Greenhouse, "Just in Time: Temporality and the Cultural Legitimation of Law," *Yale Law Journal* 98 (1989): 1640.

5. Michael Reisman, "Lining Up: The Microlegal System of Queues," *University of Cincinnati Law Review* 54 (1985): 417.

interpretations of the federal courts. Everyday life is pervaded by norms and procedures whose origins are to be found both in the rules of ordinary human interaction and in the more formal pronouncements issued from the distant centers of "sociocultural production."[6] Norms originating in diverse ways from diverse sources, of greater and lesser formality and official legitimacy, continually merge, clash, overlap, and constitute one another. Everyday life is not opposed to law, nor does it exist merely by insinuating itself into the interstices of the law. Everyday life constitutes law and is constituted by it.

In this essay, I reject sociolegal models focused on law's capacity to dominate everyday life or everyday life's capacity to resist the hegemony of law. Instead, I draw upon a perspective that emphasizes the mutually constitutive processes through which law and everyday life construct one another. Researchers influenced by this perspective have emphasized the dynamic *processes* that characterize the interaction of law with the culture of common sense and the fluidity, negotiability, and ever-changing qualities of both law and everyday life.[7] They have also emphasized the importance of identifying and studying certain *actors* who appear to play particularly significant roles in determining the influence of law in everyday life.[8]

In adopting this perspective, I intend to focus attention on the extent to which law and everyday life are mutually defining. It is

---

6. Lon Fuller, "Human Interaction and the Law," *American Journal of Jurisprudence* 14 (1969): 1.

7. E.g., Lawrence Rosen, *Bargaining for Reality: The Construction of Social Relations in a Muslim Community* (Chicago: University of Chicago Press, 1984); Carol J. Greenhouse, *Praying for Justice: Faith, Order and Community in an American Town* (Ithaca, N.Y.: Cornell University Press, 1986); Carol J. Greenhouse, "Courting Difference: Issues of Interpretation and Comparison in the Study of Legal Ideologies," *Law and Society Review* 22 (1988): 687; June Starr and Jane F. Collier, eds., *History and Power in the Study of Law: New Directions in Legal Anthropology* (Ithaca, N.Y.: Cornell University Press, 1989); Salley Engle Merry, *Getting Justice and Getting Even: Legal Consciousness among Working-class Americans* (Chicago: University of Chicago Press, 1990).

8. For example, concerning divorce lawyers see Austin Sarat and William L. F. Felstiner, "Law and Social Relations: Vocabularies of Motive in Lawyer/Client Interaction," *Law and Society Review* 12 (1988): 737. Concerning the court clerk, see Barbara Yngvesson, "Legal Ideology and Community Justice in the Clerk's Office," *The Legal Studies Forum* 9 (1985): 71; Barbara Yngvesson, "Making Law at the Doorway: The Clerk, the Court, and the Construction of Community in a New England Town," *Law and Society Review* 22 (1988): 410.

not enough, however, to say that law is fundamentally involved with and given meaning by everyday life. It is evident that law is involved in *different* ways and is given *different* meanings in different social locales. We need a way of thinking about these variations in texture, meaning, value, and behavior associated with the interplay between law and everyday life. One approach to this problem is through the concept of the *domain*.

My use of the concept of the domain is influenced by Moore's discussion of the "semi-autonomous social field," which she defines as a "social locale" that has the capacity to "generate rules and coerce or induce compliance to them":

> it can generate rules and customs and symbols internally, but . . . it is also vulnerable to rules and decisions and other forces emanating from the larger world by which it is surrounded. The semi-autonomous social field has rule-making capacities, and the means to induce or coerce compliance; but it is simultaneously set in a larger social matrix which can, and does, affect and invade it, sometimes at the invitation of persons inside it, sometimes at its own instance.[9]

A domain, like Moore's semi-autonomous social field, is an arena in which people's day-to-day interactions necessitate the formulation of a common language of ideas about the individual and the group, about time and place, about right and wrong.[10] Within a domain, people do not necessarily agree about all or even most issues. Domains may be characterized by bitter conflict as well as by solidarity. It is, however, the necessity of formulating a way of talking about common issues that gives rise to people's sense that they are within a distinctive social arena and that being in this arena requires them to cope with a particular version of common sense that pertains here but not, perhaps, elsewhere.

A domain is not a given; it is not an easily identifiable site with clearly marked boundaries, where researchers can go to study

---

9. Sally Falk Moore, "Law and Social Change: The Semi-Autonomous Social Field as an Appropriate Subject of Study" in *Law as Process: An Anthropological Approach*, ed. Moore (London: Routledge and Kegan Paul, 1978), 55–57.

10. Compare Fuller, "Human Interaction and the Law," discussing a "language of interaction."

law in everyday life. Interpretations of Moore's semi-autonomous social field have sometimes given the impression that such fields are phenomena of the natural world like towns or forests and that we need only "go there" to conduct our research. In using the concept of the domain, however, I intend to emphasize that it is the ongoing process of construcing the field itself that now engages our attention. Both law and the culture of common sense play a part in this process. Together they create a texture of everyday experience that has its own feel, its own images and vocabulary, and is distinguishable from experiences involving other people or activities in other social locales. In discussing the processes by which domains are continually constructed through the interaction of law and the culture of common sense, I will emphasize four aspects in particular.

Actors

A domain requires occupants. It is the movement and energy of social actors within a domain, like the movement and energy of gas molecules in a balloon, that give it shape. But just as the actors within a domain define its form and character, so does the domain itself shape the actors. Issues of identity are contested and determined within the context of particular social domains, as are the hierarchies of personal attributes and the principles of inclusion and exclusion.

The situation is similar to the construction of the new room in our house. Birds are no longer welcome as actors in this space (except in cages built for them by human beings), and squirrels that dared to enter would now be banished or exterminated immediately. The room is reserved primarily for human actors. Because it is a bedroom, however, and because it is attached to our house, there are implicit constraints on which humans may enter and for what purposes. The hierarchy of actors within this room—family, guests, children, repair persons, and others—is shaped by the range of activities deemed appropriate within the new space—sleeping, playing, fixing appliances, and so forth. The categories of identity correspond to the categories of appropriate activity. It is one thing for a family member to sleep in this room, but it would be considered odd for an electrician to curl up and take a nap. Guests of the family would use the room for sleeping only after appropriate rituals of invitation had been performed. Needless to say, the identities and activities of these same actors would have entirely different meanings in other rooms or buildings.

Within domains, actors are defined with respect to role and status and also with respect to their personal qualities: what is considered admirable or heroic for one person may be considered pushy or unpleasant for another person (or for the same individual in a different domain). Within domains, actors are also defined in more fundamental ways: in some contexts common sense dictates that only individual human beings should be considered significant social actors, but in other contexts ghosts, corporate groups, or even rocks and trees may have their own legal and social identities.[11]

The role of law in defining and characterizing actors varies from one domain to the next. Law and common sense have, for example, interacted continuously to constitute and reconstitute the identity and status of married women in American households. The results have ranged from a virtual denial that married women exist as legal and social actors to a view of married women as equal and independent parties in contract with their husbands.[12] This fluid and dynamic process of identity construction has important consequences for persons within the domain as they carry on their everyday activities. As we shall see in the next section of this essay, the process has been particularly significant for shaping the identities and entitlements of children with disabilities and their parents in their dealings with the public school system.

Time and Space

Time and space are constructed within domains to provide a framework for locating actors, events, and interactions. As Durkheim

---

11. See, e.g., David M. Engel, "Litigation across Space and Time: Courts, Conflict, and Social Change," *Law and Society Review* 24 (1990): 333, 337–39. For more on rocks and trees as legal and social actors, see Christopher D. Stone, "Should Trees Have Standing?—Toward Legal Rights for Natural Objects," *Southern California Law Review* 45 (1972): 450; and Justice Douglas's dissenting opinion in Sierra Club v. Morton, 405 U.S. 727, 741–42 (1972).

12. "It was often said, perhaps with more accuracy than humor, that at common law the husband and wife were one, and the husband was that one." W. Page Keeton et al., eds., *Prosser and Keeton on the Law of Torts*, 5th ed., lawyers ed. (St. Paul, Minn.: West Publishing Co., 1984), 902. Compare Marjorie Maguire Shultz, "Contractual Ordering of Marriage: A New Model for State Policy," *California Law Review* 70 (1982): 204.

observed, time and space serve as "charts" for social life. Such charts are constituted in distinctive ways by different social groups to reflect and to reinforce the activities that are most significant to them.[13] Thus, within different domains, time might be conceptualized according to a variety of cyclical or linear models, and space might be conceptualized according to models ranging from a series of concentric circles to a network of Dreaming lines that trace the mythic journeys and songs of totemic ancestors.[14]

Within the larger frameworks of space and time, many kinds of spatial and temporal substructures are possible. For example, in our society we often conceive of time as being subdivided into a weekly schedule of five workdays followed by two days of nonwork. Each work day is further divided into eight hours of labor and sixteen hours of "rest." The eight hours of labor are typically subdivided into predetermined work spans punctuated by lunch or coffee breaks of specified duration. School schedules provide their own calendrical patterns, as well as the distinctive subdivision of each day into a fixed number of class periods of predetermined length within which instruction is provided. Such temporal subdivisions, at work, at school, and in other contexts, are highly significant for shaping identities and activities within domains. They are often closely connected to legal concepts, such as labor contracts, rights and interests of employers and employees, and requirements and entitlements associated with education laws.

The role of law is particularly apparent in the social construction of space. Law is self-consciously spatial in orientation, and its first concern is to define the boundaries within which it operates. Across

13. Emile Durkheim, *The Elementary Forms of Religious Life: A Study in Religious Sociology*, trans. Joseph Ward Swain (London: George Allen and Unwin; New York: Macmillan, 1915), 10–13.

14. Barton ascribed the concentric conception of social space to the Ifugao of Northern Luzon in the Philippines. The "Home Region" was encircled in successive order by the "Neutral Zone," the "Feudist Zone," and the "War Zone." The farther from the center, the more hostile the social relationships and the more likely it was that violence and the taking of heads would occur. Roy Franklin Barton, *The Half-Way Sun: Life among the Headhunters of the Philippines* (1930; New York: Brewer and Warren, 1978), 113–17. On dreaming lines, see Richard Moyle, "Songs, Ceremonies and Sites: The Agharringa Case," in *Aborigines, Land and Land Rights*, ed. Nicolas Peterson and Marcia Langton (Canberra: Australian Institute of Aboriginal Studies, 1983), 66–93; W. E. H. Stanner, *White Man Got No Dreaming: Essays 1938–1973* (Canberra: Australian National University Press, 1979); and Bruce Chatwin, *The Songlines* (New York: Viking Penguin, 1987).

a social landscape that may include numerous social and cultural groupings and enclaves, the state imposes its own nested jurisdictional structures as well as the rules and procedures applicable at each level. The state's effort to use law to "articulat[e] an ensemble of physical places in which forces are distributed"[15] is seldom, however, an unqualified success. The gridlike spatial demarcations of the state interact with commonsense notions of where things and people are or should be. Such notions vary from one domain to the next, and so do the resulting amalgamations of spatial concepts that characterize everyday life.[16] The construction of time and space within different domains thus involves a continual interplay between legal and commonsense models, and this interplay produces both change and complexity in everyday temporal and spatial concepts.

Community

Domains are structured in time and space but are also shaped around concepts of inclusion and exclusion and of shared values and purpose. Concepts of "belonging" are sometimes expressed in spatial terms.[17] In South Buffalo, an African-American man who crosses the street and enters a traditional Irish-American neighborhood may literally be putting his life at risk. No officially recognized boundary line separates the safe from the unsafe space, but for those who live in the two adjacent communities none is needed. Sometimes, however, the integrity of physical boundaries cannot be maintained, and "undesirable" outsiders come to live on the same streets and in the same neighborhoods as those who deem themselves community insiders. In such instances, nonspatial means may be used to mark the boundaries of the community: by differentiating the saved from the unsaved, the ethnically or racially acceptable from the unacceptable, or by stigmatizing those whose values and behavior depart from what is thought to be the community norm.[18]

---

15. De Certeau, *Practice of Everyday Life*, 38.

16. I have written more extensively about the relationship between law and time in David M. Engel, "Law, Time and Community," *Law and Society Review* 18 (1987): 605; and about law and space in "Litigation across Space and Time," 333.

17. See generally Constance Perin, *Belonging in America: Reading between the Lines* (Madison: University of Wisconsin Press, 1988).

18. Greenhouse, *Praying for Justice*; Constance Perin, *Everything in Its Place:*

Concepts of community are an essential element in the construction of social domains. Such concepts are rarely accepted by all actors within a domain. They may be sharply contested and subject to continual change and redefinition. Domains are often shaped by these ongoing contests over who belongs and who does not and over the central values and goals of the group. Through such contests, the boundaries of the domain are continually redefined and its essential character continually recreated.

The role of law in relation to everyday concepts of community is often of great significance. The tension between legal and "customary" concepts of racial inclusion, for example, has been crucial in shaping perceptions of African-Americans as insiders or outsiders in many domains in American society. The law often makes explicit appeals to everyday concepts of community. It is part of the ideology of American law, for example, that a jury drawn within a given jurisdiction should apply the norms of "the community" in deciding what is reasonable, fair, or customary. Such references, however, are exceedingly problematic when viewed through the lens of common sense. Does "community" refer to the jurisdiction within which the jury was empaneled? If so, common sense tells us that there are usually many communities within a given jurisdiction, and it might take an anthropologist a lifetime to sort out the competing and ever-changing conceptions of their nature and extent.

In some situations, one finds key actors who mediate legal and commonsense concepts of community. Yngvesson, for example, shows how the clerk magistrate of a criminal court in a New England town helps to define the community by responding selectively to applications by citizens and police for issuance of criminal complaints.[19] In picking and choosing among the applications, the clerk lectures, admonishes, and praises and makes explicit and implicit pronouncements about the community itself: Who are its "true" members and who are mere "garbage"? What sorts of nonconforming behavior represent movement toward legitimate community change and what sorts represent deviance that should be sanctioned? The

---

Social Order and Land Use in America (Princeton, N.J.: Princeton University Press, 1977); David M. Engel, "The Oven Bird's Song: Insiders, Outsiders, and Personal Injuries in an American Community," *Law and Society Review* 18 (1984): 551; and Yngvesson, "Making Law at the Doorway."

19. Yngvesson, "Making Law at the Doorway."

clerk is a gatekeeper to the formal legal system, but he is also deeply rooted in the local social order. Through his everyday knowledge of the community and his specialized knowledge of the law, he occupies a key position at the boundary between the two conceptual systems and is able to manipulate both in his efforts to define the community and direct change along paths he considers desirable.

The behavior of such gatekeepers is particularly important in revealing how law and everyday life work together (and apart) to construct images and understandings of community. In addition to Yngvesson's court clerk, researchers have identified other figures, such as the police officer on the neighborhood beat or the divorce lawyer, who perform similar functions within different social domains.[20] In the activities of all these figures, we can perceive the interplay between the different conceptions of community found in law and everyday life and the processes of inclusion and exclusion that determine the form and membership of social domains.

Norms

Within domains, individuals and groups must interact. The patterns of interaction in turn contribute to normative expectations that guide future behavior, facilitate exchanges, process disputes, and even structure hostilities.[21] Domains are usually characterized by a plurality of normative systems of diverse provenance and effect. State norms often overlap or conflict with norms of a less official kind. Marriage rites recognized as obligatory in village societies may compete with state-sanctioned marriage procedures.[22] Business transactions conducted within an industry on the basis of customary practice and a handshake may also be subject to the formal law of contracts and contract enforcement.[23]

---

20. James Q. Wilson, *Varieties of Police Behavior: The Management of Law and Order in Eight Communities* (Cambridge: Harvard University Press, 1968); Donald Black, *The Manners and Customs of the Police* (New York: Academic Press, 1980); and Sarat and Felstiner, "Law and Social Relations."

21. Fuller, "Human Interaction and the Law."

22. David M. Engel, *Code and Custom in a Thai Provincial Court: The Interaction of Formal and Informal Systems of Justice* (Tuscon: University of Arizona Press, 1978).

23. Stewart Macaulay, "Non-contractual Relations in Business: A Preliminary Study," *American Sociological Review* 28 (1983): 55.

The plurality of normative systems creates both complexity and opportunity for actors wtihin domains. In Thailand, for example, persons whose ownership of land is established according to village but not state norms may find themselves evicted by those whose claims lack legitimacy in the village but conform to the rituals of state law. At the same time, persons who have been victimized and powerless within the village may be able to invoke the norms of state law to end oppression or harassment and may thereby transform relationships in this particular domain to their own advantage.[24]

Law may thus reinforce or transform everyday normative systems found within various domains. Law may also be withheld or excluded from domains that have their own distinctive systems of norms and norm enforcement.[25] In American Chinatowns, for example, there is a strong tradition of internal dispute management and a reluctance to allow state law to play a role, even in cases of potentially serious criminal behavior.[26] In sporting events such as American football, hockey, or baseball, even apparent felonious assaults are rarely viewed as subject to state law, because such occurrences are thought to be governed by the domain's own norms and enforcement mechanisms.[27]

---

24. Engel, *Code and Custom*, 154–55, 190–204.

25. Marc Galanter, "Why the 'Haves' Come Out Ahead: Speculation on the Limits of Legal Change," *Law and Society Review* 9 (1974): 95; and Stewart Macaulay, "Private Government," in *Law and the Social Sciences*, ed. Leon Lipson and Stanton Wheeler (New York: Russell Sage Foundation, 1987), 445–518.

26. Leigh-Wai Doo, "Dispute Settlement in Chinese-American Communities," *American Journal of Comparative Law* 21 (1973): 627; and Sally Engle Merry, "Going to Court: Strategies of Dispute Management in an American Urban Neighborhood," *Law and Society Review* 13 (1979): 891.

27. In a recent minor league baseball game in Rochester, New York, for example, a member of the visiting team threw his bat into the stands, where it injured a fan. In retaliation, the hometown pitcher later struck him with a beanball. Both players were then ejected from the game. The next day, however, the local prosecutor became involved. He did not bring charges against the pitcher, for dangerous and intentional assaults with a baseball were apparently considered part of the game's own system of norms and sanctions. By throwing his bat into the stands, however, the batter had gone outside the confines of the game and subjected himself to the more general norms of the criminal law. *Sports Illustrated*, 9 June 1986, 9–10. In a similar incident, criminal charges were brought against Dave Winfield in Toronto for deliberately throwing a baseball at a seagull (the late Billy Martin allegedly commented that this was the first time all year Winfield had hit the cut-off man). What is noteworthy about this incident is that criminal charges are virtually never brought—in Toronto or elsewhere—against pitchers who aim at the heads of opposing batters. Canadian prosecutors, displaying deference to the internal norms of baseball, were prepared to intervene to protect Toronto's seagulls but not to protect its Blue Jays.

In everyday life, people do not shape their conduct or resolve their disputes by referring exclusively to state law as a source of norms. As Galanter has observed, such a world would be a kind of monstrosity, comparable to a conversation in which everyone spoke "written" English rather than the language of colloquial speech.[28] Yet there are few areas of everyday life—not even the world of sports— where the norms of state law have not had some effect. Schools are often cited as domains subject to their own well-entrenched systems of rules and rule enforcement, yet school administrators in the modern era must wield their authority, however arbitrarily, with one eye on the constitutional rights of schoolchildren, tort law liability, building safety codes, and state education laws.[29]

These four elements, actors, time and space, community, and norms, are among the building materials from which domains are constructed. Within such domains people carry on many of the activities of everyday life. The term *domain* may suggest a degree of fixity and solidity that belies the protean realities of social relationships and interactions. In one sense, the construction of a domain is wholly different from the construction of a new room in a house. And yet, from the point of view of the actors themselves, everyday life *is* very often experienced in social contexts that have a sense of "thereness," where people share a common language of ideas about identity, behavior, and obligation. Whether the language is used to express agreement or disagreement, it is recognized that to function within such contexts one must have some fluency. In the discussion that follows, I will explore the role of law in shaping the everyday life experiences of actors in a particular domain: the public school system and its interactions with children with disabilities and their families.

An Example: Schools and Children with Disabilities

One needs to study what kind of body the current society needs.
                    —Michel Foucault, *Power/Knowledge*

---

28. Marc Galanter, "Justice in Many Rooms: Courts, Private Ordering, and Indigenous Law," *Journal of Legal Pluralism* 19 (1981), 1, 3–5.

29. David L. Kirp and Donald N. Jensen, eds., *School Days, Rule Days: The Legalization and Regulation of Education* (Philadelphia: Falmer Press, 1986).

I cannot risk this kind of behavior or take accountability when
he does this. If he stands alone again, I will suspend him for
the remainder of the day.
            —Letter from a school principal to the mother of a teen-
                 ager in a wheelchair who, following surgery, has
                 discovered the ability to stand independently

An unusual network of domains has emerged across the United States
since passage of the Education for All Handicapped Children Act of
1975 (EHA).[30] Because each school district has ultimate responsibility
for implementing this landmark federal statute, these local arenas of
everyday interaction have been infused with a distinctive set of legal
obligations and procedures. The convergence of education law and
everyday life nicely illustrates our concept of a domain.

Although the sweep of federal and state education law provides
for a certain degree of uniformity across such domains, there is in
fact considerable variation. This is the result of the law's interaction
with differing local commonsense notions about education, authority,
disability, children, and parental participation. Variation is also introduced by the idiosyncrasies of local actors, both educators and parents, whose behaviors and perceptions shape each domain in a slightly
different way.

The construction of these domains is not only a vivid illustration
of the role of law in everyday life. It is also a process of vital
importance for children with disabilities. Within these domains the
identity and social status of such children are formed. Their future
hinges in large measure on the process we will now consider, and so
does the future of a society whose definitions of "difference" and
whose efforts at inclusion and exclusion reflect the level of humanity
it seeks to achieve.

Persons with disabilities, asserts Murphy, are "the antiphony of
everyday life." In a society preoccupied with physical exercise and
fitness, people whose bodies look or function differently are perceived
to occupy an anomalous position:

We are subverters of an American ideal, just as the poor are
betrayers of the American Dream. And to the extent that we

---

30. Education for All Handicapped Children Act, Pub. L. No. 94-142, 89 Stat.
773 (1975). The EHA was amended on 30 October 1990 and is now titled Individuals
with Disabilities Education Act, Pub. L. No. 101-476, 104 Stat. 1103 (1990), codified
as amended at 20 U.S.C.A. §§ 1400–1485 (1990 and Supp. 1992).

depart from the ideal, we become ugly and repulsive to the able-bodied. People recoil from us, especially when there is facial damage or bodily distortion.[31]

The anomalous position of persons with physical disabilities, according to Murphy, derives from the fact that they live suspended between two familiar cultural categories: sickness and health. An individual who is paraplegic or whose gait is affected by cerebral palsy is not sick but has many of the attributes we associate with sickness—except for the prospect of eventual recovery and return to "normality." This state of suspension (or liminality) has profound implications for the social identity of persons with disabilities.

Just as the bodies of the disabled are permanently impaired, so also is their standing as members of society. The lasting inde-terminacy of their state of being produces a similar lack of def-inition of their social roles, which are in any event superseded and obscured by submersion of their identities. Their persons are regarded as contaminated; eyes are averted and people take care not to approach wheelchairs too closely.[32]

It is in childhood that many people with physical disabilities first learn that, in the eyes of others, their social identity is impaired, that a difficulty in walking, for example, somehow places them in a social category apart from and inferior to those whose gait is defined as normal. Historically, the American educational system contributed to the segregated social status of children with disabilities by sending them to different schools and classrooms and by refusing to provide support services and special programs that would allow them to participate in the mainstream.

With the passage of the Education for All Handicapped Children Act of 1975, the federal government required states receiving federal education funds to integrate children with disabilities into the "least restrictive environment" and to provide them a "free and appropriate public education" suited to their individual needs. The Act, as amended, now requires that each school district evaluate and classify

---

31. Robert F. Murphy, *The Body Silent* (New York: H. Holt, 1987), 135, 116–17.
32. Id., 135.

as "children with disabilities" those children who meet certain criteria and therefore fall within accepted categories: children "with mental retardation, hearing impairments including deafness, speech or language impairments, visual impairments including blindness, serious emotional disturbance, orthopedic impairments, autism, traumatic brain injury, other health impairments, or specific learning disabilities" (Section 1401(a)(1)(A)(i)). The parents of each child classified as disabled are to have the opportunity to meet with a multidisciplinary committee of their school district at least once a year and to help formulate an Individualized Education Program (IEP) specifically tailored to the needs of their child. In New York State, these multidisciplinary school district committees are now known as Committees on Special Education (CSE).[33]

The IEP, which is the product of the meeting between parents and CSE, was meant to provide a ticket to an "appropriate" education for each child with a disability. As a result, such children were to receive greater opportunities to interact with their nondisabled peers and to obtain educational training that would enable them to participate more effectively in "normal" society. In short, law was to be used to change the categories and behavior of everyday life and, by starting at an early age, to transform the impaired social identities of those who belonged to one of the largest and least understood minority groups in our society.

Actors: "The Antiphony of Everyday Life"

The actors whose dealings with one another structure these domains and whose identities are shaped by them include children, families, and educators. In this section, I will examine the construction of identities and attributes for each of these three sets of actors. At the center of this discussion (and of the sections that follow) are the

---

33. Mandated members of the CSE are a specialist in special education, the child's teacher, the child's parents, the child "whenever appropriate," and other persons at the discretion of the school district or the parents. 20 U.S.C.A. § 1401(a)(20)(Supp. 1992) and 34 C.F.R. 300.344(a) (1991). In addition, New York law requires that each CSE include a school psychologist, a school physician, and a parent of a handicapped child residing in the school district. N.Y. Educ. Law § 4402(1)(b)(1) (McKinney Supp. 1992). Many CSEs add numerous other members beyond those mandated by law, including social workers, nurses, and other teachers and specialists.

young children with physical disabilities who were the subjects of my research.[34] I will allude to six of these children in particular. All six had attended the preschool program of the United Cerebral Palsy Association before reaching school age and coming under the jurisdiction of their school district's Committee on Special Education.[35]

Joe DeMarco was seven at the time my fieldwork began. The son of a blue-collar worker and a "homemaker,"[36] Joe was a very active boy who walked with a limp because of the effects of cerebral palsy. Joe also had seizures and a slight speech problem. He attended a small, self-contained classroom. *Pat Dolan* was also seven. His mother was for the most part confined to her small home by multiple sclerosis. Pat walked with an uneven gait and had some behavior problems. His mother described him as "a terror . . . borderline retarded . . . not a huggable child." He attended a regular classroom, which he "hated." *Chris Getz*, also seven, was the son of a civil servant and a "housewife." Chris had limited speech ability, a seizure disorder, and severe asthma. Chris was very active and imaginative

---

34. The fieldwork on which this essay is based involved children with physical disabilities, in most cases cerebral palsy. Approximately 140 interviews with parents—and in many cases with the children themselves—took place over a fifteen-month period in urban, suburban, and rural settings in western New York. The six families discussed in this essay were among ten families whom I interviewed frequently throughout the study to explore contemporaneously their changing perceptions, experiences, and conflicts. In addition, I interviewed twenty other families twice during the 15-month period in order to trace the development and implementation of an educational program over the course of an academic year. Eight additional families were interviewed only once, since their children had just reached school age at the end of the fieldwork period, and their contacts with the school districts had just begun. A group of nineteen families whose children had physical disabilities but had *not* necessarily attended the UCPA preschool program was interviewed on the basis of their having sought legal assistance from the Education Law Clinic of the SUNY at Buffalo School of Law. Thirty further interviews were conducted in eighteen school districts throughout western New York with chairpersons and other members of district Committees on Special Education. Quoted material in this essay is taken verbatim from transcripts of taped interviews. This study and its findings are discussed further in David M. Engel, "Law, Culture, and Children with Disabilities: Educational Rights and the Construction of Difference," *Duke Law Journal* 1991 (1991): 166.

35. Since the time of my fieldwork, New York State lowered the age (from five years to three years) at which children with disabilities first participate in the IEP process. There is now a "Committee on Preschool Special Education" for children with disabilities who are three to four years of age. 1989 N.Y. Laws 243 (codified as amended at N.Y. Educ. Law § 4410 [McKinney's Supp. 1992]).

36. The use of quotation marks is meant to identify words or expressions parents used in describing themselves, their children, and their experiences.

and enjoyed physical and outdoor activities. He attended a special
school for children with speech disorders. *Laurie Hibbard*, six years
old when I first met her family, was born with a portion of her brain
undeveloped and as a consequence was unable to walk, speak, feed,
or toilet herself. She enjoyed playing with numbers and letters and
was an avid fan of Sesame Street. Laurie's mother, Christine, was a
part-time waitress, and her father, George, was an industrial worker.
Laurie attended a self-contained classroom with other children who
had extensive disabilities. *Beverly Lambert* was nine. Her father was
a blue-collar city employee and her mother was a student. Beverly,
described by her parents as fun, bright, energetic, and eager to learn,
used a wheelchair and had very limited speech. She attended a school
for children with disabilities. *Jon Mueller* was five years old and had
just entered kindergarten at a local parochial school. His mother was
an assistant in the mental health field, and his father operated a small
business. Jon's cerebral palsy affected his gait, requiring the use of
braces, and appeared to have some impact on his cognitive processes
as well. Jon was athletic and active in neighborhood sports and
enjoyed having his parents read to him.

Children such as these provide a raison d'etre for the domains
we shall discuss and for contests over identity within the domains.
The most important encounters between the families of children with
disabilities and the CSEs occur at the annual planning meeting, which
is usually held each spring or summer to formulate a program for
the coming year. These meetings were an annual event for the six
families from the time their children entered kindergarten and would
continue until they completed high school. It is during the annual
meetings in particular that the transformative thrust of the law meets
the cultural categories of everyday life.

It is a central irony of the EHA that each child who seeks to
benefit from its mainstreaming provisions must first be classified as
fundamentally different from his or her peers. Only those who have
been classified as "handicapped" (or, under the amended version of
the Act, as "disabled") are entitled to the individualized programming
and support services mandated by the EHA. Thus, the quest for a
normalized social identity begins with a determination that the child
is in some sense "abnormal." Parents seeking integrated placements
must then argue that it is nevertheless appropriate for their "abnor-

mal" child to be educated together with the children from whom he or she differs. Without the initial classification establishing deviation from the "norm," children with disabilities would be forced to do without services that may be essential to their academic survival and success. Yet if the child is perceived as differing too greatly from the "normal child," the CSE may decide to place him or her in a segregated classroom, where, in the view of many parents and critics, the child's educational goals will be drastically limited, and the child's social development will be restricted through lack of contact with nondisabled peers.[37]

Parents thus realize that much is at stake in the classification process, even the construction of their child's identity. They are cognizant of the stigmatizing effects of everyday categories of disability, and they often display uneasiness about the tendency to reify such categories through the types of disabilities listed in the Act and in the Regulations of the Commissioner of Education of New York State.[38] They need the classification for their children, but they chafe under the necessity of participating in the same process of categorization whose stigmatizing effects they are attempting to mitigate. The Getz family, for example, dealt with this dilemma by insisting on the classification they deemed least pejorative. It was acceptable to label Chris "speech impaired" because that did not imply any of the other limitations of his mental or physical capacities, which they believed the CSE was all too ready to attribute to him.

The Lamberts questioned the use of the term "multiply handicapped" for Beverly. They felt that the term was so broad and so vague that it could mean almost anything. It certainly failed to describe the reality of Beverly's circumstances as her parents perceived them. Finally, Catherine Lambert asked the chair of the CSE, "Does it mean dollars and cents in state aid by calling it multiply handicapped?" When he told her that it did, she agreed to the classification yet drew a firm distinction between the law and what was, to her, common sense: "If they want to call her multiply handicapped, that's fine. If someone is having a conversation with me about her and

---

37. Concerning this "dilemma of difference," see Martha Minow, *Making All the Difference: Inclusion, Exclusion, and American Law* (Ithaca, N.Y.: Cornell University Press, 1990); and Engel, "Law, Culture."

38. N.Y. Comp. Codes. R. & Regs. title 8, Subchap. P, Pt. 200.

they say what are Beverly's problems, I tell them what her problems are.... I say, she has CP, and she doesn't see so hot without her glasses."

The classification process involves placing children into a set of conceptual boxes mandated by law yet given a distinctive meaning, often to the children's detriment, by everyday life. Once children are perceived as subject to classification—once they are categorized as handicapped (or, more recently, as disabled)—a number of deeply rooted assumptions about the attributes and capacities of "handicapped" persons come into play. The legal entitlement to special transportation services is translated in everyday life into being a rider on the "retard bus." Children who receive supplemental instruction in a classroom taught by a special-education teacher are known to the other children as "rumps."

Such assumptions about persons with disabilities are not limited to the stereotypes of the children's peers. Suzanne DeMarco, for example, recounted a revealing conversation with her son's classroom teacher. Joe's class was composed of children from several different school districts who were bused substantial distances to study in a room that was segregated, for the most part, from the rest of the school. Suzanne DeMarco had objected to this arrangement because it isolated Joe both from other children in that school and, in a more general sense, from neighborhood children who attended a school near their home. In addition, she was frustrated that each year Joe was moved from school to school with an ever-changing set of classmates. The response by Joe's teacher suggested that she perceived Joe's identity as a "handicapped" child in terms that differed substantially from Suzanne DeMarco's perception:

> She [Joe's teacher] said within five years we'll be able to keep the kids until they are twenty-four.... And he'll be able to go into a work-study program, through GoodWill, I suppose. And I'm going, that's not my long-term goal for Joe. I mean, Basket Weaving 101 would be my last resort, and I'm pushing for college. And we're talking, you know, "We're going to put him in a work-study program, and we're going to teach him how to accept his handicap." I go, "I don't want him to accept it. I want him to go beyond it and overcome it! Forget that he has a handicap! And your philosophy is not going along with mine." And she

told me that I was prejudiced and that I was practically a bigot and that I had all these awful ideas about handicapped kids and retard buses.

Because Suzanne DeMarco viewed her son's identity as essentially similar to that of other children, she assumed that he should be attending school with his neighborhood friends and working toward comparable long-term goals. Joe's disability was a factor to be dealt with—through appropriate support services—but to her it should not be all-determinative. Suzanne DeMarco felt that the teacher viewed Joe's identity primarily in terms of his disability and assumed that the major challenge facing all of them was to "accept" Joe's "handicap" and to lower their expectations accordingly. In addition, Joe's "handicap" in the teacher's mind seemed to justify a largely segregated social existence, in separate schools and classrooms and in buses different from those used by other children (physically, Joe was quite capable of using a "normal" school bus). Joe's "handicap," furthermore, was the reason that special education administrators constructed for him a year-to-year floating existence, in which Joe and his parents were not told where he would be attending school until a week or two before the beginning of the new semester. Each year, there was a new school, with new classmates, and a new teacher. This sort of arrangement, contended Suzanne DeMarco, would never be accepted by parents of "normal" children, but the parents of children with disabilities were supposed to resign themselves or be accused of failure to "accept the handicap." Although the EHA was supposed to have made mainstreaming the norm, segregation remained the unstated assumption, and, at times, psychobabble triumphed over law.

Despite the powerful influence of everyday conceptions of disability on the special-education process, however, it would be a mistake to conclude that law is irrelevant to the struggle to define the identity of these children. The EHA itself resulted from the efforts of a grass-roots organization of disability rights advocates. It undoubtedly shaped the rights consciousness of many parents and children throughout the country. In addition, the EHA has provided some legal tools for those who have achieved full integration of children with disabilities into regular classrooms. Parents of children with autism or Downs syndrome, for example, have successfully argued in some parts of the country for placements in classrooms with nondisabled children. They have buttressed their arguments with references to the Act's requirement that

> to the maximum extent appropriate, children with disabilities [be] educated with children who are not disabled, and that special classes, separate schooling, or other removal of children with disabilities from the regular educational environment [occur] only when the nature or severity of the disability is such that education in regular classes with the use of supplementary aids and services cannot be achieved satisfactorily.[39]

Law provides an influence, a vector for change, but its open-ended terms ("appropriate," "satisfactorily") must be shaped by commonsense knowledge about disabilities and schooling. The fact that segregation and stereotyping persist despite the mandate of the Act reveals the persistence of commonsense categories of knowledge about children with disabilities. The fact that some parents—including Suzanne DeMarco—successfully oppose segregation and stereotypes reveals the potential use of law to contest these categories and to reconstitute the ways in which identities are defined in everyday life.

The interaction of law and common sense shapes the identities and attributes of parties in many other ways. The identities of parents, for example, remain problematic within this domain. When parents deal with school authorities, are they the primary parties in interest or merely the representatives of their children? Or is the parent-child unit a kind of corporate party in these situations? The Act speaks of the individual substantive rights of the children, but these are secured in large measure by procedural rights that the parents can invoke. What if the parents misrepresent the real interests of the children? School officials argue that this often occurs. But when school officials suggest, "Let's ask Johnny what *he* thinks," they appear to parents to be using their power of intimidation over the child to undercut the child's best advocates. And parents are usually not pleased when school officials assume that the parent's assertiveness is merely a neurotic coping mechanism for which the appropriate

---

39. Individuals with Disabilities Education Act (IDEA), codified as amended at 20 U.S.C.A. § 1412(5)(Supp. 1992).

response is to recommend counseling rather than to pay attention to what the parent is saying. The construction of the identity of the party at interest—is it the child, the child and parents as a single unit, the parents on behalf of the child?—thus remains an issue of considerable tension and uncertainty within this domain.

The identities of the school officials are also shaped by the interplay between law and everyday life. The CSE, for example, is a corporate actor created by law and not by custom or tradition. There is no commonsense counterpart to this group of school-district personnel who are required to confer with parents at least once a year in a cooperative effort to devise an "appropriate" educational plan for each child. Its *existence* is entirely a phenomenon of the law; yet its nature and function are largely determined by commonsense assumptions that define disability as a medical disorder requiring scientific expertise to interpret and treat.

The CSE is composed primarily of individuals who possess such expertise and who can speak the language of medicine, psychology, and educational theory. Their expertise, and the culturally based assumptions that privilege such esoteric knowledge in matters relating to disabilities, affect the interaction between parents and the CSE in two important ways. First, parents generally feel unable to participate in the specialized discourse that is used at CSE meetings to describe their child and the programming options under consideration. Second, parents feel isolated at CSE meetings. They view the other members of the CSE as a cohesive group and themselves as outsiders who sit in specially designated chairs at the end of a long table, who enter the room after all other CSE members are already present (and, parents usually suspect, after there has been some discussion of *their* child to which they have not been privy).

In the CSE discussions, parents often feel that, although they know their children best, their knowledge is of a type that carries no weight. Indeed, the emotional attachment of parents to their children may be viewed as a detriment to the planning process rather than an asset. The wishes of the parents, expressed in lay terms and overlaid with emotion, are often dismissed as subjective and irrational or are explained away in terms of the parents' failure to "accept the handicap." Several parents noted that the CSEs had brushed aside certain requests they had voiced but later adopted them without hesitation when put forward by a professional.

The identities and attributes of actors within this domain are thus shaped in distinctive ways by concepts associated with both law and common sense. For the children, there is a continual tension between normalization and the categories of abnormality, between inclusion and the requirements of special treatment. For the parents, there is the ambiguity of identifying interests within a family unit and of designating parents to be the primary advocates for their children in the IEP process. For the CSE members, there is the problem of constituting themselves as a committee that might engage in a genuine dialogue with persons they would usually regard as clients or patients. It is clear that commonsense concepts about these three sets of actors pervade the domain of special education in each school district. Yet law created the CSE, mandated the interaction between parents and CSE members, and vested the children and parents with significant substantive and procedural rights. Thus, the actors' identities in this domain are also constituted by the legal treatment of "difference" and by the tensions between legal entitlement and social disempowerment. In everyday life, understandings about children with disabilities, parents, and educators emerge out of the flux and uncertainty associated with the interaction of law and common sense.

Space and Time: Locations and Dislocations

For parents, the social space in which their child lives and forms relationships is typically the immediate neighborhood. As space extends beyond the neighborhood, it quickly becomes terra incognita. As is apparent in many conflicts over busing to achieve racial balance in schools, this terra incognita may have an ominous or threatening aspect, particularly if its inhabitants include persons of a different race or social class.

Law and government typically define space without reference to such cognitive maps. For educational purposes, the fundamental spatial unit is the school district. Within this unit, there may be many neighborhoods and communities, and the population may be quite heterogeneous, particularly in urban areas. Not surprisingly, parents I interviewed in the city of Buffalo (nearly all of whom were white) strongly opposed having their children bused to schools outside their neighborhood, whether the purpose was to achieve segregation by disability or integration by race.

For the Muellers, the neighborhood school was the local Catholic school. That was where all of Jon's friends went in order to avoid the desegregation plan mandated by the federal district court, and that was where the Muellers wanted Jon to go. For them, the boundary lines drawn by the parochial school system superseded the boundary lines of the public school district as significant social markers because the former came closer to marking off the social space the Muellers associated with their neighborhood. Because of this difference in the conceptualization of space, one of the primary subjects of contention between the Muellers and their CSE involved the delivery of special education services to a child who attended a Catholic school. Tension in the relationship between this family and the CSE originated in a clash between legal and nonlegal constructions of space.

For parents who live in smaller school districts outside the city of Buffalo, space is constructed—by law and by common sense—in a series of concentric circles. Closest to home is the neighborhood. Next comes the school district and then the larger and more inclusive BOCES district (as explained below). Somewhere within or just beyond the BOCES district is the beginning of terra incognita. Sometimes parents perceive the space within their local school district in positive terms, at least to the extent they feel that their district offers superior educational services. Some parents had deliberately decided to locate themselves within a particular school district because they expected that the quality of education for their child would be high within that space. They were then chagrined to find that children with disabilities were frequently bused to schools *outside* the school district but within their BOCES area.

The Board of Cooperative Educational Services (BOCES) is a kind of mega–school district designed to provide services and programs that individual school districts might not be able to afford on their own. In western New York, BOCES units vary in size, some serving as many as twenty-eight individual school districts (the city of Buffalo, which functions as a single school district, does not participate in a BOCES structure). Many of the children I studied attended "self-contained" BOCES classrooms staffed by BOCES teachers, supported by BOCES therapists and aides. These classrooms brought together children from many different school districts, some of whom traveled many miles by bus each day.

Parental complaints about BOCES are frequent and bitter, and often the underlying problem is related to social space or distance. When children with special physical needs, seizure disorders, or medication requirements have to ride on a bus two or three hours each day, it creates discomfort, health risks, and learning problems. Special buses often travel circuitous routes in order to pick up other children with disabilities, and sometimes they lack trained and reliable bus aides. One parent complained that her child's head was not adequately supported by the bus seat and, because of weak muscle control, tended to flop from side to side. The next, day, her child came home with a noose fastened to the side of the bus and tied securely around her neck!

In addition to the hazards of long-distance busing for children with disabilities, some parents complained that BOCES classrooms were composed of children from distant communities. The classrooms were usually reshuffled from year to year, so that even if friendships formed there was little opportunity for continuity of relationships. It was difficult to get together with classmates whose homes were far away. In many interviews, parents asked why their children had to attend schools outside the spatial boundaries of their communities simply because they had disabilities. These, after all, are the children *least* able to cope with the demands of distance and constant change and are the children who find it *most* difficult to form friendships. In addition, parental contact with teachers and service providers needs to be more frequent and intense for children with disabilities, and the problem of distance means that such contact becomes difficult. In this way, too, competing conceptions of space create concern and frustration. The solution for an increasing number of parents (outside the city of Buffalo) is to insist that a single spatial unit—the school district rather than the BOCES unit—be used for all children whether they have disabilities or not. These parents want their children in the neighborhood school.

In the conceptualization of time, there is a similar tension between categories created or sanctioned by the state and categories reflecting everyday common sense. The construction of time has relevance both to short-term programming and to long-term development of children from infancy to adulthood.

Within the special education system, time is marked in yearly cycles. Each year, usually in the spring or early summer, the CSE must meet to assess progress toward educational goals and to develop a new IEP. Every three years, the CSE must provide a review with additional testing and reassessment. Each fall and, for some children, each summer, an assignment is made to a particular classroom and a particular teacher and group of classmates. Thus, educational programs and social relationships are shaped within the yearly cycles mandated by state and federal law.

The annual educational cycle is not a fact of nature but a human construct. The process of human learning could be carved into larger or smaller segments or could be conceptualized as an unsegmented continuum. Likewise, the formation of peer relationships or teacher-student relationships need not occur within time units of nine or twelve months. The annual cycle was devised by educational administrators to reflect their conception of human growth and development and their policies as to how educational services should be delivered.

Within the span of a year, educators subdivide time into smaller units: the semester and the school day itself. The school day typically consists of a specific number of class periods of fixed length. Learning segments do not usually expand or contract to fit the subject of study or the learning styles of the individual students. Rather, learning takes place *within* time segments of thirty, forty, or fifty minutes, the length of which is predetermined by school policy.

The rigid time boundaries of the school day inevitably constrain the process of teaching and learning. For children with disabilities, whose programs have been individually tailored around their special educational needs, these constraints can lead to difficulty. Consider Jon Mueller, for example. As his parents contemplated the transition from half-day kindergarten to full-day first grade, they asked how an "appropriate" program of physical therapy would be scheduled. Generally, therapists schedule their sessions in half-hour time blocks. This raised two problems. First, the Muellers felt (and some therapists would agree with them) that a half hour was less beneficial than sessions of forty-five minutes to an hour. Parental requests for longer therapy sessions, however, are seldom granted because this would depart from convention and would disrupt therapy schedules. Second, the Muellers were concerned that Jon's therapy would conflict with regular class meetings. The problem was especially acute for the Muellers because Jon was in a parochial school and the school district required that his parents transport him to a "neutral" site away from his school building to receive physical therapy. Transportation back and forth took additional time from his academic work. One solution would have been for Jon to receive his therapy after school, but the Muellers were not optimistic about this possibility. Some districts and BOCES providers refuse to offer therapy outside "school time." This frequently means that there are time conflicts between therapy needs and academic needs, and such conflicts must be reconciled within the temporal segments created by the school. Parents and children are thus presented with a Hobson's choice of *either* adequate therapy *or* adequate instruction.

Parents, as well as educators, tend to accept school routines, including the rigid time blocks of the school day, as givens, as facts of the commonsense world in which they live. Yet in some interviews, parents spoke in idealized terms about the kind of educational programming that would really benefit their children. The conflict between these ideal programs and the conventional conceptualization of school time suggests that the problem goes beyond disagreements over therapy schedules and class periods. Some children are hyperactive, have attention deficit disorders, or are affected by seizure medication. Others require longer to absorb what is being taught. A truly individualized and "appropriate" education would disaggregate commonsense notions of time within the school day and restructure it for each child.

If time were individualized in this way, it would strike at the heart of the routines developed to provide mass education. No one suggested to me that this should be done in order to meet legal requirements that each child's IEP be individualized, nor is it clear how it could be accomplished without transforming the entire school in the process. At best, time variances or limited exceptions were granted (e.g., extra time to take an exam, less time for homeroom in order to accommodate therapy). If "handicapped" children are to take part in "normal" classrooms, it is clear that most school districts will require them to sacrifice a significant measure of their right to individualization in order to squeeze their education into the time segments of the public education system.

The construction of time in terms of an annual cycle has further implications for children with disabilities. Academic achievement as well as other aspects of human development are conventionally measured in terms of chronological age. Children with disabilities, who are perhaps the most frequently tested of all humans on earth, are constantly compared to "age-appropriate" norms. There is thus an important time dimension to the concept of disability itself. A child with a disability is not simply a child who has difficulty with math or who cannot cut accurately with scissors. Rather, a child with a disability is defined as one whose math skills or dexterity with scissors deviate significantly from those of the average skills of other children at the same calendar age.

When children with disabilities work their way through a school system, the process of temporal comparison continues. Attention is typically focused on whether a child is able to do, for example, what is considered third-grade reading or fifth-grade science. Yet this time-conditioned view may be particularly inappropriate for some children with disabilities, whose learning styles and ability profiles differ significantly from those of children without disabilities. For children with disabilities, the concept of a linear temporal progression from one annual grade level to the next may have little relevance to the way in which they experience the world and add to their store of knowledge and ability.

Parents may thus experience frustration in attempting to integrate their child into mainstream classrooms because the child in some ways is "out of time" (as time is constructed for educational purposes) and unable to participate in the standardized progression from one temporal stage to another. Being "out of time" may be interpreted by some educators as lacking in academic aptitude or learning potential, yet many parents feel that conventional evaluation procedures tend to overemphasize their children's deficits and underestimate their abilities. Their child is learning different things in a different way, and the importance of that learning process should not be entirely discounted because of an overly mechanistic attachment to standardized testing.[40]

Ironically, when classroom placements and routines are altered to reflect the sense of being "out of time," parents feel that a different set of risks may be created. When children with disabilities are placed in segregated special-education classrooms, time-related expectations are sometimes abandoned by teachers and administrators. Although in one sense this introduces flexibility to the education of children with different learning styles, in another sense it can serve as an

---

40. Compare Oliver Sacks, *The Man Who Mistook His Wife for a Hat and Other Clinical Tales* (New York: Summit Books, 1985), 181.

excuse for the abandonment of meaningful educational goals, as defined in terms of conventional temporal categories. Parents are disconcerted to see their children falling further and further behind the academic work of other children who are the same age. They ask how and when their child will catch up through the intervention of special education. In fact, however, it is not at all clear that the special-education system is capable of helping children with disabilities (at least those in self-contained classes) to "catch up" to the standardized temporal achievement levels of the "average" child or even of benefiting such children in any significant way.[41]

Lou Brown, in his public lectures, tells of parents who were informed by an educational specialist that their three-year-old child was already two full years "behind" in development. To the specialist's surprise, the parents expressed relief rather then concern. "That's not as bad as we thought," they observed. "By the time she's twenty-one, she'll be like a normal nineteen-year-old." The specialist then explained to the parents that things didn't work that way. Their child's education would be structured in such a way that each year she would fall further behind. The longer she was in special education, the more "retarded" she would become. By the time she turned twenty-one, she would be closer to the level of an eight-year-old than that of a nineteen-year-old. "That's what special education is all about," he concluded.[42]

For parents of children with disabilities, the humor of the story is also painful. Even though age-related measures of development may seem irrelevant to their child in many respects, they provide the only means by which parents are able to insist that their child's educational needs be taken seriously. They provide a means of quantifying progress that is sometimes useful to the parents for purposes of advocacy. If progress is not being made from year to year, if their child is indeed falling further behind others in the temporal grid

41. "There is no compelling body of evidence that segregated special education programs have significant benefits for students. On the contrary, there is substantial and growing evidence that goes in the opposite direction." Alan Gartner and Dorothy Kerzner Lipsky, "Beyond Special Education: Toward a Quality System for All Students," *Harvard Educational Review* 53 (1987): 367, 375.

42. Lou Brown teaches in the Education School of the University of Wisconsin at Madison. I heard him tell this story—or one pretty close to it—at a lecture in Williamsville, New York, on 7 April 1990.

constructed by educational specialists, then parents can argue that programs and services are not accomplishing their purposes.

Thus, as inappropriate as normalized age-related measures might be for children with disabilities, neither parents nor educators are able to conceive of some other commonsense system that might serve as an alternative, and there are genuine risks associated with placement in programs and classes that are simply "out of time." Although parents might resist the Procrustean bed of conventional time concepts because such concepts are in some ways inconsistent with legally mandated individualization, there is also a contrary danger that the child will float through a timeless academic never-never land in which expectations are low and progress is irrelevant. Such an eventuality would not represent the emergence of a child-appropriate conceptualization of time but a failure to redefine time to develop each child's unique potential to the fullest possible extent.

Community: The Path to Inclusion

In the domain of schools, parents, and children with disabilities, there are two interrelated problems of community. The first problem is whether children with disabilities are to be included in everyday society, for which the school-district domain serves as a microcosm. The second problem is whether there exists a broader, overarching community of children with disabilities (and their parents) that could advocate the interests of its members and could act as a force for inclusiveness within particular domains such as the public schools. The first problem involves (in Goffman's terms) the inclusion of stigmatized persons in a community of the "normal." The second problem involves the formation of a community of the stigmatized, a "community of disability."[43] Both types of community, as we shall see, are important in the shaping of everyday understandings of children with disabilities. Both are significantly affected by law.

The interrelationships between these two problems of community can be illustrated by comparing the differing responses of the Lamberts and the Hibbards to the issue of scarce resources for their

---

43. Erving Goffman, *Stigma: Notes on the Management of Spoiled Identity* (New York: Simon and Schuster, 1963).

children in the school system. Before the Lamberts moved from California to the town of Bentley in western New York, Beverly had
been receiving physical therapy three times a week. Upon placement
in her school for children with disabilities, however, the Lamberts
received a new IEP stating that Beverly would receive therapy only
twice a week. Knowing that the reduction in therapy was a concern
to Beverly's orthopedist, Catherine called her CSE to ask why the
service had been cut back. The reason, she learned, was that Beverly's
school was short of staff, and if Beverly were to receive three sessions
per week then another child's therapy would have to be reduced.
Catherine's reply was, "I feel real bad about that, but that's not my
problem, that's your problem."

Christine Hibbard's daughter, Laurie, was also assigned a physical
therapist twice a week. Christine felt that Laurie, who was on the
verge of independent ambulation with a walker, should receive therapy between three and five times per week. But, unlike Catherine
Lambert, she was unwilling to question or challenge the CSE on this
point. She knew that there was a shortage of therapists, and to ask
for more therapy sessions for Laurie would be "selfish . . . because
that's thinking of my child and not of other children."

Catherine Lambert and Christine Hibbard approached the same
problem with fundamentally different perspectives on the question
of community and the individual. Catherine Lambert's response was
based on her ultimate goal of having Beverly included in the community of the "normal." She understood that the law supported this
goal by requiring an individualized determination of the unique needs
of each child. Therapy levels for her child were not to be determined
by reference to what other children with disabilities needed or could
obtain. State and federal subsidies could defray some of the costs of
services required by each child. But even if resources were insufficient
for all children to receive the services to which they were entitled,
then, according to this perspective, the school district would have to
find a way to obtain more resources or face legal action by the
parents.[44] Children with disabilities would ultimately attain inclusion

---

44. In the influential case of Mills v. Board of Education of the District of
Columbia, 348 F. Supp. 866, 876 (D.D.C. 1972), which was decided before passage
of the EHA, the federal district court stated:

> [T]he District of Columbia's interest in educating the excluded children clearly
> must outweigh its interest in preserving its financial resources. If sufficient funds

in the community (in this case, in the public school system) only if each individual set of parents insisted on each child's full legal entitlements.

Christine Hibbard, on the other hand, viewed herself and her child primarily in terms of their membership in a community of children with disabilities—a community of the "stigmatized"—whose circumstances were interdependent. She did not perceive the pool of resources, particularly physical therapists, who were in chronically short supply, as expandable. Her perception was that available resources should be allocated to advance the community of children with disabilities as a group. If any one parent sought a disproportionate share, then the interests of other children in the community would suffer. If Laurie learned to walk, it would mean some other child was still crawling.

Catherine Lambert's version of common sense would probably be identified as the "correct" one under the law. The EHA was premised upon an individualistic view of children with disabilities and their families. Each child is a rights-bearing person whose programming and progress can and should be determined without reference to other "handicapped" children served by the CSE. In this sense, connections among all children with disabilities and their families have no place in the legislative scheme of things. The statute was designed to promote greater inclusion of each child in the "normal" community but not necessarily to foster a sense of community among its beneficiaries. Each child was to come before each school district as an individual case to be decided on its own merits. The EHA did not contemplate that CSE officials or parents like Christine Hibbard would determine individual service levels with reference to the welfare of other children with disabilities. The law, which was created in large measure because parents *had* formed effective political alliances and promoted a new sense of community, spoke only in terms of individualism.[45]

---

are not available to finance all of the services and programs that are needed and desirable in the system then the available funds must be expended equitably in such a manner that no child is entirely excluded from a publicly supported education consistent with his needs and ability to benefit therefrom.

45. The activities of the National Association for Retarded Citizens (NARC) and the Council for Exceptional Children (CEC) were especially influential in the political processes leading to passage of the EHA. See Erwin L. Levine and Elizabeth M. Wexler, *PL 94-142: An Act of Congress* (New York: Macmillan, 1981), 27–33.

As school district officials attempt to comply with their responsibilities under the law, they are affected in somewhat inconsistent ways by these variations in everyday perceptions of community. On the one hand, they often approach the provision of services with a community-of-disability perspective on apportioning available resources rather than emphasizing the individualized needs of each child. On the other hand, they rarely take affirmative steps to foster a sense of community among the children and families they serve.

In the districts I studied, school administrators never brought together the families of children with disabilities within a given school district or held group meetings for all the families served by the CSE. They did not attempt to organize parent groups and, in several instances, they actually discouraged the parents themselves from doing so by citing legal requirements of confidentiality to justify their refusal to facilitate contacts.[46]

In Christine Hibbard's case, a strong sense of the "community of disability" tended to make her less insistent upon services for her child. Yet school district officials seem to understand that this might not always be the case. Parent organizations might actually increase and sharpen the demands for services, challenge existing routines, and cost the district more money. The possibility of parent-instigated change can present problems for professionals who have operated with relatively little parent involvement in the past.

Thus, neither the law nor those who implement it tend to promote a sense of community among the families of children with disabilities. It is interesting to consider why the sense of community does not emerge spontaneously in everyday life, quite apart from the individualizing effects of the EHA. After all, one sees such communities among many other minority groups in our society. Why not a community of children with disabilities and their families? I have attended gatherings where parents of children in special education discovered one another with great excitement and have asked myself why these are rare and atypical events.

One explanation lies in the absense of a spatial nexus around

---

46. The usual procedure for formation of such parent groups would be for the district to distribute information about the groups to the parents of every child receiving special education services. In that way, confidentiality need not be breached but interested parents could choose to contact the parent group if they wished to become members.

which such a community might form. Children with disabilities who live with their parents are not usually clustered in particular residential areas. A town may have neighborhoods that are primarily African-American, Hispanic, Irish, or Italian, but there are no neighborhoods that are primarily composed of people with disabilities.[47] The reason is obvious: children with disabilities are not necessarily born to parents with disabilities. Membership in this minority group is in most cases a random occurrence that may appear in *any* family or neighborhood.

Furthermore, the fact that the parents often do not have disabilities themselves means that they may be unfamiliar with the needs, life-styles, or experiences of people with disabilities. Often their own child is the first person they have known well who has a childhood disability, and the parents, at least initially, may be prone to the same stereotypes and misconceptions as those held by the general population. As they learn over the years about their child's disability, they may remain ignorant about other kinds of disabilities. All of these factors tend to diminish the likelihood that parents of children who have many different kinds and degrees of disability will readily view themselves as members of a single community.

The dissimilarity of individual circumstances suggests another kind of obstacle for the creation of a sense of "community of disability" in everyday life. The terms *disability* or *handicap* are used in everyday speech as if they have some actual social referent. Yet being blind, having a learning disability, and being emotionally disturbed (to cite three examples) are very different things. We think of them as one thing because we have an everyday word and a legal category, disabled or handicapped, that has been applied to them all. The existential reality of raising children who are disabled in these three different ways, however, requires some attention. Parents of these

---

47. I am not speaking here of neighborhoods in which there are group homes or residential institutions created specifically for persons with disabilities. Even in such cases, however, the residences would not usually create a sense that the entire neighborhood had become a community for the disabled, comparable to the racial or ethnic neighborhoods mentioned above. Jessica Scheer describes an exception to the general observation that there are no neighborhoods primarily composed of people with disabilities in her article, "'They Act Like It's Contagious': A Study of Mobility Impairment in a New York City Neighborhood," in *Social Aspects of Chronic Illness, Impairment and Disability*, ed. Stephen C. Hey, Gary Kiger, and John Siedel (Proceedings of the Twenty-Fifth Annual Conference of the Western Social Science Association, Albuquerque, N.M., 1983).

three categories of children may have little in common beyond the shared experience of social stereotyping, discrimination, and having to cope with the bureaucratic structure created by the Act. In short, it may be unrealistic to expect the formation of a community around a single category, disabled or handicapped, that embraces radically different realities for those whom society classifies in this way. The very law whose individualism tends to "unform" communities of parents of children with disabilities may also, by reifying the concept of disability, create unrealistic expectations that there is a group out there waiting to be formed at all. Perhaps this helps to explain why sporadic attempts to form special education parent organizations were unsuccessful in several of the school districts I studied.

In law and in everyday life, conceptualization of a community of disability is problematic. What is the significance of this fact for inclusion in the first type of community we have discussed: the community of the "normal"? We have seen that the Act encourages entry into the community of the "normal" on a one-by-one basis by each child with a disability within each school district domain. Handler has suggested that such a process will not succeed unless the parents of these children view themselves as a group with common interests and a common strategy of advocacy.[48] My research also supports the conclusion that individual parents are generally unable to carry the burden of advocacy that would lead to meaningful inclusion of children with disabilities on a case-by-case basis.[49]

The experience of the Lambert family suggests how important the formation of a community of disability may be for parents who hope that their children will eventually be regarded as insiders in the community of the "normal." The Lamberts moved to western New York from California where, by the Lambert's description, persons with disabilities were far more organized and active. In California, the sense of community among persons with disabilities was much stronger. The Lamberts recalled that when Beverly was born, they were immediately directed to a regional center where a long-range perspective on Beverly's growth and development was provided and continuing advocacy and support were available. Catherine and Robert Lambert were made to feel that they had become members of a group of similarly

48. Joel F. Handler, *The Conditions of Discretion: Autonomy, Community, Bureaucracy* (New York: Russell Sage Foundation, 1986).
49. See generally, Engel, "Law, Culture."

situated families and that this community would provide emotional support, useful information, and political clout. They believed that the effects of group solidarity were everywhere apparent in the town where they had lived, from accessible buildings to genuinely helpful social service agencies and school officials.

As the Lamberts reflected on their changed circumstances, they acknowledged that the people in Bentley, New York, were no less kind and well-intentioned than those in California:

> There are a lot of groups around that are overwhelmingly kind to disabled kids. They visit schools, or they have a circus, and they have things that you would only dream about in California.

Yet in their new home town the Lamberts were continually faced with inaccessible buildings, hostile social service agencies, reluctant school officials, inadequate resources, and uncertainty as to where they might turn for help. Bentley was a friendly small town: the neighbors were kind and generous. The problem was not a lack of kindness but a culture of common sense that defined children (and adults) with disabilities as outsiders to the community, as persons to be pitied but not to be included in the mainstream of society.

Although the details of the Lamberts' account could not be confirmed, nor could the causal connections it implies, the contrast between California and western New York is at least suggestive. The Lamberts had moved from a society in which they perceived that disability rights activists had created a strong sense of in-group awareness and political consciousness. They had moved to a society where such a feeling was almost totally absent. The difference, they believed, was not in the law—at least not in the law of special education— but in the degree to which political organization and activism had pervaded everyday life and reshaped societal assumptions about the boundaries and the core values of the community. Law was a necessary part of this transformation of everyday life, but so was the formation of a community of disability that could influence the way the law worked and could assiduously guard the distinction between difference and exclusion.

Norms: Authority and Participation

Within the domain of schools, parents, and children with disabilities, there is considerable overlapping and interaction of norms originating in law and in everyday life. The interplay between these various norms is most apparent in the annual IEP meeting. This unique encounter between parents, teachers, specialists, and administrators is one of the most striking and significant innovations of the EHA. The annual meeting brings into play norms of decision making as well as norms related to the basic rights and entitlements of children with disabilities. Particularly in its procedural aspects, the thrust of the EHA was to introduce new rules and hence new relationships among the actors involved. If ever a law was drafted with the intention of transforming everyday life, it was the EHA in its guidelines concerning parental participation in the IEP process.

In everyday life, parents would not ordinarily expect to sit down with a group of educators each year to tailor an educational plan specifically for their child's needs. For one thing, "common sense" would suggest that public education, on the whole, must be delivered en masse rather than individual by individual. Furthermore, parents would not expect to be regarded as a member of the educational team that makes decisions about methods of instruction and related support services. Common sense would reserve such decisions for the teachers, who have both authority and expertise in these matters. That parents might participate as partners in producing an Individualized Education Program and that they might be placed at the center of the decision-making process would seem to violate both common sense and time-honored traditions concerning the roles and prerogatives of educators.

The Act is, however, unambiguous about the pivotal role of parents in the decision-making process. The IEP, according to Section 1401(a)(20), must be developed by a group of which the parent is specifically listed as a member. The House version of the equivalent provision in the original EHA was rejected in conference. It would have provided only that the CSE develop the IEP *"in consultation with* the parents or guardian of the child."[50] In the final version of the EHA, it was made clear that parents were not simply to be consulted but were to be partners with the other CSE members in developing the IEP.

The parents' role in decision making is further safeguarded by their right to invoke an elaborate appeals process when they feel that

50. S. Rep. No. 455, 94th Cong., 1st Sess. 30, reprinted in 1975 U.S. Code Cong. & Admin. News 1484 (emphasis added).

their interests or those of their children have been violated. The parents may initiate an impartial due process hearing whenever they disagree with a school district decision as to "the identification, evaluation, or educational placement of the child, or the provision of a free appropriate public education to such child" (Section 1415 (b)). Parents in New York State, when dissatisfied with the decision of the impartial hearing officer, may then appeal to the state commissioner of education.[51] If dissatisfied with the commissioner's decision, they may initiate a civil action in a state or federal district court.

The parents' due process rights under the Act are not empty formalities. Local attorneys told me that parents who invoke the hearing and appeals process have a very high success rate, and favorable settlements are frequent. Thus, parents should feel secure in the knowledge that their right to participate in the decision-making process is protected by law, that they have the right to appeal decisions with which they disagree, that dispositions of such appeals are subject to further administrative and judicial review, and that their overall chances for success in opposing school district decisions are relatively good.

The procedural and substantive norms of the Act are clearly designed to empower parents within this domain. Yet the parents I interviewed did not experience the decision-making process as one in which they were genuine partners or in which their preferences carried special weight. As legal norms interact with commonsense understandings, the distinctive outlines of the statute become blurred. The contrast between legal norms and the norms of everyday life was forcefully expressed by Rachel Dolan:

> I don't have a choice. They just come and tell me, "This is where he's going. This is the kind of class that he's going to have. This is what we're going to do." And I have to say, "Okay." You know, I don't have any option. They don't give you any option, that you could even, say, put him in a different classroom or something with the teacher. This is what he's offered, and it is what

---

51. 20 U.S.C.A. § 1415(c) (1990); New York Education Law § 4404(2) (McKinney Supp. 1992). The EHA (now the "IDEA") leaves it to the states to choose between a "two-tier" impartial hearing process like New York's and a "one-tier" process in which every hearing would be conducted at the state level. See 20 U.S.C.A. § 1415(b)(2) (1990).

you're going to get. It's not multiple choice. You're told; there you go.

Rachel Dolan's perspective was perhaps affected by an illness that limited her ability to go out and participate actively in conferences and school visits. Yet her observations were echoed by many other parents. It should also be observed that she felt far more skilled, knowledgeable, and effective in her dealings with the state welfare system, although the participatory norms of special education law seemed more to her advantage than those of the welfare bureaucracy. Rachel Dolan did not feel empowered by the Act, nor did she seem to understand the extent to which the provisions of this law might be used to meet some of Pat's needs. Why, she asked, should he be getting speech therapy in the first place? After all, he did not speak with a lisp. And when she realized that he was having emotional problems, she did not consider raising this as an education-related concern for which her CSE might provide help. Rather, she set off on her own to arrange a meeting with a private psychologist whom her father helped to locate.

Rachel Dolan, like many parents, did not participate effectively in the decision-making process. She did not understand the law or how it might serve her child's needs. The technical complexity of the statute is not the only factor that limits parental participation. There are also factors related to the culture of the domain itself. In their dealings with school officials, some parents are influenced by the memory of their own experiences in the school system. From their own childhood experiences, parents recall the normative system of schools as rigid and hierarchical. They think of the teachers and administrators as persons of great power and themselves as persons without power. For parents who have not gone on to college or graduate school, this was their last impression of the educational system. They have no concept of a decision-making process in which educators actually share power with students or parents. Furthermore, some of the parents still live in the school districts where they attended school as children, and the CSE process thus brings them into contact with some of the very people who were their own teachers and authority figures when they were growing up.

Images of authority and of decision making from above color these parents' perceptions of the public school system. Such images are deeply rooted in their personal experiences and also in the culture of schooling that is a part of everyday life. To understand the actual working of the IEP process, it must be remembered that a legal model of parental participation was legislatively established in a social domain where all of the actors had been conditioned to view decision making as a "top down" affair. Parents who attend IEP meetings have no imagery to draw upon that would correspond to the role the law has given them. They find it difficult to imagine how they might express their feelings or wishes in a way that could shape the decisions of the group. Many find it difficult to believe that their feelings or wishes are actually relevant or important, for they are neither educators nor experts on "handicapped" children.

CSE officials feel equally uncomfortable in sharing their decision-making authority with laypersons. To grant parents a genuine role in the process would seem to call into question the importance of their own professional credentials. If *anyone* can make good decisions about the education of children with disabilities, then their own special training and years of experience seem to be devalued. Furthermore, they feel that parents tend to be emotional and irrational when it comes to their own children. Several CSE chairs told me that they always kept plenty of Kleenex on hand during the IEP meetings, and that an important part of their job was to be sensitive to the particular emotional stage through which the parents were passing as they attempted to cope with raising a child with disabilities. Common sense tells us that Kleenex are not needed by CSE members, however, and that their emotional stage or circumstances (e.g., recent marital problems, a death in the family, or difficulties with their own children) will not be deemed relevant to the decision-making process. Thus, even when CSE members attempt to be sensitive and sympathetic, there is a lack of symmetry in the roles and relationships that suggests an imbalance in what was to have been a working partnership.

For the educators, the emotionality and subjectivity of the parents (generally, but not always the mothers rather than the fathers— imagery of women is highly important in these perceptions of parents by the CSE) contrasts significantly with their own neutrality and objectivity. CSE members tend to believe in the scientific foundations of knowledge about children with disabilities. In the decision-making process, those who have access to this objective body of knowledge are viewed in a very different light from those whose knowledge is subjective and exclusively experiential.

Given these realities of everyday life, one might think that the EHA norms of parental participation would inevitably fail. It is true that most parents simply do not participate in a meaningful way in the decision-making process. Yet the exceptions are intriguing. Suzanne DeMarco typified some of the maverick parents who were increasingly assertive about their roles and their children's rights:

> I just think they [the educators] should be in a partnership with these parents, because we're the ones that have been with these kids all this time and we know what they're doing. Just last year I got the feeling that "once your kid comes to our school, you're not anything anymore. It's what *we* say." . . . It was so hopeless, or helpless, that "once he gets on that bus he's ours, and you don't have anything to say about what we do with him." I think they should have a partnership with the parents.

Suzanne DeMarco became increasingly dissatisfied with the yearly routine of busing Joe to a distant segregated classroom and not knowing until shortly before the beginning of classes which town or school district would be his new home. She finally decided to send a written notification to her CSE announcing that next year she would expect to have Joe placed in an integrated classroom in his own school district. In her letter, she observed that, although the BOCES classrooms were located in school buildings serving non-"handicapped" children, Joe was effectively isolated from contact with them. He entered a different door, studied only with children who were "handicapped," and never participated in plays or other school events with his non-"handicapped" peers. She argued that his academic growth was being stunted and that his social environment was overly restricted. She wanted Joe "to grow up to be as normal as possible." This, her letter concluded, could best be accomplished in an integrated classroom.

Significantly, Suzanne DeMarco cited the EHA in her letter to the CSE. She observed that the law guaranteed Joe an education in the "least restrictive environment," which was, in her view, a regular classroom. Thus, she cited a substantive norm guaranteed by the Act in opposition to what had become a customary or commonsense norm of segregated classrooms under the BOCES system. Furthermore, implicit in Suzanne DeMarco's letter was the threat to challenge any future CSE decision that did not accede to her request. She was announcing, in effect, that she would invoke her right to an impartial hearing and, if necessary, further review proceedings, if the CSE did not agree to an integrated placement for Joe next year. This was not an idle threat. A few other parents in her district had already pursued this strategy successfully and had obtained full integration for their children. The CSE knew the DeMarco's well enough by now to realize that they would do the same.

Suzanne DeMarco had no illusions about her role in the decision-making process. Asserting her rights under the Act did not really make her a partner with the other members of the CSE as the drafters of the EHA might have envisioned. Instead, her letter was an assertion of legal power and an implicit threat to use it if the CSE ignored her position. The law enabled her to challenge commonsense norms of decision making and to force the CSE to consider her views of what was best for Joe. The result was something less than the cooperative partnership suggested by the Act but something more than the de facto exclusion of parents that had become the customary norm for everyday decision making even after the passage of the EHA.

Because of the activities of parents like Suzanne DeMarco, Joe's school district has become known as one that has integrated children with disabilities more extensively than any other district in the region. What was originally a confrontational process involving legal challenges by parents has gradually taken on a more cooperative aspect. The school district itself has explicitly adopted the policy of integration and has received favorable publicity as a result. While tensions between parents and educators persist, particularly over issues of implementation, it is interesting to observe a convergence of interests around the concept of integration. The school district has discovered that it, too, can benefit from moving in the direction that had originally been favored by the parents alone. Because a small number of parents invoked their legal rights under the Act, the prevailing norms were reshaped and the status of children with disabilities within a particular domain was dramatically changed.

Conclusion

What is the role of law in everyday life? I began this essay by rejecting attempts to answer this question in terms of the extent to which law is able to control everyday life or everyday life is able to resist law. Instead, I adopted the perspective of those who see law and everyday life not necessarily in oppositional terms but as elements that are interdependent and together help to shape social domains. Law and everyday life, I argued, are mutually defining in the sense that neither could exist or have meaning without the other. The emphasis of this essay was on the dynamic processes through which law and everyday life interact to define social actors, to construct understandings of time and space, to make and unmake communities, and to shape norms.

Although I believe that this characterization of the role of law in everyday life is less misleading than those that portray law and everyday life in oppositional terms, it may also seem less intellectually satisfying. If the research enterprise no longer aims at measuring the extent of law's capacity to control everyday life or the power of everyday life to remain autonomous, then must every analysis of law and everyday life end in mushy inconclusiveness? Is there nothing distinctive about the role of law? Is it not significant that the features of law are more apparent in some situations than in others? Is it not possible to generalize about the consequences of law's influence in the constituting of social domains?

The example of schools and children with disabilities provides us with some answers to such questions, and these answers may be applicable to other domains as well. To begin with, law in the example we considered did *not* appear unequivocally to have some of the qualities that are often attributed to it. It is often said, for example, that law acts as a force that radically individualizes social actors, isolating them from one another and inhibiting the formation of spontaneous communities in everyday life. In our example, however, the situation seemed to be far more complicated than this. It is true that the thrust of the EHA was individualistic. Yet its emphasis was on inclusion of children with disabilities in the mainstream, and to this extent its aim was to bring them into a community from which they were excluded rather than to isolate them. Ironically, however, its method was to grant them a set of rights that were premised upon their difference from other children, and thus the creation of a sense of common ground was undercut from the very beginning.

Furthermore, the creation of a sense of community among all children with disabilities (a "community of disability") proved to be equally problematic in law and in everyday life. It was the values and assumptions of the educators and parents as much as the provisions of the Act that prevented the children and their families from forming communities around the concept of disability. In fact, the evidence from some school districts and from states such as California is that law may be quite useful and important in mobilizing persons with diverse types of disabilities through grass-roots organizations that provide advocacy, support, and a sense of solidarity. Thus, it is not accurate to assert simplistically that the role of law in this domain has been one of radical individualization or that its tendency has been to crush the spontaneous communities of everyday life.

It would also be inaccurate to assert that law has been a force for the linearity and uniformity that typify the late capitalist system to which it has often been linked. In the construction of time (if not of space), in the framing of educational plans, in the validation of different learning styles and needs, law has, if anything, acted in opposition to linearity and uniformity. Special education law, at least, has insisted on approaches that are shaped around *each child's* distinctive needs and abilities. It is everyday life, and the "commonsense" justifications that underlie the relentless routines and disciplines of mass public education, that have been the forces for uniformity in this domain. Law has been subversive and, if the logic of the EHA were taken to its extreme, has suggested a world in which public education would be individually tailored for every child.[52]

Nor does it appear that law has been an unambiguous force for formalism in opposition to the more natural, affective, and informal processes of everyday life. It is true that the elaborate due process guarantees and appeals mechanisms have made the educational process and the relationships between parents and school officials seem more formal in some respects. Yet the more formal procedural aspects of the Act are rarely invoked or even considered by most parents. Their effects are felt indirectly, if at all. And it should not be forgotten that the thrust of the EHA was antiformalistic in the sense that parents were now to be included at an earlier and less formal stage in the decision-making process. By placing them at the table where evaluations were discussed and alternatives weighed, the EHA was meant to foster informal discussions and exchanges of views that included

---

52. Gartner and Lipsky, "Beyond Special Education."

the parents. This was surely a less formalistic approach than one in which the parents were simply presented with the educators' final recommendations and were told that their only recourse if they did not agree was to initiate a due process proceeding.

If we are to generalize about the distinctive role of law in this particular domain, therefore, we must be very cautious about relying on some of the more frequently cited attributes that law is supposed to possess in opposition to everyday life, attributes such as individualism, anticommunitarianism, uniformity, linearity, and formalism.

Instead of searching for law's distinctive role in such innate characteristics, it might be more helpful to reconsider one of the most obvious facts about "official" law in relation to everyday life: its externality. Although the impetus for new law may come from local-level movements and organizations, the norms, procedures, and sanctions of law are generally extrinsic to particular social domains. In this sense, law differs from the customary norms and processes associated with interactions and relationships within domains.

The externality of law does not mean, however, that actors inevitably experience it as a foreign or obtrusive element in comparison with the other elements of everyday life that constitute their domain. Within particular settings, law can be "domesticated" in ways that assimilate it to the values and perspectives of the local order. For example, when the law is used to punish criminals or to collect debts, residents of American towns may see it as a powerful positive force to preserve the traditional community and its core values.[53]

When law is domesticated within a social domain, it plays the role of preserving harmony between external and internal sources of power. It contributes to a sense of stability, at least among those who benefit from the preservation of the status quo. On other occasions, however, law takes on quite a different aspect. When law is used by the "wrong" people for the "wrong" ends, then its externality is seen—at least by local elites—as the essence of the problem. For example, when parents exercise their due process rights under the Act, educators decry the "legalization" of their domain and lament

---

53. See Carol J. Greenhouse, Barbara Yngvesson, and David M. Engel, *Contest and Community: The Meanings of Law in Three American Towns* (Ithaca, N.Y.: Cornell University Press, 1994). See also, Engel, "Oven Bird's Song"; and Engel, "Law, Time."

the loss of personal, affective relationships with parents and children. The irony, of course, is that many of the parents and children had traditionally experienced such (nonlegalized) relationships as highly formalized, rigid, and impersonal. The difference between the new system and the old was not one of greater or lesser legality, formalism, or impersonality but rather of who was empowered and how.

The law has an alien, intrusive character when it is used to change power relationships and to assert norms and invoke procedures that have no antecedents within the domain. In such situations it contributes to a sense of disharmony between internal and external realms. It creates a feeling on the part of some, at least, that the state or the large-scale institutions of mass society are "taking over" and the traditional authority figures within the domain (and the traditional values and practices associated with them) are under attack.

When law takes on this second meaning within a domain, when it is associated with foreign and invasive forces, there are serious implications for those who seek to use it. Children with disabilities and their parents have much to gain by invoking the rights and procedures of the Act in opposition to their local school districts, but they also have much to lose. The path to social acceptance, integration into the community, and to a meaningful education leads through the mainstreaming provisions of the Act and through the support services and accommodations it guarantees. Yet parents who insist too strenuously on their legal rights also risk alienating themselves and their children from the community. Their stance in opposition to local authority figures may brand them as troublemakers or as selfish people who seek a disproportionate share of the district's resources for their own children. And their reliance on the law as a source of empowerment provides the children with a far more tenuous claim to citizenship in the community than those whose status is secured by other, locally grounded indicia of achievement. There is a suspicion of those whose claim to personhood is founded on a legal right that has no counterpart in the local system of values and beliefs.

The role of law in everyday life can thus be read in dramatically different ways, depending on the extent to which it is assimilated to the purposes of particular groups or persons within a domain. These different readings are in themselves of great interest to researchers.

But their significance is not merely academic. Perceptions of the role of law in everyday life are closely linked to understandings of social order and disorder and to the processes by which the identities and the fates of human beings, including children with disabilities, are determined.

Law and Everyday Life

Patricia J. Williams

The Unbearable Autonomy of Being

On the front of the J. Edgar Hoover FBI Building in Washington, D.C., there is a big sign that reads: "A Drug Free America: The Right Choice." There is something boldly epigrammatic about this sign, stern yet permissive, tersely delivered as though by the Marlboro Man. This call to chosen sobriety suggests vague tests of mettle, images of ultimate worth and pioneering effort—"the right stuff"— and resistance to the forces of gravity.

As I speed by the J. Edgar Hoover FBI Building in a taxicab, I am touched by the evocative bravura of this minotaur singing the siren's song; by this new world order's kinder, tougher love potion of just choosing rightly. I feel frail and female somehow. I feel faintly threatened, as by a nascent toothache, the autonomy of my life-style welling up like a loneliness.

As my taxicab bounds through the stoplight and speeds up Pennsylvania Avenue, my head fills with ruminations about force and law enforcement, about the boundary between choice and lack of alternative. It is a powerful image that chases me down the street, these walls of the FBI fortress guarded and adorned with the blue and gold filigree of lettered choice. It is a timely rumination, I suppose—I am on my way to a conference addressing just such paradox, during which there will be presentations on all aspects of women's reproductive rights. One of the chief concerns will surely be the growing prosecution of pregnant drug users, who, regardless of addiction, are found to harbor the requisite intent to commit themselves to (or choose) criminal behavior. In my own research, I have been considering a range of activity, in and out of the criminal justice system, in which control of women's minds and bodies is a major theme—from abortion to surrogate motherhood to court-ordered birth control.

With the advent of a variety of new technologies, women's lives and employment are increasingly defined as body-centered. Women live in relation to their body parts, the dispossession or employment of ourselves constrained by a complicated pattern of self-alienation. Increasingly, I hear about cases that reason away women's bodies as assets that may be wilfully disposed of; I read about judicial pronouncements that refer to our wombs as "fetal containers"—as though women were packing crates or petrie dishes or parking lots. Increasingly, whole ranges of paternalistic intrusion and outright coercion are placed beyond the bounds of either legal or humanitarian remediation by labeling them the outcome of either "bad choice" or "irrational acts."

A good liberated female, according to this new-age script, should be able to sell her assets or rent the space of her available containers or make improvements on the premises with nary a second thought. Needless to say, many of us do have second thoughts, but the Orwellian powers-that-be tell us that if some bodies are valued more than other bodies, it's not because we are called assets or containers. It's just that in the weird territory of law and economics-speak applied to the property of bodies, certain preexisting valuations become all the clearer, more apparent.

Who can argue with that logic? Certain races are worth more in the marketplace. Pretty faces are worth more in the mating game. Certain hairstyles and clothing fashions just don't sell. And if it all sounds more like a meat market than a market of ideas—too bad, that's life and that's death, so stop your bellyaching, go out and get a job, buy a better nose job, a better baby, a better skin tone, a better life. Just say yes, dial rent-a-womb NOW, and give that unwed teenage mother-to-be a job.

In the following discussion, I want to recast and even intentionally mystify certain valuations that inform those life paths purporting to be choice—valuations that are too frequently nothing more and nothing newer than medieval obsessions, a kind of obsessive eugenics. Perhaps only in their mysterious contradictory power over us can these valuations be seen as the real irrationality in our lives—

as almost religious beliefs and even hatreds, rather than "simply economic" or "observably scientific" taxonomies. My other project in this paper is an attempt to trace a connection between the bizarre, even hallucinatory, self-partialization that afflicts these times and the necessity for rethinking the relentless abstraction and word violence of particular legal taxonomies.

Incorporating Incorporeality: The Paradox of Prelife

Flipping through the pages of a book on dreams, I read: "In archaic times, a person who stood outside the law of a culture was considered dead by ordinary people."[1] It is instantly riveting, this idea of illegitimacy as a form of death, of legality as its own life force. It makes me think of a weird case in Los Angeles some years ago. An elderly woman, desiring immortality, entered into a contract with cryonics practitioners to have her old grey head severed at a predetermined opportunity and then frozen until such a high-tech moment that it could be defrosted and attached to younger, healthier body parts. Predictably, the event of her decapitation precipitated murder charges against the cryonics practitioners. Their defense was an interesting one: they asserted that the prosecution could not prove murder except by an autopsy. That particular deduction of Truth, however, would necessitate defrosting her head during our still-archaic times, thereby, they alleged, enacting the true murder by depriving the head of its chosen mode to immortality.

My remembrance of this case was reawakened by Carolyn Walker Bynum's book *Fragmentation and Redemption*, in which she aligns the cyronics case within an entire Judeo-Christian tradition of debate about the life and resurrection of dismembered bodies.[2] Professor Bynum looks at voluminous medieval theological debates— serious legal debates no less than our own—about what will happen on Judgment Day if, for example, the leg of a Moor is grafted onto the body of a white man. (Since this particular experiment coincided with only the very crudest beginnings of European medical art, the subject of resurrection presented itself with necessary immediacy.)

---

1. Hans Peter Duerr, *Dreamtime: Concerning the Boundary between Wilderness and Civilization* (New York: Basil Blackwell, 1985), 61.
2. Carolyn Walker Bynum, *Fragmentation and Redemption: Essays on Gender and the Human Body in Medieval Religion* (Cambridge: MIT Press, 1991).

And what will happen if a man fathers a child, then eats said child, the child's body thus becoming part of the father? Whose body will rise on Judgment Day? Will one body rise or two?

As outdatedly macabre as these cases may sound, consider the legalities of resurrection in the recent case of Angela Carder, a young woman who had battled cancer for many years. When she became pregnant, her condition worsened, and eventually she lapsed into a coma that doctors deemed terminal. It is unclear from where the idea first cropped up to save the "life" of her "preborn child," but, however and whenever, Angela Carder ultimately was subjected to the Solomonic intervention of a court-ordered caesarian, over the objections of her husband, her family, her doctors, and the lawyers appointed to represent her—everyone, that is, save the hospital's insurers, apparently determined to slice the mother in half in order to show who best loved the child.

Angela Carder died within days of the operation; her twenty-six-week-old fetus died within hours.

Another case that captures the degree to which life and death in our society are not merely biological but are sanctioned events, is that of Nancy Cruzan, a young Missouri woman who, after having been injured in an accident, remained in a coma for eight years, kept alive by means of a feeding tube. After an internationally publicized battle, Cruzan's family and friends finally obtained a court order permitting her feeding tube to be removed.[3] Particularly interesting were the comments of the nursing staff at the hospital, who had only known her comatose body. They cried and spoke of her as their friend. They were, they said, content to nurse her forever, as long as her body housed its soul—perhaps longer, inasmuch as some of their protestations made Nancy Cruzan's body sound like a reliquary. Of what is this body a relic, I wondered from the mythos-spinning positionality of my own agnosticism. What do they imagine her soul to be that they revere the altar of her prostrate form, washing away patiently the daily corruption of the body's composition.

It is true that the hospital where Cruzan's body lay was Roman Catholic, as were the nurses, but I do not mean my comments as a particularized observation about their belief. Rather, I am interested by the way in which the Judeo-Christian notion of a community

3. Robert Sternbrook, "Comatose Woman Dies 12 Days After Life Support is Halted," *Los Angeles Times*, 27 December 1990, sec. A.

demarcated by the form of a communal body makes itself felt in our general sociological and legal discourse. The symbol of Nancy Cruzan's helpless innocence not only served a religious need but also underlay much of the secular debate about the medical ethics of her treatment. In this sense, Cruzan's body was no longer her own, nor even her nurses' (in the body of Christ) but ours (in the corpus of law).

In the transformation from worshipful community to industrialized collective, however, I think that something insidiously complicated has taken place. If there is in our culture nothing we love so much as a suffering body to idealize, then we should not underestimate the ability of our profane, mechanical age to transform that metaphor into a biotechnological enterprise. If there is a fascination with the holiness of our incorporeality, we may want to be on guard for the extent to which new technology literally sells us a brand of tenuous corporeality—bodies hovering in that deliciously exotic state just between life and death.

The new technology is itself so incorruptible in its clean plasticity, in its nonbiodegradable promise of immortality. I wonder sometimes if it is not the Leviathan of technology itself we are empowering even as we rush to create new rights to life and prelife. I wonder, in fact, if any of this has anything to do with "real" life, at least as lived in a wakeful consciousness. The contemporary adoration of the fetus, for example, has taken on a legal life of its own. The fetus has become an abstract, technologically separable life-that-is-not-life: the pure future of infinite potential combined with an impeccable past, the absence of a present presence.

This impossible hunt for purity. The terms of its pursuit demand that all else is impure: all else therefore justifies a quantum of rage at the autonomous corruptions erupting all about, and at the imperfect communion of bodies that is the only fate we can ultimately ever own.

Perhaps what connects these stories is, as a friend of mine writes, that "there are no bodies (nobodies?)—only ciphers for the will of other entities. They do not exist except as markers of narrative transactions."[4] Consider the case of *United Auto Workers v. Johnson Controls*,[5] a so-called fetal protection case, in which a workplace rule

---

4. Wahneema Lubiano, letter to the author, 6 March 1991.
5. United Auto Workers v. Johnson Controls, 886 F.2d 871 (7th Cir. 1989), rev'd 111 S.Ct. 1196 (1991).

barring all women of childbearing age was upheld by the Seventh Circuit, employing a standard of review that looked only to the "business necessity" of the employer. While the U.S. Supreme Court reversed the Seventh Circuit, it is interesting to examine the two opinions for the contrasting ways in which both make the material conditions of men's and women's bodies disappear.

The Seventh Circuit Opinion

The case of *United Auto Workers v. Johnson Controls* grew out of a union challenge to the employer's policy of barring all women of childbearing age from working in those parts of a plant that manufactured lead batteries. The policy was motivated by an expressed fear of exposing not the women but their fetuses to lead poisoning. That much of the story conforms to a perfectly laudable public interest goal, but upon closer examination the record reveals that under conditions at the Johnson plant some lead was likely to be absorbed into the blood of all workers. Johnson Controls admitted that all actual, living employees risked exposure to elevated levels of lead in their blood, yet it was fetuses and *potential* fetuses that were given protection, rather than actual, living employees, whether women or men. (The plaintiffs in this suit included a woman who had "chosen to be sterilized in order to avoid losing her job, . . . a 50-year old divorcee, who had suffered a loss in compensation when she was transferred out of a job where she was exposed to lead, and [a man] who had been denied a request for leave of absence for the purpose of lowering his lead level because he intended to become a father.")[6] In fact, with the irresolute logic of the Rule against Perpetuities' concern for the fertile octagenarian, disenfranchising all women of childbearing age without regard to their intent to have children was deemed purely incidental to the goal of fetal protection.[7]

The Johnson policy superficially resembled the cases in which canaries are brought down into mining shafts: when the canary stops singing, you know the gas is leaking. While it is true that fetuses are more quickly susceptible to the ravages of lead poisoning than

---

6. "Excerpts," *New York Times*, 21 March 1991, sec. B.
7. Only a medical certificate of sterilization would exempt a woman from the bar.

adult humans, this particular bar seemed unconcerned about the debilitation from prolonged lead exposure in adult workers. Rather, it amounted to a righteous ban of canaries in the interest of canaries and all future generations of canaries—perhaps not a bad cause—but a diversion from the fact of mineworkers dying in explosions below.

In upholding this outcome, the court employed "neutral" but extremely loaded vocabulary, describing its ruling as affecting not women in particular but merely the "offspring of all employees" without regard to gender—while at the same time asserting that it is only women who are capable of transmitting the harm to the fetus.

Furthermore, the opinion referred throughout to "the unborn child," thus making present and palpable something that is at best hypothetical. The court upheld a demand for medical proof of sterilization and disposed of all alternative ways of protecting fetuses—even as it said that it would leave room for consideration of other, less restrictive alternatives: it disposed of them by saying that the other alternatives must be "equally as effective" in preventing harm to the unborn child as barring all women from the workplace. But what alternative could possibly be equally as effective as a total bar? Why not simply confine all women to the home, keep the liquor under lock and key, and feed them a constant diet of whole grains and antibiotics like a flock of brood hens?

The Seventh Circuit's opinion in the *Johnson Controls* case accomplished the following: it did not establish a social interest in healthy future generations, as it purported to do, but a property interest in the fate of fetuses, belonging to Johnson Controls, a corporation. Johnson literally owned an interest in the fetus, through its ability to control all women who might be the bearers of fetuses—that control premised upon shielding its stockholders from being sued. This property interest was explicitly expressed as the court allowing Johnson to exercise its "best business judgment" in fashioning an exclusionary rule. Thus it was the business interest, rather than any notion of the public interest, that ultimately governed the rule in this case.[8]

As the court created this bizarre equivalent of fetal ownership, it simultaneously disowned the employees of Johnson Controls, in

8. Patricia Williams, "Fetal Fictions: An Exploration of Property Archetypes in Racial and Gendered Contexts," *University of Florida Law Review* 42 (1990): 81.

particular the female workers who were the so-called risk factors to the ideal, nonexistent, unborn, uncarried, unconceived, unthought-of child. (I am reminded of a cartoon my colleague Professor Alta Charo mentioned seeing in a German magazine: in it, a man and a woman were depicted each with a ray of white light streaming from their eyes. The caption read: "The gleam in the eye of the mother + the gleam in the eye of the father = the new definition of conception." Unfortunately, that gleam can also now be said to conceive not a public interest in the fate of that child-to-be, but a tangible property right in the employers of the biological parents.)

The Supreme Court Opinion

The good news about the Supreme Court's holding in *Johnson Controls* was its insistence that Johnson's "professed moral and ethical concerns about the welfare of the next generation do not suffice to establish a B.F.O.Q. [Bona Fide Occupational Qualification] of female sterility."[9] The bad news is that the decision relied upon a brand of libertarianism that lurches the workplace back to the most problematic form of caveat emptor. Rather than frame the issue as one of public interest in workplace safety, the court styled it as one of worker choice and assumed risk. "The bias in Johnson Controls' policy is obvious," said the Court. "Fertile men, but not fertile women, are given a choice as to whether they wish to risk their reproductive health for a particular job."[10]

Thus, while the court effectively recognized a general, rather than a gendered, risk of danger, it squarely placed responsibility for the costs of such exposure upon the individual employee, not the employer. "Decisions about the welfare of future children must be left to the parents who conceive, bear, support and raise them rather than to the employers who hire those parents."[11] (Note that while the Seventh Circuit implicitly upheld a standard in which the fetus symbolically represented the only part of either the man or the woman that would be held not able to consent, the Supreme Court actually situates future *children* within a sphere of absolute parental control.)

---

9. "Excerpts."
10. Id.
11. Id.

The implications for suits involving dangers to health are clear: "John-son Controls . . . complies with Federal job-safety standards on exposure to lead and warns women of the hazards of exposure. Unless an employer is negligent . . . the basis for holding an employer liable seems remote at best."[12]

In summary, if the Seventh Circuit opinion disempowered employees by narrowing the range of recognizable or actionable health risks of the workplace to those affecting fetuses rather than real men and women, the Supreme Court's take on the same facts eliminated any possibility of employer liability for workplace-related birth defects. A distinct if hidden premise in both the lower and the higher court opinions is that workers who stay in poisoned environments "choose" to do so and therefore consent to anything that happens to them. These opinions excluded, in other words, a range of economic realities about a market that is not as free and option filled as theory would have it. They exluded the real conditions or real workers while establishing a prima facie case of consent for them in highly toxic situations. They disowned a range of arguments that all workers might try to make on behalf of themselves.

How peculiar and contradictory are these images: the corporatizing of the body as a way of making it incorporeal. The completely tamed body as one without will, controlled, obedient, perfectly malleable, having made all the right choices after all.

Johnson does control.

Johnsons Controlled

In July 1991, Jennifer Clarice Johnson became the first person in the United States convicted (not just prosecuted) for drug dealing by umbilical cord. On 18 April 1991, her conviction was upheld by the Florida Fifth District Court of Appeals employing a law intended to punish the sale of drugs to minors. Writing for the majority, Judge James C. Dauksch concluded that Ms. Johnson "*voluntarily* took cocaine into her body, *knowing* it would pass to her fetus, and knowing (or she should have known) that birth was imminent" (emphasis added).[13]

---

12. Peter T. Kilborn, "Employers Left with Many Decisions," *New York Times,* 21 March 1991, sec. B.

13. Tamar Lewin, "Court in Florida Upholds Conviction for Drug Delivery by Umbilical Cord," *New York Times,* 20 April 1990, sec. 1.

Judge Dauksch's language of attributed knowledge and voluntarism are increasingly commonplace in criminal courtrooms as well as in general legal discourse. Increasingly, such words of consent and autonomy affixed to almost any event instantly transform into "private choice" what used to be matters of some social consensus, or, at least, matters of public debate about the limits of power, force, and individual integrity.

In fact, Ms. Johnson chose to tell doctors of her addiction to cocaine and expressed her concern about the birth of her child. Acting on this information, doctors were prepared to deal with the particular risks of her delivery. By pitting the health care of the fetus/child against the criminalization of the woman/mother, the state actually imposed an irreconcilable tension between the desperate plea for help that Ms. Johnson's informing her obstetrician represented and the threat of prosecution and custody removal that resulted. Judge Dauksch's opinion brings into high relief the distinction between treating addiction as a criminal act and treating it as a health problem.

Writing for the dissent, the lone woman on the court, Judge Winifred Sharp, took issue with the simplification of addiction as knowing choice, observing further that "once Ms. Johnson went into labor, the only way she could have prevented the delivery of the drug to the newborn would have been by severing the cord before the baby was born, probably killing both herself and the baby in the process." Expanding upon this, Rutgers law professor Dorothy Roberts observes that pregnant addicts, for whom drug treatment is virtually nonexistent, are actually

> penalized for choosing to have the baby rather than having an abortion. In this way, the state's punitive action may coerce women to have abortions rather than risk being charged with a crime. Thus it is the choice of carrying a pregnancy to term that is being penalized.[14]

On 23 July 1992, Jennifer Clarice Johnson's conviction was overturned by the Florida Supreme Court, citing Judge Sharp's dissent at length, on the grounds that the Florida legislature, in its attempt to

---

14. Dorothy Roberts, "Punishing Drug Addicts Who Have Babies: Women of Color, Equality and the Right of Privacy," *Harvard Law Review* 104 (1991): 1445.

outlaw drug trafficking and sale of controlled substances to minors, had not anticipated the use of that law to "criminally prosecut[e] mothers for delivery of a controlled substance to a minor by way of the umbilical cord." The Supreme Court opinion was supported by a broad consensus of health care professionals, including the American Public Health Association, who fear that "prosecutions of women like Ms. Johnson are misguided and serve more to scare women away from the health care they need than to stop them from using drugs." A similar case in Connecticut refused to extend the statutory definition of "drug dealer" to include pregnant women only a few weeks later. Yet despite an overwhelming professional consensus, political sentiment has fueled the zealous prosecution of drug-addicted pregnant women in twenty-four states.

In an unrelated case, Darlene Johnson, a twenty-seven-year-old mother of four, was ordered by a judge in California to use a new, long-term birth control drug after she pled guilty to beating two of her children with a belt. The drug, Norplant, is particularly controversial because its ingestion requires the implantation of capsules in the upper arm; the capsules release the hormone progestin for a period of up to five years. Although Ms. Johnson's sentence purportedly came about as the result of her "consent" to a plea "bargain," Ms. Johnson was "completely taken by surprise by the judge's decision. In a plea agreement arranged earlier, Ms. Johnson was to be sentenced to one year in jail and three years of probation."[15] At the actual sentencing hearing, however, the judge presented the unexpected term of temporary sterilization.

Her lawyer, who was not at the hearing,

> said she had agreed to the judge's order only because she was afraid that if she refused, she would go to jail for four years. . . .
> A Dec. 12 editorial in the Philadelphia Inquirer . . . suggested that because of growing poverty among blacks, welfare mothers should be offered incentives to use Norplant. . . . Ms. Johnson's status as a welfare recipient may have played a role. "According to the transcript, [the judge] asked Darlene Johnson whether she was on welfare," [her lawyer] said. "She is. I think that's what's going on here."[16]

15. Tamar Lewin, "Implanted Birth Control Device Renews Debate over Forced Contraception," *New York Times*, 10 January 1991, sec. A.
16. Id.

According to the National Coalition against Surrogacy, fifty percent of surrogate mothers are on welfare. The archetype of poor (non)-relation has plagued a series of women in recent years, women who—like Anna Johnson, a poor black woman in California who bore a Eurasian child to whom she was not genetically related—enter courtrooms with the already diminished status of "surrogate" mothers and, with increasing commonplaceness, leave reduced yet further, as mere "fetal containers."

In the years since the New Jersey Supreme Court ruled that surrogate contracts were illegal and against public policy in the so-called Baby M case, surrogate contracts have nevertheless proliferated around the country, generating ever more immaculate conceptions of biological relation. Yet the severe economic constraints that describe the lives of so many of the women who enter into these breeding contracts is rarely seen to legally problematize the issue of choice.[17] And the question of choice itself is, I think, too often a diversion from profound moral valuations—and devaluations. When Anna Johnson lost custody of the child she bore to the child's wealthier genotypes, my class ruminated briefly about the prospect of a black woman not merely caring for, but adopting a nonblack child as her own—"it would be like Romulus and Remus being raised up by wolves," was the enigmatic suggestion of a student of mine.

Of Human Harvest

Standing in the line at Kohl's grocery store not long ago, my eyes happened to fall upon the front pages of a jumbled miscellany of show-biz magazines. In one sweeping glance, I read: a doctor has recently implanted a whole pint of silicone in each of Dolly Parton's breasts, Cher is sporting a new tatoo, and Oprah is considering liposuction. And then, there, right on the front page of the *National Enquirer*, second only to a headline about how Trump Is Trumped by Another of Maples' Sugar Daddies—there on the front page of

---

17. Indeed, some commentators have stretched it to reprehensible lengths: "In a regime of free baby production and sale there might be efforts to breed children having desirable characteristics and, more broadly, to breed children with a known set of characteristics that could be matched up with those desired by prospective adoptive parents." William M. Landes and Richard A. Posner, "The Economics of the Baby Shortage," *Journal of Legal Studies* 7 (1978): 345.

the *National Enquirer* was a story about the Amazing Donna Shalala, Chancellor of the University of Wisconsin, and Tiny Human Dynamo. Shalala, who by this account measures a miniscule but mighty five action-packed feet, is pictured shaking hands and dispensing diplomas to Big Men twice her size. I do find this story amazing, and on a number of levels, not the least of which is the implication that, somewhere on the campus of the University of Wisconsin where I work, there is running loose a reporter from the *National Enquirer*, looking under every stone for freaks of nature. I am amazed and just a little terrified that that reporter might be lurking just outside my office door, for example, and might see me in one of my wild, intense, postcommittee states—and I'll end up plastered in next week's grocery stores: "Weird Alien Intelligence Posing as Disembodied Black Law Professor."

I take this possibility seriously, partly because I have been reading too much trashy literature lately. Yesterday, I read an article in that slick mag, the *George Washington University Law Review*, entitled "Increasing the Supply of Transplant Organs: The Virtues of a Futures Market."[18] In it, the author, a professor of law and economics at that foremost producer of science fiction, the University of Chicago, proposes a market of efficiently "harvested" human organs in which the sale of "salvageable" organs marks a ritual of exchange made sacred by the miracle of technology, a duty whose service is attended by the ministry of medicine. The body becomes the sum of its physical by-products, something that can be mined, excavated, worn, rendered immortal by the profane circulation of excision and transplantation. In this equation, immortality becomes not the equivalent of the immanence of the human spirit, but instead mortality extended by an indefinite trail of pieces and parts, an engulfment of organs, an extension of limbs. Life everlasting, mortality without end.

And just last week I was reading an article by two more literary moguls from the Chicago school, Elizabeth Landes and Judge Richard Posner: in their short opus, "The Economics of the Baby Shortage," newborn humans are divided up into white and black and then taken for a spin around a Monopoly board theme park where the white babies are put on demand curves and the black babies are dropped off the edge of supply sides. "Were baby prices quoted as prices of

18. Lloyd Cohen, "Increasing the Supply of Transplant Organs: The Virtues of a Futures Market," *George Washington University Law Review* 58 (1989): 1.

soybean futures are quoted, a racial ranking of these prices would be evident, with white baby prices higher than nonwhite baby prices."[19] The trail of the demand curve leads straight into the arms of the highest bidder; the chasm of oversupply has a heap of surplus at the bottom of its pit.[20] In this house of horrors, the surplus (or "second quality") black babies will continue to replicate themselves, like spoors, unless the wise, invisible, strong arm of the market intervenes to allow the wisdom of pure purchasing power to clear away the underbrush.[21] These authors conclude, in a not surprising rhetorical turn, that the current "black market" for adoptive children must be replaced with what they call a "free baby market."

Stabat Miss Mater

In February 1990, I took a trip to Eastern Europe with about ten other people generally associated with critical legal studies. Our Samsonite luggage packed full of trail mix and Talking Heads tapes, we took off for a conference on rights theory. In Poland, the embrace of freedom of expression has resulted in such odd trade-offs as the open practice of Catholicism enabling a spirited movement to repeal laws permitting abortion;[22] and pornographic images becoming sym-

---

19. Is not the very pricing of babies like soybeans the whole problem? Perhaps the pricing of soybeans like soybeans is part of the problem. It invites, indeed necessitates, the ranking. It perpetuates it and makes it an indispensible part of our vocabulary and how we deal. Landes and Posner, "Economics of the Baby Shortage," 344.

20. "The thousands of children in foster care . . . are comparable to an unsold inventory stored in a warehouse." Landes and Posner, "Economics of the Baby Shortage," 327.

21. "By obtaining exclusive control over the supply of both 'first-quality' adoptive children and 'second-quality' children residing in foster care but available for adoption, agencies are able to internalize the substitution possibilities between them. Agencies can charge a higher price for the children they place for adoption, thus increasing not only their revenues from adoptions but also the demand for children who would otherwise be placed or remain in foster care at the agency's expense. Conversely, if agency revenues derive primarily from foster care, the agencies can manipulate the relative price of adopting 'first-quality' children over 'second-quality' children to reduce the net flow of children out of foster care." Landes and Posner, "Economics of the Baby Shortage," 347.

22. "Late last spring, the Ministry of Health imposed new rules restricting access to legal abortions. The regulations, which were passed with no parliamentary debate and little notice in the media, require women to get permission for an abortion from three doctors. Any who find fault with their patients' reasons for wanting an abortion can refuse to sign the 'contract.' If one does, women must see a state-sanctioned

bolic of the new order, their own form of religious icon.[23] The first
day, we were given a moment of rest in the offices of the Institute
for Social Prevention and Resocialization (sort of like the Sociology
Department of the University of Warsaw, but somehow, untranslat-
ably, different). I sat down at a desk and allowed the jet lag to swirl
up in my head. In the intoxication of my fatigue, I stretched my neck
in a graceful 180-degree swoop to remove some of the kinks; and as
my head careened past the northeast corner of the room, my eye
was caught by a gigantic, 4' × 3' calendar. Well, a thin strip of it
was calendar, the months of the year in Polish in a narrow band
down one side; the rest was given over to a glossy photo of a mam-
mothly endowed young woman in a cheerleader crouch, her hands
crisscrossed coyly to cover her crotch.

I was amazed. I turned to Professor David Trubek, with whom
I had traveled from the cheesy innocence of Wisconsin to this most
complicated of places, and I was prepared to say something like "Do
you believe this?" But David, who was seated 63 degrees to the
southwest of me in the neckstretching, headswooping order of
things—David was sound asleep. His toppled head, I noticed, was
haloed by another gigantic poster, this one enshrining Miss Ginger
Miller, 1989 Pet of the Year. She had her arms akimbo, her legs
spread wide for the camera, and no doubt in deference to some illusion
of modesty, she was wearing a nice pair of fuzzy black Alaskan
tundra boots.

I was amazed. Later, when we asked our hosts about this, they
explained that the whole office, male and female, went out together
in the wake of the revolution and shopped carefully for symbols of
their new expressive freedom. They explained that "women here are
not prudes like in the United States, where people bathe in their
clothes." An American professor observed that it seemed not simply

---

psychologist. Most often, these, like the church, try to persuade them to give up
their babies to overcrowded orphanages, run by nuns. . . . The most serious threat to
abortion rights, however, has arisen in Parliament. Last summer, Senator Walerian
Piotrowski proposed a bill that would outlaw abortion, saying it would help Poland
lead the way to a more moral Europe." Gabrielle Glaser, "New Poland, Same Old
Story," *Village Voice*, 2 April 1991, 19.

23. "'Poland is at a turning point, and we are turning to the right and into the
dark,' says Hanna Jankowska, a Warsaw feminist. 'We are trading a red regime for
one that wears black robes. Things are moving in the direction of an absolute clerical
state, like Khomeini's Iran. And naturally, women are left behind.'" Id.

an issue of nudity, but of the sexualization of the workplace. The response from one man, exuberantly unleashed from the oppression of Communism, was again, "We are not like you Americans; we are proud of their bodies."

Now I know those possessive pronouns are really tricky in English, but, again, giving the language barrier every benefit of the doubt, I think it was the notion of possession itself that was trickiest of all.

The complicated iconography of *Penthouse* centerfolds was everywhere we went, in a war of imagistic oppression and proclaimed liberation.[24] Pinups on buses, in the telegraph office, in department stores, on walls filled with political graffiti, in the monastery where our conference was held. Jesus dying on the cross hung above every doorway. Perhaps most peculiar of all was the bookstore we walked by, an ordinary bookstore, like B. Dalton or Waldenbooks, full of computer manuals and recent fiction and textbooks and how-to-fix-your-car. There in the window, sharing center stage, were two spotlighted pictures. One was of the Polish Pope, a good, kindly, and sanctified man, leaning on his holy shepherd's staff, his eyes cast upward to heaven. The other was of the February 1990 *Playboy* centerfold, who wore her hair streaming on the waves of some gentle wind and a demure though extremely long string of pearls. Her bunny ears were flopped forward in a shy downward cast, as were her eyes; a perfect madonna of the First Amendment.

Self-Effacing Choice: The Politics of Plastic Surgery

Strange story: there I sat, glued to the television as usual, scanning the Oprah Winfrey show for moments of redeeming social value. One of the featured guests was a travel agent who described herself as "ugly." Apparently she was slightly overweight, and she had dark skin and a broad nose that turned under rather than up. She was extremely proficient at her job but found herself passed over for higher-paying client-contact jobs in the front office because her employer felt that image was one of the qualifications for front-office

---

24. "'Poles want to believe that they have a free, modern society,' says Hanna Jankowska. 'The truth is that unfortunately we are a Third World country, especially when it comes to women. But we have the Catholic Church and the legacy of Communism, both of which foster passivity, to contend with.'" Id., 21.

jobs. Image was supposedly related to consumer tastes and expectations. The "ugliness" with which she was afflicted, in other words,
turned out to be the inability to please hypothetical clients desiring
the exotic—clients whose keenly acculturated consumer appetites
were better whetted by flat tummies, little noses, golden but not
brown skin, and long hair tousled as though by soft tropical rainfall.

Another panelist on the Oprah show was the requisite psychologist—the expert whose presence always assures us that closet can-
nibalism with a taste for lizard blood (or whatever) really is a treatable
condition but the first step of Reaching Out is up to you. In this
instance, the eager psychologist was reassuring the Ugly Black Travel
Agent that more self-assertion, more self-confidence, and more aggres-
sive sales techniques, were all she needed to turn the situation around.
"Just say yes to yourself," she glowed happily.

Eager for comparative data, I switched channels. In two flicks
of the wrist, I was beamed aboard the world of Joan Rivers. Joan,
it turned out, was having a plastic surgery sweepstakes: prizes were
being awarded for the most complete surgical makeover by a member
of the audience. Again there was a panel of people, all of whom
were testifying that they had been going nowhere in their jobs until
they decided to get liposuction, rhinoplasty, a nice Armani suit with
big shoulderpads, and some cheek implants—and now they were
running the company. Over by the edge of all these testimonials,
sitting in more or less the same seat occupied by the psychologist on
Oprah, was an eager plastic surgeon. He too was preaching the
virtues of self-assertion and self-confidence that flow from the choice
to go under the knife. "Just say yes to yourself," he glowed repeatedly.

As I searched for a moral in the middle of this morass, it occurred
to me that what linked my discomfort about both women's shows
was the underlying espousal of the very worst kind of assimilationist
platitudes. I don't simply mean that they were advocating assimilation
into a particular cultural aesthetic or ideology, although that was
obviously an important part of the shows' push. What made it the
very worst kind of assimilation was that it took women and men *out*
of the very right to coexist in the world with that most basic legacy
of our own bodies. What made it so bad was the unselfconscious
denial of those violent social pressures that make so irresistible the
"choice" to cut off that perfect replica of one's grandmother's nose in
favor of a trendier, more acceptable model.

Both programs redirected attention away from the powerful, if petty, call to conform—absolutely, in these cases—that is the perpetual risk of any socializing collective, whether family or polis. Rather than acknowledge that this is an interactive problem, both styled the issue as a mere matter of individual appearance, attitude, control. Neither program effectively addressed how the politics of prettiness comes to be so dominating that ordinary people's economic survival depends on anesthetized self-mutilation, or that "image" has shaken itself free of illusion and become a power concept, or that David Duke and Michael Jackson win hero status for transforming themselves overnight into identically featured, middle-aged, middle-of-the-road white people.

Put on a happy face was the bottom line of both programs—literally, according to the Joan Rivers show, and figuratively, in the Oprah Winfrey version.

This erasure of ourselves is so pervasive a force. But the pressure to banish our bodies and banish ourselves in the competitive race to become Ideal has too much cost ultimately, I think, and perpetuates social divisions it is time we healed rather than exacerbated.

Ordering around the World

During my short visit to Poland, I was astonished by how often I heard the term "social parasite." It came up as a reason both why Communism had failed and why capitalism was so desirable: with a free market, each would be on his own, working hard and reaping the fruits of his labor, aligned with the "normal" world, unconstrained by parasitic "elements" who would fall by the wayside and finally learn the bittersweet lesson of fending for themselves.

I was very worried by this rhetoric of social parasitism, this holdover vocabulary from the old-world order of the Nazi lexicon; I remain worried. It sounded—it is—profoundly fascistic and racist. Here's what I read between the lines: an unquestioning nationalism in which Russian domination (in the case of Poland) equals parasitism, but in which, in the rush to embrace American-style capitalism, all shortcomings are dismissed as being caused by or limited to said parasitic elements, to wit, "Stalinist peasants," Romany nationals, African-Americans, or others. (On several occasions, people actually announced that in their opinion the only reasons problems like homelessness and unemployment existed in the United States was because of African-Americans.)

At the same time, there was in Eastern Europe a ubiquitous sense of embarrassment. As we exuberant Americans came marching into the Polish winter, with our Pepsi Cola and our nasal sprays, our Batman ballpoint pens and our pump 'em up running shoes, we had every reason to be embarrassed; and yet it was they who were. The Poles apologized constantly for their standard of living, for the condition of their houses, for not having answering machines, for not living lives like ours, as they imagined them to be. They seemed intensely self-conscious about, even ashamed of, a life-style that, though considerably simpler than the American, is a perfectly hospitable one and considerably above the global norm. As we were shown around Kracôw, our hosts proudly pointed out historic buildings that had been sold to West German and Canadian hotel chains. I felt as though I were bearing witness to the so-called sale of Manhattan Island—this nation of sensible subsistence farmers rushing to trade their lives and land for the baubles of MacDonald's burgers.

I worry as well that in the massive influx of capital to Eastern Europe there is a quality that feels like a throwing-of-dollar-bills-at. I don't mean that the money isn't needed or deeply appreciated by the recipient countries. Rather, I'm referring to the spirit in which it is given by the donor countries. It felt imperialistic and condescending in the same way, if not to the same degree, as the West's financial condescension in other parts of the world, particularly the Third World. Yet at the same time I was able to see, during my trip to Poland and, later, to Czechoslovakia, more than I had been able to see in other parts of the world, that this condescension operates as a complicated form of seduction. On the airplane to Warsaw, for example, I heard three young Polish-Americans with strong Chicago accents talking about how great it was that all their friends and relatives were finally beginning to see the light and embrace the free market. There was a profound scorn in their voices, having nothing to do with ideological discontent with Communism, at least as they expressed it. Rather, it was scorn for Poland and its standard of living. It was comparative scorn, like relatives who have done well and are determined to rub it in. It was like some complicated sibling rivalry.

It reminded me of a friend I once had, a classmate from my tenure at Wellesley College, whom I invited to my parents' home in Roxbury, Massachusetts, for dinner. Afterwards, she came away saying over and over, "Oh I'm so sorry, I didn't know"—as though my material circumstances were so inferior to hers that I needed to be *consoled* about them. And I confess that, in the smarting wake of her comment, I was tempted to a certain shame about myself and my home; her careless, simple disrespect so profoundly devalued me that I was tempted to reassess everything that was solid, sustaining, and comforting in my life as something to be "overcome."

Similarly, Western flashing of cash and its ability to generate massive realignments troubles me less as ideology than as a deep discourtesy, a seductive humiliation, which teaches that self-worth derives from appearances and material possessions.

Again, it is worth understanding that I do not mean these observations as specific ideological commentary ("neo-Marxist," I'm told, is what many readers mutter to themselves when reading my work). I would rather they be understood as referring back to my initial observations about more general and ancient traditions that permeate and configure not merely the so-called new world order, but the old world, the Third World (whatever happened to the Second?) and, of course, the still-to-be-conceived future world of our best longings and imagination.

I began this essay from mystical exile, feeling a stranger in a strange land. Let me end now in contemplation of the prosaic everydayness of these ruminations on great power. I suspect that these stories are, to varying degrees, similar to the histories and experiences that propel most of us in our daily lives, and that we share, even in our difference. I suspect that these are the paranoias and embarrassments and pressures to conform for which we must be ever vigilant, in our own lives and in the coercive social power we give to the consensus of our legal institutions. I suspect that these are the living, actual, ongoing dangers that describe our collective reality, not just our individualized imaginations, and for which we stand, in hopeful coalition, ever on guard.

Autumn Weekends: An Essay on Law and Everyday Life

David Kennedy

I was asked to write an essay on law and everyday life shortly before departing for Lisbon to attend the establishment of the International Jurists Platform on East Timor. I completed the draft several weeks later after returning from a trip to Madrid for a meeting of the Academic Council of the Royal Complutense College, established some months previously. My reflections on law and everyday life were focused by the contrast between these two experiences—a moment of international institutional establishment in a project of advocacy and a moment of institutional management—and by my movement from one to the other.

In the first, the law and the everyday seem separate, struggling for connection. This was a weekend of organization for legal activism, of earnestness about justice and cynicism about politics and the bureaucratic form, a weekend sharpened by awareness of the distance between law's promise and performance, between the pain of every-day life and law's imperfect tonics. Ours was the work of the metropolis, a machinery of international norms and institutions mobilized for deployment on the periphery. In the second weekend, law and the everyday seemed complacently intermingled. This was a weekend of international legal routine, calling for neither idealism nor realism, through which law and everyday life might stroll untouched by the

I would like to thank everyone mentioned in the text as well as Nathaniel Berman, Dan Danielsen, Ioannis Drossos, Karen Engle, Gunter Frankenberg, Jerry Frug, Marge Garber, Barbara Johnson, Duncan Kennedy, Rose Moss, and Henry Steiner for their comments.

heroism of norms or the spectacle of a life beyond law's order. This was a cosmopolitan weekend, in which the courtesies of international management displaced the awkward political realism of an activism preoccupied with (opposition to) local sovereignties.

Together, these weekends present a movement from the isolation of expertise, with its anxieties about effectiveness and complicity, its rigid roles and stereotyped relationships, to the looser pragmatism and contentment of membership in a constituted institutional environment. The first, preoccupied with its effort to bring law to bear on social life, may interpret the second as law unmoored from the "realities" of everyday life, or as a bureaucrat's everyday unmindfulness of law's higher normative vision. The second is likely to see the first as either quixotic or ideological.

Each traditionally offers a place for the skeptical modern observer/participant and each forms part of the modern international lawyer's everyday life. As international lawyers, we rove between them, struggling to merge normative and institutional identities. As observers of modern culture, we hoist each on the petard of the other. The activist's faith seems foolish, his cynicism bitter; the bureaucrat's routine uninspired, his complacency immoral.

I. The First Weekend

Scene One: Setting It Up

The establishment conference for the International Jurists Platform on East Timor, a smudged xerox affair from the start, unfolded as a cantilevered jumble of lawyers, activists, local and international metropolitans. As I understand it, the project began with Pedro, a Portuguese lawyer working in the Netherlands as an academic of some sort. Pedro had been interested in East Timor since his days at law school in Lisbon, had written about the human-rights violations that had taken place there since the Indonesian occupation and had identified a network of human-rights activists committed to East Timorese self-determination.

East Timor had been a Portuguese colony until the revolution of the midseventies and continues to figure in the political imagination of the Portuguese as a nonpartisan and rather distant test site for the nation's honor and humanitarian commitment. The struggle for

East Timorese liberation from Indonesia might somewhat redeem Portugal's colonial experience, both confirmed (for East Timor is distinguished from the hundreds of other cultures and islands within Indonesia by the boundaries of Dutch and Portuguese administration) and cleansed by righteous defense of self-determination and international human rights.

In an elaborate bank shot, Portugal had recently sued Australia in the World Court over Indonesian treatment of East Timor. The legal issues are probably too procedural to ignite the imagination: does Portugal, as the ex-colonial power, have standing to bring a claim on behalf of the East Timorese; does Australia's entry into a treaty with Indonesia to divide the seabed resources lying between East Timor and Australia give rise to a claim against Australia for recognizing an illegal occupation, and so forth. Nevertheless, it seemed reasonable to establish the Jurists' Platform as a legal person in Portugal in part to situate international legal work on such issues in a knowledgeable cultural milieu. I quickly discovered that everyone in Portugal, like longtime activists, knew to drop the "East" when referring to Timor. In Portugal, moreover, Pedro could implement his plan for an international institution among old friends.

Pedro's idea for a Jurists' Platform borrowed a leaf from the international nongovernmental human-rights community, an assortment of nonprofit foundations, research centers, advocacy groups, and religious organizations. Some of these groups are general, some issue focused, some academic, some litigious, and many are focused in the Netherlands. All circulate around the large intergovernmental organizations of the U.N. system to one degree or another, and all share a number of institutional features: an international membership, an international board, an executive director, a small staff, and so forth. There is a great deal of overlap among the players in this community—the members of one organization may well be the staff of another and so on. The Platform of Jurists for Timor, as Pedro imagined it, would replicate these features to provide a focal point for what would become "our" activity on behalf of Timor.

To inaugurate the effort, Pedro had worked for over a year to identify potential participants and fund an opening conference. I first heard about his efforts from a former doctoral student of mine at Harvard Law School who had returned to Lisbon to teach international law. Paula had called some months before to ask if I and a colleague from Boston would be willing to come to Lisbon to participate in a conference on East Timor. I had said yes in large part out of friendship and respect for Paula, although I suppose also at least partly because I had never been to Portugal.

I had not participated in the more activist side of the international human-rights movement for some time. During the international human-rights boom of the late seventies and early eighties, I had experienced much of the international conference scene as somewhat tawdry and disappointing, had written up my skepticism about international human-rights institutions and advocacy and departed the field. Much of my frustration stemmed from the oscillation between private cynicism and public piety that characterized many of the international lawyers and bureaucrats I had met in the field. My expectation that either the solemn declarations would be fulfilled or the private criticisms be made public was disappointed often enough that I developed a jaded professionalism and lost interest.

I agreed to go to Lisbon partly to see whether things had changed, whether there had come to be others frustrated with the traditional professional posture who might connect with one another at such an event. Substantial criticism of human rights had meanwhile reached the academy from the Left and the Right, and I wondered whether any of this had reached the activist community, whether there was, or might come to be, a different form of activist culture in the international law.

Paula had also invited a Boston area specialist in self-determination who was completing a study of cultural modernism in international law. We enjoyed one another's company and often found ourselves reflecting similarly on our profession. It seemed an ideal opportunity to rethink my relationship to international law advocacy. As for Timorese self-determination, there seemed many reasons to favor it and little to be said on the other side.

It is hard to get very far thinking about such an experience in terms as abstract as *law* and *everyday life*. From the vantage point of my Cambridge everyday, there is always, of course, an element of fantasy in such events. For activist missions, there is the fantasy that trips to the site of law's deployment will be magic journeys, full of fabulous characters and novel engagements, escapes from the routines of everyday life in the academy. This sort of fantasy distracted my focus from the establishment of a Jurists' Platform toward the advocacy for which it was the intended vehicle. This is a simple fantasy—law promises to get you there, take you higher, make it real. Be there or be square.

For the earnest advocate, law relates to the "Timor situation" as norms to facts, a simple program for action: international human rights norms are to be translated into everyday practice in Timor. Where everyday life strays from the law, activism will bring them together. Of course, for the cynical advocate pondering the stilted language of "self-determination" or "human rights" and the daily life of Timor, the same normative vision may seem half empty. In either case, the fantasy of law's application frames law as something fabulous, abstract, even magical: words that become deeds. Law as an instrument of social change, a force for freedom, and so on.

This fantasy touches the institutional work of establishment that precedes direct advocacy. The constitutional moment is always a mystical one, lawyers gathered to make law and constitute themselves as activists in its service. Thinking about going to Lisbon, I couldn't help feeling that even if I did not participate in the normative mopping-up operation of later advocacy, having been present when lawyers came together as members of a Jurists' Platform, united with a calling, I would have been part of, prior to, whatever activism ensued. At the very least, this sort of thing can sometimes be cashed in for political correctness points with students and collegues.

Focus on the conference itself brings law's internal mechanisms into the story, contrasting the directly apprehendable language of international norms with the elaborate institutional machinery of international law's interpretation or implementation. The contrast suggests a chronology, progress forward from the everyday clarity of norms to a more speculative institutional site for their interpretation, application, and enforcement. An establishment conference straddles these two moments, providing the link between a normative everyday and future institutional pragmatism. Forward ever, backward never.

Focus on the international lawyer himself shifts the image of law and the everyday yet again. I think about myself going to Lisbon— I may become magic, an objective expert, a professional agnostic, a temporary interloper, a generalist, formalist, bringing world public opinion, world public order, the rational and the reasonable into the continuing everyday of Timor activism. As a lawyer, I will be more than my everyday. Of course it is not so simple. I remember past experience. Even with daily discipline the law often disappoints, becomes a messy affair of airports and fax machines, doctrines, and deadlines. Still I can be hopeful.

Lawyers remain divided between the transcendent idealism of their normative vision and the institutional grind of legal practice as well as between the programmatic aspirations of legal institutions and the tedium of doctrinal interpretation or document drafting. And like other professionals, the international lawyer earns his keep as a ventriloquist, throwing his legal idealism forward from the realism of his everyday.

Characters in a Jurists' Platform might stabilize these internal fantasies by reference to the ground of a "Timor," the client, the base, the terrain of interpretation, application, sanction, and struggle, perhaps especially to the touchstone of visible violence. This can be prurient, it can be pornographic. The activist arranges his polemics and tactics, his righteousness and his realism, to assure the transparent representation of a struggle at another site, the site of the Timorese everyday. For this, St. Timor in agony must be seen. And Timor also sees us, imposes self-discipline. For the lawyer, the mystically receding client operates as a reader of last resort.

As I look back, the Platform seems a kaleidoscope of form and fancy: lawyers and activists, doctrines and institutions, dreamers and tacticians, all refracted against the backdrop of another country and culture, a Timor beyond the exchange of word and deed. Of course, all this was a bit unfocused on Saturday morning when I arrived in Lisbon. Having had tickets for Natalie Cole the preceding Thursday, I left only on Friday and arrived in Lisbon after a somewhat disorienting stop in the Azores just as the conference was starting Saturday morning. The meeting was held upstairs in a downtown religious cinder-block kindergarten from the sixties—ubiquitous Papal insignia, institutional walls and food, dozens of Portuguese children. Inside were perhaps a hundred jurists and activists.

Scene Two: The Entrance

Although Paula reassured me with a wink from the dais, as I entered the conference site to begin my weekend with these people I had the uneasy feeling of arriving in an ongoing conversation among strangers. My cross-cultural anxiety was probably heightened by the fact that they were already there and I was arriving a bit late. And by the unexpected presence of so many Catholic children in what was to have been a project of secular professionalism. As a law professor new to Timor, I imagined the others as committed lawyers and activists, sharing a canon of histories, doctrines, and atrocities that I would come at best to recognize, if not learn, by the end of the conference.

As I walked in, it would have been hard for those already in the room reporting their "work" on Timor not to have had a more immediate and ongoing relationship to Timor-the-conference-topic than I. Although I had asked some students to pull together a packet of legal literature on Timor to read before dozing on the plane, I was still pretty much a blank slate as to Timor. In a way, this relative ignorance came naturally to me as a lawyer. Nothing like ignorance, blind justice, to distinguish the law from everyday plays of power, passion, and prejudice, and I have often been asked to participate in things because I don't know much about them or haven't written about them. Human-rights junkets to places like the Mideast are always looking for someone who is neutral but whose sympathies can be predicted.

In such events, professionals typically start off serious about roles, loosening ties or removing jackets only later. I entered the room as an attorney, interested to begin a relationship with a group of clients. If there turned out to be any Timorese in the room, I could be their lawyer. For the activists, I might be law to their politics. We might think of the jurists in the crowd as in-house counsel for Timor and I as outside counsel. At the threshold, I constituted the group against my identity as a lawyer, a generalist, an internationalist, above all, someone who legitimately didn't know much about what was to go on. Perhaps this is how it is whenever the lawyer enters the everyday, a man at an airport with a passport.

This messianic or metropolitan posture—a lawyer gone to activism, the general arrived in the specific—brings with it some predictable, even clichéd, resentments. The lawyer not as midwife to justice, but as formalistic distraction from activist passions, agnostic in his commitments, apologetic for imperial power, complicit in things mundane. The first thing we do is kill all the lawyers, etc. At this early stage, the international lawyer has two strong defenses against these entailed resentments. On the one hand, one may simply assert expertise, the power of the objective, the scientific, the broader reality of an international community, of a law that renders any everyday petty. On the other hand, and hopefully simultaneously, one may search for common ground with activists and specialists in an earnestly shared commitment to our clients in Timor.

Harmonizing these defenses may be difficult, a matter of discretion more than valor or expertise. Professional ethics for lawyers is largely a matter of juxtaposing mandated disclosures and confidentialities to reconcile fealty to law and client. Tensions remain, and in my experience it is good to get beyond these early moments of "lawyers" and "activists" as quickly as possible. Well-established and mannered participants leave such roles at the door, background to conversation.

The next morning, when I thought we had long since put such things behind us, a peach-skinned activist responded acidly to a lawyer's description of the local disco by mentioning her own evening at a "solidarity meeting." It was a bit rude. But we lawyers could always think of this as naive, and I suppose they could always think of us as cynical or parasitical. At the start, I was reassured that the lawyers were thought needed and had been invited. This was after all to be a Jurists' Platform, constructed as a focal point for legal work on behalf of the Timorese, a site for representation rather than solidarity.

If such differences usually fade only after roles have given way to interpersonal reconciliations that merge private ambitions and public commitments, amused cynicism with shared polemics, sometimes, if only briefly, a more public reconciliation may seem possible. I felt that flicker in the person of Pedro—earnest, activist, lawyer, mobilizer of the metropolis, link to the periphery, Portuguese and Dutch, at once lawyer and client. He was more than just a role and seemed to yield no purchase for cynical connection. Could we ever be that committed, that certain of our direction? In a way he seemed to have achieved personally what we hoped to achieve as a group over the course of the weekend together—to become one with our mission and with one another. Perhaps, together in a Platform we might find the determination and clarity that eluded us alone.

It seemed right that he should be extremely busy, somehow always just a bit unavailable, attending to some detail that would keep the conference afloat, to some dignitary who would grace our meeting with meaning. It wasn't necessary to speak with him, it was fine that he was kept busy. It was enough that he was there, had brought us there, that we were all his guests, his friends. I knew Pedro only as a name at the end of a fax machine when a good friend of his from the Netherlands picked me up at the airport. He provided a first conversation for any two arrivals, how had we come to know him, what was he really like. If he had conceived the Platform to multiply his advocacy, our goal in joining was also clear: to become more like Pedro.

Scene Three: The Early Work of Establishment

I had come in and sat off to one side just as the first plenary broke into "working groups" to consider litigation, human rights, education, drafting a constitution for the Platform, and some forgotten fifth topic. Having done the constitution drafting at another such conference some years before, I joined the litigation group, thinking, in the light of the ongoing ICJ case, that it might be more interesting. Besides, the constitution-drafting group seemed a distinctly dull crew of Pedro's more earnest Portuguese acquaintances.

A few minutes after we started, Pedro pulled me out of my working group for an interview with Portuguese television. Through the authority of expertise, I would establish the Platform in the media somewhat in advance of our own constitution by reference to two vague alternative sites: world public opinion and Timor. A charming reporter said she would have a few question about the U.S. position on Timor and my sense for the legal issues underlying Portugal's position in the ICJ. Such an interview at this stage would have to be a very generic performance. It would only be later, much later, late the following afternoon at the closing press conference that nuanced expertise, the formal opinions of the Platform and results of our deliberations, would be available to be voiced.

Her camera man turned on the lights. What was my assessment of the U.S. position on Timor? Looking back on it, I should admit that I had no idea what the U.S. position on Timor might be—where were we on Indonesia these days anyway. I flashed rather unhelpfully on nuclear ships and New Zealand. But even if a lawyer is supposed to be neutral, he is not supposed to be totally in the dark.

I said I had, of course, wished for a more forthcoming attitude from the State Department on Timor (don't they always disappoint), but that in light of the newfound enthusiasm for international law and institutions in Washington (brief invocation of Kuwait, the Berlin Wall, the New World Order) we might see more. This is what made initiatives like that of Portugal in the ICJ all the more timely and important. Did I expect Portugal would win its case? There were certainly a number of crucial procedural hurdles, and the case would need to be pursued diligently, but the importance of the norms involved could hardly be overstated. And so on.

We had to repeat the whole thing with the camera pointing the other way and without sound, so I asked her a number of questions about life in the media, in Portugal. And later that evening, there I was, a talking head—not savvy, it was really too early in my Timorese immersion for that, but on TV all the same, dubbed into Portuguese and discussing, somewhat prematurely, the work of the International Jurists Platform for Timor.

As the conference got going, it would surpass and confirm these media highlights. At the start, it was quite explicitly the work of the Platform and of its establishment conference to connect with Timor and the outside world precisely by narrowing the gap between the law, with its norms, and the everyday, with its violations. On this, each of the plenary speakers was more earnest and eloquent than the last. We would take law to Timor, make the international law regime practical, demonstrate its relevance, milk it for all it was worth. By about 11:00 A.M. on Saturday morning, of course, these statements had lost much of their punch, and speakers turned like sunflowers at midday to increasingly practical points. And it was in this spirit that we moved to our working groups.

Nevertheless, a general activism was our shared and public agenda. We had put it on grant applications to fly to Portugal, and we would promise at least ourselves to do something about it later. The conference working groups reflected this sentiment: we might choose to assist in litigation, devising tactics of enforced compliance. Perhaps we could get an injunction, or start a shareholders suit involving some oil company. In the education group we could harness the great sanction of public opinion. The human-rights group could feed the institutional reporting machinery. And we all thought of Kuwait—why shouldn't the Security Council take this matter in hand and pursue a collective war?

When we were all home writing up our reports, we would try to remember our work in the terms of these opening flourishes, as an instance of law's application to fact. Only in these terms may international lawyers situate such events in the narrative conventions of their discipline, for whom international law arose from the chaos of politics in a great social contract three hundred and fifty years before, becoming in this century, after three hundred years of philosophy, a matter of institutional pragmatism, sanctions, obedience, payments and compliances on a great ledger of legal relevance, responding to international conflicts in conferences such as this, a thousand points of pragmatism, law returned with the power of the norm through our work in the here and now.

By reference to these opening ambitions, it was not surprising that the Platform constitution group, so self-absorbed, should have the last refuge of the lawyer's lawyer, the nerd's nerd. Pedro's drafters seemed stuck in a moment before the conference, when it was still necessary to bring us together—perhaps Pedro had become himself too occupied with organization to see the importance of getting on with the substantive work at hand. And perhaps we knew, as we fantasized ourselves constituted as collective action, what constitution would in fact entail.

Bringing us together would require more than a simple allocation of tasks among lawyers or activists. As we settled into the petty routines and relations of our conference world, the everyday media world would fade, and so, for that matter, would Timor. Our earnestness would be corroded by the sharing of private doubts. As we came to live ever more in the conference, we would live somewhat less for Timor. By the end, a coincidentally simultaneous massacre in Dili on Timor would barely break into our everyday.

Although we would want to remember the conference as constitution for action, the Platform would need to be established against the background of our experiences in Lisbon as much as against our disciplinary idealism. In the middle of all the working-group rooms stood the plenary session, where we began and where the conference would end. And circulating around it were tables with stray literature—many participants had brought their reprints, notices of other conferences, cultural survival T-shirts, human-rights studies, bibliographies, recent publications of the professional press, concert announcements, maps of Lisbon, tourist brochures on the southern beaches. Nothing much was for sale, but the milling crowd situated the plenary in a new petty mercantile atmosphere, smoking, joking, parishioners at a cathedral. The conference plenary had become a shrine, a tourist monument, an Eifel Tower, with its own bustling everyday.

Scene Four: The Platform Really Takes Off

The bustle in our little Papal kindergarten would be the site for the social relations that would emerge as by-products of our earnest work for Timor. It began in unimportant ways—a sharing of pasts, tiny fragments of a shared present, the ride in, the bad coffee, my ex-student was the former wife of your government's U.N. representative, and so forth. We recognized one another in a mutual remove from the client, situating ourselves in a common tactical terrain. We shared a common project, participants in a broad division of labor, some of us formalists, some administrators, some political tacticians, experts in local or metropolitan knowledges, some doctrinalists, others more practical—all tacticians for the real, together a magnificent pragmatic machine.

And we shared a method, a fantasy of institution building, a process by which to constitute ourselves as a membership with a leadership. Indeed, from our own diverse institutions, nationalities, and professions, we shared Pedro's idea: a council, a secretary general, a resolution, a preamble, a resolution, points of order, plenaries, working groups, drafting sessions, all the modern technologies.

Was there any conflict not subject to reconciliation in the metropolis? In plenary, one fashionable Latin American woman from New York stood up, feet together in rather high pumps, held her copy of our draft resolution before her and asked if she might make a few suggestions from her experience in the U.N. Shouldn't our preamble rather say "taking note that" where we had written "deeply deploring that" and shouldn't the operative paragraphs of our resolution be clearly numbered?

As to the second, she was clearly correct. We all knew we should clearly distinguish the perambulatory recitation of norms and facts from the operational engagement with the everyday. Numbering would do the trick, indentation would help. The differences that had separated us—between law and activism, norms and facts—had migrated to a common text where they might, indeed should, be expressed with increased clarity. As to the preambulatory point, we would need to vote. We quickly agreed, voted, to delegate the "taking note"/"deeply disturbed" issue back to the drafting committee for resolution, and having found consensus, we moved on.

What, in our little metropolitan world, had become of Timor, the collective fantasy with which we had kicked off the exercise? At first we heard the Timorese participants speak with the authority of authenticity. For me the moment of transition occurred early on Saturday when I shared a taxi with one Timorese fellow, a young lawyer from Macau on the make, who announced his hope to meet an American lawyer or law professor who might know how one of his clients could purchase a small U.S. bank. Could I help him in this venture, locate such a bank for him, for Timor, for his client whose identity could not be disclosed? My native had abruptly disappeared into professional courtesies and confidentiality. In our little conference spaceship, Timor became a screen on which we could project our common fantasies and anxieties about the real.

To many in the metropolis, of course, this comes as no surprise. When I shared my taxi-ride encounter with a young Canadian friend, he smiled and nodded and we began a friendship. Isn't the client, in a way like the earnest activist, the technical lawyer, indeed, the entire public zone always a disappointment, an immaturity? International sophisticates have come to see the technologies and actors in our public spaces and national realities as more or less shrewd manipulations, constructions. In large part, that is what it means to be cosmopolitan, to have transcended the pull of unreasonable local specificities and passions.

Of course this stance can bring cynicism, a corrosive split between private commitment and public realism, public polemics and private doubts. Participants in the international activist milieu often bond around this sort of split, as I did with my Canadian friend. As narrator, I am also tempted by such split moments. If I present them correctly, readers will share the alienation of my observation as one might the bemused observation of a newscaster at a political convention ("Well at this point Jed, he needs to make a strong appeal to women between thirty-five and fifty-five, yes and here it is, we go now live to the appeal"). Perhaps we will laugh together about the fragility of institutional forms and the pettiness of activist work.

In the metropolis, although we are moved by invocations of the real and the client, and are careful to orient ourselves toward the practical or the redemptive, as representation displaces the represented, we find ourselves ambivalent—has our everyday displaced their culture, or has our law finally achieved its relevance for their project? Sometimes the ambivalence seems more than a routinized cynicism, the bonding more than complicit passivity.

This ambivalence was embodied in Portugal for me by a quite urbane and sexy lawyer from an international nonprofit that had styled itself the "Unrepresented Nations and Peoples Organization." She seemed smart and savvy, and a new Australian friend and I determined to recruit her for our evolving affinity group. We asked about her organization. They (a small office in the Hague, a "General Secretary," three lawyers, a membership, a board, a newsletter) were present for the absent. They had correspondents in Tartu and San Francisco. Although they had recently lost three clients (Estonia, Latvia, Lithuania), they hoped for continued Baltic financial support out of solidarity with all the places where boundaries, nations, ethnicities, tribes, or governments had been insufficiently coordinated to perfect the transparency of international representation through statehood.

It was noble work, rendered more palpably significant, if strangely doubled, by their lawyer's assertion that she was herself unrepresented. As I recall her account, she had come from a minority ethnic group in Bangladesh, or perhaps Pakistan, grown up the child of diplomats, become a lawyer, worked for a big Washington law firm, pierced her nose, and moved to Holland, where she had been representing the unrepresented now for almost a year. She told her story with a light ironic touch that made it impossible to respond with either earnest relief that the unrepresented had found their spokeswoman or with any doubts about why this form, why here, why her?

I liked her immediately and when we discussed the work of her education group over lunch, I proposed that her organization sponsor a gigantic blimp, like Goodyear, which would travel around the world labeled with one or another unrepresented people, tethered outside the Olympics or the Clarence Thomas hearings, wherever. Others joined in as we developed a comprehensive blimp-based program for human-rights protection. She wrote me some months later to ask whether I had encountered any "blimps hanging outside campus," and reported that "I went off to Estonia for a conference on Population Transfer, which was quite an experience. Very interesting place. There was something surrealistic about Tallinn, reminded me a bit of that weird bar we went to in Lisbon. Which was lots of fun." She was a cosmopolitan all right.

Was this cynicism or irony, destructive or delicious? The routinization of enthusiasm, too many hours together in a small building, we looked to one another for hints of private doubt, small islands of relief from earnestness. A Scotsman who seemed in working group to have memorized the procedural details of every ICJ case for his dissertation turned out to be an extremely ironic devotee of British punk culture. He joined our clique and followed up on our acquaintance in Lisbon with a package of trashy British comics.

At lunch, smoking by the tennis court, drinking with age cohorts, national cohorts, private in-groups, we recognized with a wink or a chortle that our public idealism would not be supported by the realism of our common projects. We entered the zone of flirtation. Of course this brought with it a turn away from the public narrative of law engaging the Timorese everyday, a turn from activism to narcissism. True enough. There emerged the tawdriness of all conferences everywhere. If we could bring law to bear on Timor together, wouldn't we also sleep with one another? Indeed, who would sleep with whom, who befriend whom, who would promote, hire, help whom? Who would reveal their loneliness, exasperation, sexual orientation?

How can laughter in Lisbon be defended when people were being slaughtered in Timor? We could say it's only human, that we should blame the naive idealism of our common project, that laughter is the best medicine. Perhaps it is efficient—it might be these social strands, the tears and fears of the everyday rather than our textual productions, which would hold us together after the conference closed. In this, the promise of the social and the sexual functioned as an idealism, an aspiration, a promise. And I hoped, if only vaguely, that more might come of our affinity cohort than it seemed possible to expect from the official working groups.

This growing private social sensibility offset the sensible, if sterile, formality of our public debates. As the social verged into cliché, the conference plodded along its familiar route: introductory exhortation, working groups, working-group reports to the plenary, working groups, plenary to adopt constitution and resolutions, press conference, social event. Every meeting begins with a recollection of past work and ends with a promise of work to come, two moments that pull us back from the sexual to the social and render the private cynical. Indeed, this is the very function of the agenda.

At one point my litigation working group flagged, wandered on the patio, suspended in the idea of litigation, having been unable to identify anyone actually working on any actual case. We were left only with duty to the meeting, remoteness from our own individual everydays, and goodwill for the ultimate cause. We traded anecdotes, discussed the weather, and experienced our situation as confusion about the agenda. We asked one another who had brought the agenda. We waited for leadership and were quite good naturedly ready to follow anyone with a plan.

And along came a young Australian lawyer whom we told about our lack. She sprang into action, jotted a few notes, urged us to return to the meeting room, and simply began the meeting, intoning in the flat locution of all U.N. debate everywhere that it would be good to begin with a restatement of where we had been, and sure enough everything each of us had half mentioned the day before reappeared as a subject discussed, an observation made, a point taken. In the passive voice of recounting we became alive as a collective. What, we wondered, would she have for us for today. And she posed some issues, and we threw them about, and she did it again, and now we were in a hurry, needed to get our report together for the plenary, and off we went to hear from the other working groups.

When we got there, there wasn't time for our report, but it hardly mattered. As a plenary we needed to work on our resolution and our constitution, prepare for the press conference. We didn't want to waste time reporting what had, after all, already been accomplished in the working groups. As it turned out, only the constitutional group really needed to report.

Scene Five: A Constituted Life

When we look back on the Platform's establishment as an institutional narrative, we focus on the final moments, when the constitution drafters returned with their document. But inside the conference, focusing on our substantive accomplishments and objectives, the constitution drafters had come to seem quite beside the point, the terms of our constitution almost trivial, the procedural disputes predictable.

Every platform must apparently have a council, every conference must pass a resolution—regardless of the terrain upon which law acts, these are its points of access. And so we recreated here in the Platform our own model U.N., complete with compulsory geographic distribution—for shouldn't the seats on the Platform's Council be distributed among the continents? As soon as it was proposed, we knew it had to be so. And we had one African, one European, one Latin American, one Asian, and before someone forgot, one Timorese. Even, we were pleased, or surprised, or bemused, someone from the world's largest democracy.

Nevertheless, we focused our determination increasingly on texts, the most practical suggestion often a textual one, as in the case of our dignified Latin American U.N. delegate. We revised resolutions, elected a board, published polemics, committed to doctrinal inter-pretations, rendering our experience more visible, also to our own memories. The leadership had the constitution read out by a jovial legal activist, bringing our international locutions alive in his some-what ironic English translation. There were a few open questions. Were corporations to become members, for example, would they receive extra votes in the Council? All this seemed secondary, legal, the usual technical details, and the urge in the plenary to delegate these issues back to the committee or to vote quickly (either would do) was irresistible. By Sunday afternoon there were too many issues to deal with, each crowding for the plenary's attention. We would soon need to face the press again, mobilized into a platform with a resolution. Time in our little world had sped up.

In a way this acceleration was precisely the point—as we moved through stages of mutual recognition and institution building, each hour had seemed suspended, filled with new people, new institutional developments. In such a small space, by the end of the first day the gossip circle could run a full round in well less than an hour. Each hour would find us days, even centuries ahead of the last in the evolution of our common everyday. We had been strangers, now we almost had a constitution, we had been normative, now we were almost pragmatic, we had been generalists, now we were almost specialists. The acceleration of centuries had slowed the conference to a snail's pace.

By the end of the weekend, we each thought increasingly of our return home, to what seemed a jumbled fusion of two scenes—the scene of our origin, the workplace realities from which we had come to the conference, and the scene of Timor, the object of our endeavors. The two had become somehow fused, or confused, in the course of the weekend. Here, we were being productive, enjoying one another, liking our jobs. Somehow, after it was over, we would have been changed, would be Timor activists and members of a platform. That, after all, is the point of an establishment conference, a great collective narcissism in the name of empathy, a culture of representation which held out Timor as aspiration, a promise of pragmatism, where our work would have bite, effect, relevance. Like successful conferences everywhere, we would end with a call for action. The idea that "we" would be carrying on "work," each in our own way, on behalf of Timor had become a collective fantasy, at once insistent and worrisome. Indeed, I suspect that only those already dedicated, enacting the resolutions of some earlier establishment, could think about their own workplace realities and Timor without anxiety.

Late in the conference, these underlying doubts and shared anxieties came to rest on Pedro and the constitution drafters. Looking back on it late Sunday, it seemed I had felt uneasy about them all along. Five somewhat somber Portuguese men of indeterminate age, suits right out of the Chicago twenties. I wondered what they were putting together for us. Why had Pedro really brought us here? He seemed so earnest about it all, so insistent, more serious across a year's work than we could maintain even for two days. Why didn't he participate in the tiny flirtations of the weekend. Was he really that busy? If it had been somewhat reassuring on arrival to find someone who so clearly knew what we were supposed to do, now it seemed almost ominous. What if we didn't live up to our platform, couldn't bring law to the everyday, if our everyday could never be as unified with Timor as had been his? Would we still get our travel money?

Pedro and his friends had an experience different from the removed disputations of the working groups on education, litigation, or human rights. Their reality was here, with us, however much Pedro sought to project the moment of establishment into the past, onto our agreement to come, or into the future of our rather open-ended commitments to cooperate. He was not promising to be pragmatic, he was being pragmatic. Our narcissism was his empathy.

Our groups had done less well, some had not even found it necessary to report. The human-rights group had foundered on what seemed a choice between the self-determination and human rights "approaches" to Timor, the education group boldly decided to establish an as of yet unfunded prize for student writing on Timor. At best we projected future action, contented ourselves that the purpose of our being together was fulfilled by the establishment of the platform—by the work of the constitution group. As everywhere, talk is suspicious of action.

And to some extent, we had become cynical. By the final plenary, I found myself in an ad hoc affinity group with my Boston colleague, our Scottish, Canadian, Australian, and unrepresented friends and a few other young law professors. We had become the only mobilized group in the meeting other than the team of would-be founding fathers. Although generally earnest in group, we had become caustic in private and could be off-putting. A young German woman who seemed desperate for an alternative public rhetoric, frustrated by the law's increasing distance from her own fantasy of contact with the Timorese everyday, nonetheless found our alternative corrosive, biting, impolite, unhelpful.

She was right to be worried. To my mind, the most likely direction for our group would be simply to abstain from the main action of the platform and enjoy the hilarity of voting as a bloc on one after another absurd amendment or proposal, modern spectator participants in a social contract repeated now as farce. We would then go home, remembering pleasant private times but without more than the old earnestness to link us professionally with Timor. The question for this group seemed whether any sense of personal commitment to the cause could survive the private cynicism of activism in these tired institutional and doctrinal forms. Pedro was also right to be worried. Pedro balked at the idea that some of us might not wish to "join" the Jurists Platform. Had we not always already joined, by coming? I began to fear that we were all in Timor for the duration.

I had tried once over lunch to connect with the German woman. Couldn't she see us as a symptom of a frustration she must surely share? I hoped she would teeter between the temptations of the discipline and joining us in recognizing the truth of her own experience. The latter seemed too scary, without direction. What was our little group, where was our commitment, what was our program? As it happened, we seemed in control of the plenary voting and were careening madly from one position to another—table that, adopt that, reject that, allying now with one, now with another faction, with Paula, still chairing the meeting, with the Director of the Unrepresented, our friend's boss, and so forth. It was fun.

Somewhat offhandedly, as we debated our final resolution, I made a proposal of my own. In part, I thought it might link us back to the group as a whole. And in part it might disrupt the proceedings sufficiently to throw those who would constitute us off their guard. I stood up and made a little speech, proposing that we delete the carefully numbered operative paragraphs in our resolution, following the concerns of our preamble with the statement "1. express our frustration at the limitations of traditional institutional and doctrinal means of addressing our concerns."

I argued that we might thereby leave a mark in the public space of an experience we had shared, an experience of exhaustion, boredom, frustration. Didn't we all feel worn out by the prospect of yet another resolution from some international institution? Hadn't we all been here before? Rather than allow the parallel narratives of public speech and private pleasure to resume their separate paths after we leave, rather than find our doubts disciplined into fealty to a common program, I propose acknowledging the social experience of our weekend together and learning to live as international legal activists for Timor without the dream (or the excuse) of a law that might be brought to bear for social change.

It was a quixotic moment—I hadn't done the work necessary to mobilize my constituency nor to lay the groundwork for such a suggestion. And I had formulated the proposal so awkwardly that many heard only an exhortation to renewed earnestness—and found it moving. I don't think anyone thought our formal resolution would "have an effect," or that the institution we constituted would be much beyond a shell within which Pedro would raise money to carry on whatever activism he had already begun. Still, unable to think of anything else to do, it seemed absurd to abandon our standard operating procedure. We unanimously adopted the resolution as originally drafted and opened the meeting to a press conference on our conclusions. When the plenary was over, my Boston colleague and I were vaguely down. Perhaps we had been too seduced by cynicism, or immobilized by jet lag to render our faction effective as a cultural alternative to the Platform's closing pieties. We resolved to strategize more self consciously in the future—perhaps we could build a cosmopolitan culture outside the clichés of private irony and public activism.

The weekend ended that evening with a collective excursion to see native Timorese folk dancing. Gestural primitivism. I passed it up for dinner with friends. The next day I intended to rent a convertible and ride around the Portuguese hills with an old friend and a bottle of wine. The conference would slowly recede into the background. We would come to take it for granted, see its petty social dimensions, its anxieties and erotics as part of our individual private and professional lives, its institutional achievements part of the broader constellation of human-rights machinery grown up around the discipline of international law. This had been one weekend in the metropolis: by turns pragmatic, earnest, and cynical. Whatever possibilities our psychosocial dynamics had opened for a renewal we had not managed to exploit.

I still get the occasional jaunty card from one or the other Platform friend—they've started calling it IPJET (pronounced ip-jet) and the Council has duly met to review the first year's program of action. I don't suppose I'll hear much more about Timor. Every month or so now I receive notice of some solidarity demonstration, but in my experience those trail off. If I see a news story on Timor I read it with more interest—it reminds me of good friends in Lisbon. And I am glad to have been able to help Pedro continue his work, now proceeding on the firm pediment of an International Jurists Platform.

II. Between the Weekends

On the plane coming home I sat with my old friend and colleague, now also a member of the International Jurists Platform. While we waited for the steward to bring a first drink, I told him I had been asked to write something philosophical about law and everyday life and asked for his help. As the drinks arrived and we relaxed into conversation about our Portuguese weekend, we decided to catalog things that might be said in such an essay and began a list of associations, more or less as follows:

The everyday as the zone of routine,
law as the code or order for the routine.

The everyday as a zone of violence,
law as a social contract to end violence.

The everyday as peaceable kingdom,
law as violence, both structural and immediate.

The everyday as a field of reality,
law as the sign of power over reality.

Law as agent, the everyday as field.

Law as norm, the everyday as fact.

Law as reason, the everyday as politics.

Law as will, surprise, intrusion,
the everyday as obvious, inert, taken for granted.

Law as honor, the everyday as shame.

The list got longer and longer:

Law acts on the everyday as:

    culture upon nature,
    official on private,
    narrative upon fact,
    vision on the quotidian,
    public on personal,
    written on spoken,
    desire on experience,
    logic on desire,
    force on fear
    order on chaos,

Loosening up, we challenged ourselves: is there any set of alternatives, any cultural movement or contrast not implicated by the law and the everyday?

> Law might be time, the eternity of wisdom and order on the everyday space of the here and now.

> Law might be space, the mapped topology of the state, on the rooted, progressive, or cyclical time of culture.

As we got the hang of it, our associations came in matched pairs, and we sparred with one another to find the reversal:

> The Challenge: Law is to the everyday as the dead hand of the past is to the spontaneity of daily life: As then is to now.

> The Riposte: Law is to the everyday as legislative innovation is to the eternal cultural verities of the everyday: As now is to then.

> The Challenge: Law is to the everyday as high culture is to modernist consumer kitsch.

> An Easy One: Law is to the everyday as formal bureaucratic idiocy is to the complex romance of traditional rural or small town culture.

> How about: Law is to the everyday as the conjectural imagination of the urban planner is to the steady empirical reality of the frontier.

> Too Complex: Law is to the everyday as formally knowable rule, objective authority, collective cultural illusion of Norman Rockwell is to the surprising spontaneity of the cultural avant garde.

Things had gotten out of hand. We limited ourselves to one more.

> A Bonus Rematch: Law is to the everyday as the voice of the other is to the subject's own experience or desire; as there is to here, them is to us.

> The Winning Response: Law is to the everyday as shared value is to deviance, as the rules of the center to application at the periphery; as we are to them, here is to there.

But the possibilities kept multiplying: maybe it was just the alcohol.

Law is to the everyday as

male is to female, woman is to man,

creativity is to the clay of experience, history is to innovation

the plan or leader is to the mass, friction is to genius or the routinization of charisma is to leadership.

illusion is to truth, reason is to fantasy.

It was vertigo, an amusing delirium.

To get our bearings, we turned back to our weekend together in Portugal, joking easily about activist pretensions. Here we were, international legal activists on a junket—we'd been stranger places together, played odder parts. With strangers one might couch critique in a field of disclaimers, but no need with an old friend, just thank goodness this conversation is not being recorded. Back in the plane it seemed safe to be paradoxical and postmodern and politically incorrect.

Still, too much ironic detachment and the delirium refuses to stabilize, cynicism beckons. I think we both may have felt vaguely unsatisfied about the weekend and wanted to redeem it somehow. I wondered, moreover, how I could write about law and everyday life in such an ironic and paradoxical spirit when the naughty shock of transgression had come to seem just another tired intellectual routine, outdated, banal. However pious our Platform colleagues, hasn't law lost its innocent commitment to untroubled notions of the real, the self, the word, the deed?

My friend agreed—a modernist intellectual avant-garde has been rebelling for close to a century against the clean separation of norm and fact in law, as elsewhere in philosophy or science. In the legal academy, this had been the stuff of legal realism, backbone for the judicial and institutional innovations of the welfare state. I felt silly for a moment, philosophically unsophisticated. Assembling a book on law and everyday life may be no more than a naive rotation through the standard modernist moves. Why should I get involved?

But the everyday still sounds the siren call of a new site for legal scholarship: someplace hip, passionate, private, personal, the privilege of purple prose. Concern for the everyday remains a sign for good liberal political commitment to laws relevant to the everyman. Between work and family, choose family; between capital and labor, labor; man and woman, woman; producer and consumer, consumer. . . .

And what's wrong if legal scholars want a shot of pragmatic earnestness in their aging, but still humane, project to place law in the service of social change? A harmless little charge of meaning in the old Warren Court dream, law gone to the everyday. Or if they need a reminder of law's power, the fate and importance of lawyers, the consequences of judicial power or legislative choice. Or if they want to look once more at the damage done, the scars, the victims. Cheap thrills. Maybe we should just lie back and enjoy it when we see them straining to remind us that law "takes place" on a "field" of pain and death.

Besides, I asked, who wouldn't want to redeem these politically correct objectives from the many assaults of modernism? Who has not experienced the importance of a redemptive law, the sanctity of contract, the reliability of property, the centrality of rights to progressive politics? We would not have gone to Portugal were we not in some sense moved to legal activism. In this system, whatever you may think philosophically, if you don't stand with the everyday, you probably stand with the law—or maybe you just don't care.

I may have gone a bit too far, but he tolerated my polemic and proposed, in a tone at once indulgent and sadistic, that we look more closely at this return of piety. I thought we might start by thinking more emphathetically of those who would revisit law's relations with the everyday. Their work might be a cry from the heart, a redemptive gesture of resistance against the modernist vertigo that had corroded faith in law as the social project of law's engagement, begun in the world of politics, had come to rest in the world of language.

We determined to spend the flight thinking empathetically about some current legal traditions that might support such a cry from the heart, stabilize our earlier associative vertigo, even redeem our weekend of representational activism. We settled our empathy on three broad slogans: pragmatism, narrative, and policy.

In a way pragmatism seemed the great framework for such redemptive efforts. Low to the ground, always already skeptical,

innoculated against doubt, forward to action. And modest, a theoretical bumbler, down home good sense. So much legal scholarship
rides loose in the saddle, objectives out front, off camera. Don't get
lost in distinctions that don't matter, rather light a single candle.
Don't wallow in feelings like some self-indulgent little bugger, produce
some results. Pragmatism as anti-intellectual modernism, the tradition of technocratic realism with all its anti-Semitism and
homophobia.

That's the tone, but how do they do it? How stabilize the law
and the everyday, each at once both visionary and practical? As my
friend saw it, pragmatism was a form of social work with words that
begins by situating both law and the everyday—"norms and facts,
words and deeds, speech and writing"—in two registers. First, as
extremes, embodiments of social differences: nature vs. culture, man
vs. woman, and so on. Second, as more middle-of-the-road terms,
associated with a move away from these extremes to a common
ground of reasoned procedures, civilized institutions. Each term both
illustrates an extreme to be avoided and promises a temperate middle
position.

We tried to work this out for nature and culture and thought of
claims by both law and the everyday to be culture to the other's
nature. Law as norm, the everyday as fact. The everyday as civilization's custom to the fact of law's intrusive form or force. And of
claims by each to be nature to the other's culture. Law as objective
rule against the subjectivity of the everyday, the everyday as mute
fact, a bulwark against the cultural experimentations and pretenses
of the law. For the pragmatist, it's not so important to determine
which is which—it's the relationship that counts.

At the same time, both law and the everyday could shed extremist
opposition to build a middle way against the more dangerous claims
of either nature or culture. Both claim to be culture against a broader,
more archaic, more immediate, more frightening real. Law as reasoned government against the specter of totalitarianism. The everyday as the wisdom of the reasonable man, of cultural order, against
the specter of anarchy.

And both claim to be more reliably real than a hyperbolic or
ideological culture. The everyday as the taken for granted against
the temptations of ideological commitment, the apparent against the
dreams and nightmares of individual fantasies and collective illusions.

The law as objective anchor (the law of gravity), whether from God or science, against sacred illusions and democratic seductions.

As a result, law and the everyday provide both an arena for struggle and a comfort zone against a real we find only in its invocation. Much like our Lisbon kindergarten, full of contrasts, debates, stabilized by our representation of Timor, a collective Cheshire smile, soothing as it loses focus. But such a pragmatism could hardly sustain a cri de coeur against modernism, for this is the rhetoric of modernism, turned from substance to process, from reality to rhetoric. Moreover, this structure was taking us quickly back to the vertigo.

My friend nevertheless insisted that for the pragmatist, the point is less to fix a relation between law and the everyday than to sketch a plausible, defensible series of relations, to harness them in a dynamic argument against the extremes they threaten to embody. In such a pragmatic space, the work is less political or philosophical than rhetorical, the play of paradox stabilized by an articulate vacuity. To criticize pragmatism for its logical gaps and circularities misses the great claim of liberal legal science, to have beaten the swords of political conflict into the ploughshares of argument.

As we pursued this line, I remembered hearing it all before—a structuralism gone apologetic. Our analysis lost its empathy as pragmatism took us out of vertigo and into apology. Soon we would be insisting that all normative associations could always be reversed, turning what had been a joint creative project into a machine of philosophical necessity. I knew what could happen next, the beauty of the rhetorical system a powerful addictive, deflecting our attention from the split between private cynicism and public performance experienced in Lisbon, leading eventually to the literatures and conferences of "autopoesis." Not socio- but rhetero-biology.

Pragmatism had its points, to be sure, but we had not found stable ground for a redemptive struggle on behalf of the everyday. Neither had we found relief from the special and awkward emotional residue of our time in Lisbon. The next great slogan, narrative, promised a departure from pragmatism, an embrace of the modern turn from action to language, as well as a redemptive gesture against the dark side of the modern.

In the spirit of much recent legal scholarship, I proposed we might think of ourselves not as philosophers or politicians, but as strategists or storytellers in a project of social narration and legitimation, using law and the everyday as terms from which to weave a social fabric. He didn't like *legitimation* (a hopeless reification of agent, object, and interest) and thought *strategic* too wedded to an intentional subject. But I asked his indulgence and we pressed on.

Pragmatism's vices are narrative's virtues, seizing the rhetorical playfully, earnestly, creatively. If this is all there is, so be it, let our stories be just and true. Stories in which real people struggle for real consequences, not the phony reality of representation, the hyped presence of others, but the immediate reality of our own work, woven now into a broader cultural project. If it seems tawdry, rewrite it. Should vertigo dawn, focus on your characters, sharpen your plot.

A tone more easily the object of empathy, we thought to exercise it on the central stories of our discipline: stories to liberate public international law from the everyday politics of sovereignty, a noble struggle of centuries to establish an autonomous legal culture, removed from politics and the vagaries of princes and peoples.

I began. In the traditional period, this was the work of philosophy. It was the struggle of naturalism: to identify enduring values, a coherent reason, a transcedent humanism of general principles against the ebb and flow of political practice and the haphazard forms of international relations, legal content from social form. It was also the struggle of positivism: to develop a legal contractual practice that would simultaneously liberate the legal sovereign from cultural inertia or religious value and liberate law from the everyday whims of sovereign desire, legal form from social content.

In the modern era, this has been the project of international institutions: to develop a normative and administrative regime detached from periodic intersovereign conflict. Why not renew the great cosmopolitan dream that international law might attain its freedom from the everyday to become a profession, a logic, a system, the story of law's struggle against deviance and conflict and of law's efforts to pacify the processes of social change? Why not renew the narrative of struggle to liberate the legal process from the rigidities of a professionally embedded formalism and the fickle commitments of nation-states?

Over dinner, my friend reminded me of stories from the other direction, of equally noble struggles to distinguish the everyday from law. He began with the important histories of liberation, retold every time politics seeks to free itself from the law of one or another ancient regime. Here were enlightenment stories of citizenship and popular resistance as well as romantic stories about peasant cultures, natural harmonies, primitive forces, whole wheat bread. And stories sympathetic to deviance, defiant of law's regularizing ambition. In the traditions of international relations, this reminded me of the repeated valorization of the political as "real," a realism that aims to liberate the sovereign as the ultimate embodiment of the cultural everyday. And of claims about the cultural margin, the religious, linguistic, or racial minority, the indigenous, the South, the East, or the Third World, as concrete poles of resistance to the generalizing project of international law.

He began to get carried away: a thousand new orders have been launched in the name of the everyday against law. In this century, a history of political extremes—unite the volkish forces of national identity, the everyday of the petty bourgeois against the cosmopolitan, Jewish aristocracy of legal ideas. This has been the project of isolationists and imperialists, of progressives and conservatives. In the academy, he insisted, we constantly find this "struggle" in "play": the pitting of experience against reason, the fetish of the empirical, the trendy invocation of phenomenology against logic. Thinking of narrative as a rooted social gesture, he concluded, demonstrates rather than escapes interpretive fluidity and may as well get you in political hot water.

This seemed right to me—you'd have to admit as many narratives of liberation from law as of law's liberation. If these were cries, they were hardly all from the heart, nor might they stabilize our empathetic aspirations for the everyday. Must we always return to the vertigo we had left behind before dinner, dueling chronicles, blind to one another's insight, each the other's dark side? Of course, there still remained important narratives of reconciliation between the law and the everyday. For our narrative catalog to be complete, we would have to add stories that needed the distinction only to elide it.

Think, I said, of international lawyers who insist on law's reconciliation with the everyday—think of our Lisbon comrades, chiding the law for its isolation, insisting that it become relevent, get real, practical, and pragmatic, return from its cosmopolitan space to enter the everyday either as history (contract) or as promise (sanctions), as a norm to be applied or a program to be implemented. This is what it means for international law to be binding, and no claim, other than perhaps the claim to be autonomous, is as important as the claim to return from autonomy as a binding norm. If law is culture, this is the story of its search for an audience. If law is fact, this is the account of its return to culture as sanction, a terrible swift sword.

He interrupted to remind me of compelling reconciliation narratives in which the everyday seeks to become law. Narratives accompanied by disturbing accounts of the everyday as desire, chaos, enigma, struggling for legal expression. The everyday as experience, reaching for interpretation. The everyday as chaos, reaching out for order. These are the narrative gestures of liberation movements searching for recognition and of politicians and sovereigns hoping to transform their deals into contracts, their imperium into a regime, the repressed struggling for repetition as rule.

He was right, of course. For the international lawyer, little is as striking as politicians' continual return to the law they have scorned. The strong and the weak, the hegemony and periphery, all pressing their claims in the language of law. These are the stories that fuel international law's proliferation—ever new rights, new remedies, new states, new regimes. As often as we hear resistance to law's distinctive claims, we hear claims for a new law and struggles for assimilation. Perhaps it would just have to be vertigo all the way down.

Before we left narrative altogether behind, I wondered if we might not judge the narrators who told one rather than another tale. There might be differences of character, if nothing else, that could sustain our empathy for the cry against modernism. In a way we liked that— an identity politics in which the characters were scripts searching for the narrative conditions of their dramatization. So Pirandello. The activists who called out in Lisbon for law's arrival in the everyday were honorable characters. Perhaps, my friend chided, but wasn't it also they who had told of international law's emergence as an autonomous discipline, justifying their entitlements, their standing, by law's autonomy? What sort of "characters" speak in such different ways? And it was clear from the narrative range that the turn to character, from narrative to narrator, would support more than simply our new empathy for the everyday.

We were through with supper, but the Atlantic still stretched out hours before us. We considered watching the movie—but decided against it. As we reviewed our lists of contradictory claims and narratives, cognac in hand, I had to admit he was right about their fluidity, their political undecidability.

I thought I'd try another turn, to policy, to larger arguments woven together less as narratives than social practices and institutional structures. Perhaps our clichés and polemics are as much history as literature, identities to be lived as much as narrative characters. The realm of policy is practical, even pragmatic, yet retains the mystery, vision, and strategy of narrative. It speaks a twinned language, technocracy and renewal, nostalgic postmodernism. Revenge of the vision nerds, the sovereign is dead, long live sovereignty. This is an insistent frame, full of facts and figures, moving, like pragmatism, forward to a better society, but rooted in the real, in choices, values, consequences.

We turned again to our own discipline, for the history of international law presents a great movement as well as a great narrative: law wrests itself from the chaos of religious conflict in 1648, spends two hundred and fifty years clarifying itself in philosophical autonomy and returns to the international community in this century as an institutional and doctrinal regime. If we look at the doctrines in the field, we find an elaborate division of labor between those that work to establish law's autonomy by locating its origins in the everyday— primarily rules about the "sources" of law—and those that provide some substantive (and usually quite modern and pragmatic) bite to the legal regime. In between are the procedural rules establishing a legal process at once cut off from sovereign prerogative and deferential to it. Here is a space for policy, management, balance. In a strange way, every judicial case repeats this movement, first away and then back towards the everyday in the cycle from jurisdiction to the merits to remedies.

Even granting that each of these turns is written in the unstable distinctions and polarities we have discussed, surely this is more than literature. To convince him, I talked about war, but we might as well have spoken of development in a world both "delinked" and "interdependent," of trade and aid, sanctions and sovereignty, of the New World Order, or of the European Communities split between "subsidiarity" and "cohesion." International policy is both myth and science, in which a hypothetical world of "free trade" or "internal market" might be translated into an architecture or an expertise.

I reminded him of work we had once done together on international law's three rhetorics about force, three moments in relations
between law and the everyday, three sides of war. Think of the "law
of war," a primitive affair of norms and definitions developed into a
quite modern vocabulary of contextual justifications for intersovereign
intervention, blurring distinctions between war and peace, norm and
deed. In this modern tradition, war is a matter of sending messages,
establishing definitions, setting boundaries, peace a process of political consolidation and competition. This is a vertiginous space,
uprooted from the violence it defines.

This realist vision is coupled with two bold idealizations: the
"law in war" and the "law of collective war." The first, governing
military conduct in permissible conflicts, aspires simultaneously to
perfect the military machine by restricting its ambit to the militarily
"necessary," to actions "proportional" to the military objective, and
to open it to the "humanitarian" through quaint rules evoking a
sputtering Red Cross ambulance on some Crimean or Flanders field,
nobly distinct from the everyday of warfare. The law of collective
war dreams of an international institutional regime that could enforce
law in the everyday of international relations.

Military force in three rhetorics is more than felicitous phrase
making, and it is in policy, or perhaps strategy, that these rhetorics
are brought into the service of politics, brought to bear together as
means in actual combat. I found myself earnestly reminding him that
it was easy for us, floating across the ocean, to see these traditions
as narratives, but people die for this, and it all does, in some sense,
happen on a field of pain and death. He laughed. All your war
stories, the particularities of disciplinary convention, so reminiscent
of our Timor platform pieties.

He was right to take me back to Lisbon, where international law
and Timor had been the ground on which we stood, the reality we
knew. Like an audience, they had reassured us of the drama and
stakes in our uncertain situation. In this they functioned like other
great modern stabilizers: power, base, phallus, woman, community,
autonomy, contradiction, expertise, models and their empirical con-
firmation, transactions and their costs, the unconscious, the real,
family values, choice, voice, difference, blindness and insight, the
violent, the sacred, the profane, the list seemed endless.

I was only briefly annoyed when he laughed, less that he should laugh at suffering, than that I should not have recognized myself teetering from policy to polemic. I guess I liked the conversation better when we didn't focus too precisely on the meaning of either law or the everyday, when we permitted ourselves to enjoy the reality of our metaphors. Making the rhetoric real, after all, was the work of the artist, of the warrior or statesman, or of the manager, judge, or legal scholar. Perhaps policy less supported than restated a gesture against modern skepticism, redeeming the tawdriness of its deployment and stabilizing the terms of its elaboration only as a gesture, a pole of attraction for our empathy.

Perhaps these were but statements of faith in the possibility of policy, of narrative, of pragmatism, as also of identity. A great gesture, a contemporary humanism, grounded in an illusion whose only future is repetition. Yes we can realize the precognitive in social life; our characters, however dramatic, are earnestly acted. You can say what you will, but for the victim the torturer brings law home as pain, irreducible, inexpressible, inarticulate. Property rights might be unbundled, traded, relativized, mortgaged, dispersed, be lost in rhetoric, but for the welfare mother a car repossessed is transport lost, rent not paid yields, inexorably, predictably and often cruelly, eviction, and why hesitate to call this law?

The danger was clear—that we'd back ourselves into all the earnest clichés, back to familiar politics, the legal process and liberal commitments, a process for speech. We'd soon seek movement from code to communication, to a place where judges think like defendants and act like legislators. We'd be back to the politics of representation, a stable process on which to project the exotic, calling always for a turning of the tide from speaking to listening, from abstraction to difference, from man to women, projector to project, law to equity, dialogue to polylogue. Soon we'd be envisioning a new judicial style, fragmented, sensitive, a dispersion of power to groups, disempowering, decentering the state. We could call it all dialogue or republicanism.

But after being in Timor, or anyway Lisbon, why not let the primitive reinvigorate a law gone flaccid, pragmatic openness energized by the exotic? Why eliminate nostalgic pleasures, rather play those old scripts one more time. We could keep it modest and self-effacing, eschewing the traditions of idiosyncratic programs and grand theoretical claims. If we wanted to join empathetically with those who turn to the everyday, we might best begin with narrative, telling stories, every legal theorist a Studs Terkel, every lawyer a novelist. We'd have time for pragmatism, policy, program.

The flight was almost over, after all, and I wanted to come up with something for my essay, a life-style, or perhaps a management style, that could firm our opening delirium. Not all the elements went well together, and it was all amazingly familiar, lacking the charge of transgression and the addiction of insight. There were pragmatic protests against modernist anxieties on behalf of history and character. There was the modern avant-garde, with its irony and critical sensibility. We had bits and pieces of narrative—the specificity of the abstract everyman or a camp sensibility that in turn could seem complicit, apologetic, a cop out. There were the great pediments of policy, representational structures calling out to clients, citizens, customers. There was worry about the prurient, the pornographic, the self-confidence of nostalgia and the marginality of the primitive. And there were thoughts of sovereign missiles, of aged spinners and noble savages, of the holocaust and the electrocution of tabloid strangers that we were reluctant to deny their magic, glamour, and grit.

As we clapped our tray tables up for landing in Boston, these all seemed voices of modernism—those, perhaps, of the metropolis, with the rooted mechanics of secular humanism, and the cosmopolis, with its deracinated agnosticism. All claims, promises, and procedures. My narrative about Lisbon, begun, in a way, as the classic metropolitan story, had moved from an activist's call for the reconciliation of law and the everyday to the more confused zone of the cosmopolitan lawyer's own everyday life, struggling to relate the diverse calls of its experience.

Two weeks later, over a second weekend, I would trace the reverse trajectory, from a cosmopolitan everyday towards disentangled legal and social gestures that could renew metropolitan virtues, locations, and characters. This story would not end in an anxious riddle of empathetic gestures. And it would begin, not with the anxious metropolitan separation of law and the everyday, but with the easy everyday of the legal cosmopolis.

III. The Second Weekend

In 1385, the King of Spain established a Royal College in Bologna. In the ensuing 500 years, the College, living lavishly off its surrounding properties, has hosted the cream of Spanish postgraduates for a year or more as fellows. Former fellows of the Royal College have formed a tight elite in the Spanish academy, in the liberal professions, in business, in politics. In 1991, the King of Spain established a second Royal College in Cambridge, Massachusetts, to continue the tradition over the coming centuries by hosting the cream of Spanish postgraduate students in residence at Harvard.

The second Royal College would be a modern affair, funded by bankers and businessmen rather than land rents, and managed by an array of joint Spain-Harvard committees, councils, and administrations. I had been asked by the outgoing Harvard president to serve on the Academic Council for the new Royal College. The Council meets a couple of times a year to set academic policy and distribute grants. Our autumn meeting this year was held in Madrid on the Tuesday morning before Thanksgiving. I left for Madrid the preceding Saturday evening.

I embarked on this cosmopolitan weekend with no fantasies about law's application, no sense of myself as a lawyer moving onto the terrain of law's engagement with the world. There was no primitive waiting to be civilized, no narrative of law's autonomy or of my special role. In a way, nothing dramatic was supposed to happen: I was a functionary rather than an activist. I would sit in the Academic Council, represent the Harvard Law School to some alumni, and perhaps do some fundraising for a European Law Research Center we were in the process of establishing. At best I would squeeze in a couple of hours at the Prado. At worst it would be hotels and taxicabs, meetings and meals. I traveled as an academic and as an administrator.

I can see that this may all seem to have taken place somewhere other than in the "real world" of "everyday life." Perhaps. At times it all seemed a bit unreal to me. The cosmopolitan world is distant from both everyday life and the dream of a law that might come into that life as sovereign. In the cosmopolis, management replaces activism as institutional pragmatism replaces social engineering. If the cosmopolitan urge had made the Lisbon weekend seem tawdry and provided the ground for my private affinity group, in Madrid, the absence of any purport to participate in a great project of legal activism removed the tawdry feeling. In a way, the cosmopolis exists in and for itself, pursuing a project of recruitment and proliferation.

In Madrid, I was confident on arrival that I and my American and Spanish colleagues would all be insiders together, living the dream of an autonomous professional culture. Over the three coming days, we would repeat a dozen familiar institutional behaviors and have conversations familiar from others I have had in many other cities. Our bureaucratic encounters in meetings of the Academic Council would only dimly echo the establishment conference in Lisbon two weeks before—the routines of membership, voting or adjourning now routinized into the normal practice of an ongoing institution.

I had traveled with the Spanish director of the Royal College, and we shared a taxi to my hotel. Having not been to Madrid in seven or eight years, I was grateful for his informed commentary on the striking architectural changes in the city. We agreed to meet for lunch after a brief nap, and he offered to show me a bit of the old town. On checking in, I received a message from an alum inviting me to dinner that evening with some of his friends.

Lunch proved the first of six lengthy and enjoyable meals I would have over my three days in Madrid. It also provided the opportunity to get to know a bit more about both Spain and the Royal College. We ate in an old inn, a bit touristic, but still authentic in feel. Most of the guests that Sunday afternoon were vertically integrated and apparently prosperous Spanish families. My friend urged me to take along a copy of the menu, helpfully presented in English. As we wandered a bit in the old town, an elaborate outdoor market for stamps and coins was underway in the Plaza Mayor. Everything looked tidy, everyone well dressed. My companion apologized for having taken me to a largely working or middle-class milieu, he hoped we would go to a better district the following afternoon. I had to admit I had pegged our surroundings to the upper middle class, at least a notch higher than he, but it may have been my expectations, my experiences in Spain before the new regime.

This, he explained, was the new Spain. And it soon became apparent that little could be seen in Madrid except through the optic of the new and the old Spain. The new Spain meant everything since democracy, modernization, membership in the European Communities, prosperity. It meant a palpable sense of a country on the move—everyone on the make, optimistic. It meant miles of new construction on the barren hills outside the city and blocks of dramatic postmodern office buildings superimposed on Franco's grand modern metropolis. It meant thousands of Timberland shoes.

So I was in a foreign country. The mood, the food, the history, the architecture, thousands of details reminded me that I was learning about Spain. That Spain was modernizing, developing, returning to Europe, reaching out to America. Despite the enthusiasm for American fashion, the desire for American legal education, the engagement with Brussels, the Benneton on every corner, it could not have been more clear that I was not in Boston any longer. My own private cosmopolis was situated here, in a Spain on the move between its national past and its international future.

And it was an exciting time to be in Spain. It appeared that the national process of renewal had set in motion a dramatic circulation of elites. This was most evident as a generational phenomenon: relatively young people seemed to be running everything. There were new career opportunities in business and administration, many apparently open to the educated middle class. There was new status in going abroad, working for a foreign company, studying at a foreign university, learning about European law. There were new educational paths—business schools and private law schools springing up beside the public universities. A new business sensibility held together a modern commercial elite, savvy about things international, liberal in sentiment, conservative in fiscal management.

On my second afternoon in Madrid, I had been invited to visit the law faculty at Complutense University and to meet with members of the faculty for an informal discussion in an enormous modern conference room around what was surely the largest trapezoidal table I had ever seen. Around the walls hung about three dozen nineteenth-century, life-size standing portraits of ex-rectors and ex-professors. The dean, a rather bland middle-aged figure, introduced me and my Spanish colleague from the Royal College to his faculty quite warmly, and we described the work of the College.

The assembled teachers were mostly young and seemed primarily interested in one question: how can I get funded by the Royal College to go to Harvard Law School to study or pursue research? They were quite sophisticated about it and had somehow accumulated a fair amount of information about a college and a law school with which they had had, until that point, absolutely no direct contact.

I had hoped for some more intellectual exchange and asked a few questions about approaches to legal scholarship at Complutense, the ideas or debates that moved the faculty or animated their teaching. In the ensuing discussion, as far as I could tell, no one over forty spoke. Those who spoke presented a sense of frustration and disappointment—teaching was a dismal science of rote lectures, there was no time for research, subject matters were rigidly departmentalized, there was no pattern of shared experience or discussion, they could identify no canon of non–law books or materials with which everyone on the faculty might be expected to be familiar, the genre of writing they were expected to produce struck them as formal and uninteresting, and so forth.

These criticisms were linked to an enthusiastic and insistent call for pragmatism, for real-life business concerns, for the abolition of legal history and legal philosophy and their replacement with more practical subjects. My interlocutors valued legal education in the United States for its pragmatic and anti-intellectual spirit. To find a Spanish law faculty so furiously pursuing a move to reason and pragmatism was perplexing and quaint, like finding an Enlightenment preserved in amber. For two generations, legal scholars in the United States have tried just about everything to counter the tide of pragmatism, enlisting economics, literary theory, sociology, psychiatry, anthropology, legal history, and a great deal more. And yet here I provided the lightning rod for a renewed assault on philosophy and formalism in the name of business reason.

Just when I thought I had the group pegged in an early twentieth-century struggle for modernization, one man sheepishly indicated how few of his colleagues—perhaps less than a dozen—were really familiar with Coase. Another explained how tired he and others were of Habermas. Someone else complained that his own work on Ely and Critical Legal Studies was simply not generally understood by his faculty. Could I explain where one might best pursue the study of leveraged buyouts using a law and economics approach? And I was back in Cambridge, the same names dropped, the same mainstream feelings that everyone's own work is misunderstood or undervalued. The great struggle for modernism seemed suddenly to have been not only won but routinized.

I thought about this encounter in terms of the new and the old Spain. Younger faculty strutting their discontent with the old regime,

encouraged by the presence of a foreigner to articulate their desire
for something new, their fealty to all that was already new. The battle
between history and pragmatism may even have been a set piece in
the presentation of that difference. Don't young law faculty everywhere bemoan the rigidity of the old pedagogy, defend themselves
by reference to the needs of business and commerce, appeal to the
student's interests in practicality? And what could be more modern
and up to date than to tinker with the academic legal debates being
pursued in the United States.

In a way, presentation of these stereotypical arguments worked
to mark generational differences. Styles in the rotation of legal academic fashion had become postures identifiable as modern, ways of
confirming and pursuing the project of national renewal. Far from
transcending the clichés of modernism, the banal enthusiasms of a
universal metropolitan culture, the cosmopolis was being built on
their reiteration.

The possibilities for conflict between the new and the old Spain
seemed ever present—in relations between old and new faculty,
between the new, largely private professional training schools and the
traditional faculties, between the new commercial interests and the traditional bureaucratic elites, between the new lawyers and the old civil
service, or the new civil servant and the old bar. I spoke with a
young cosmopolitan alum who was an associate in a leading Madrid
firm about the possibilities for cultural conflict. He had a very good
part-time position teaching law at an increasingly prestigious private
business academy and felt the difficulty of moving into the traditional
law faculties with either his commercial pragmatism or his intellectual
postmodernism. But conflict, no he really didn't see any. He felt that
the new Spain was experienced by the older generation as the fruit
of their sacrifice—having built this utopia, they were simply happy
that their children had inherited a country on the move. I was skeptical, but the next day, at lunch, I felt there may have been something
to what he had said.

My best meal in Spain was in the private dining room of a
leading Madrid law firm, where I lunched with a senior partner, an
emeritus professor at Madrid who had recently retired as director of
the Royal College in Bologna, and a young associate in the firm who
had studied at Harvard while I was practicing law in Brussels. The
food, table service, wine, and decor were superb in the small formal

dining room off the senior partner's richly appointed sitting area. The conversation was cordial and professional. The only possible glitch was the opening soup of baby eels, but we were able to share a laugh at my inauguration to Spanish cuisine, and indeed, they turned out to be delicious.

We described our various institutions, compared plans for the new Royal College with the experience of the old, considered changes in the Madrid bar, spoke of the food, the city, the desirability of foreign study, the importance of postgraduate academic training, the role for a legal background in the upper reaches of government, commerce, and university life. Whatever differences might have separated us, we found common ground in the vocabulary of a cosmopolitan law. The narratives of law's progress towards the international, towards the modern and the technocratic rendered the move from Bologna to Cambridge, from liberal arts to the professions, inevitable, untroubling. We were all carrying on each other's work.

And I wondered again what it meant to go to the law, as I puzzled over the meaning of Spanish renewal. The same familiar narratives that structured relations of development, discord, and cordiality in the Spanish cosmopolis seemed to play a role in the development of the cosmopolitan. I reflected on characters I had known in Harvard's graduate program. Young lawyers from peripheral capitals, Madrid, Vienna, Kuala Lumpur, Santiago, come to Cambridge. Where they encounter hundreds of middle-class Americans in the process of professionalization, struggling with hopes for fulfillment, class advancement, assimilation to the establishment, practical skills, and savvy reflections.

To come to the law, to come to Cambridge, was, for some of them certainly, to make a bid for the cosmopolis. Imagine a young man from Spain, brought up in a wealthy environment, well connected to the old, familial and corporatist establishment, offered numerous ways of assimilating to a Spain which was disappearing. How to escape, to join a world ahead of his milieu, a combination of escape from his everyday and commitment to pursuit of its dreams, perhaps to return with new skills for a new society, having passed his contemporaries, perhaps not to return, to live no longer in the periphery but in the cosmopolis itself. With such ambitions, one might well study the EC at an institute, perhaps in Italy or Belgium, and then move to Brussels to become a Community functionary. But one would remain a civil servant—what if you wanted to hit a home run, becoming simultaneously a world-class intellectual and a player in the commercial world of international business. You might think about law school in the United States, perhaps even a doctorate.

Of course these are just cosmopolitan fantasies about the law: the new aristocratic modernizer. Imagine the children of *comprador* traders in a Third World capital dreaming of a more honorable calling, a more secure place in the world of the *Financial Times*. Fantasies that combine elements of escape with promises to return. Or the children of diplomats with no place to which they might return. The Brazilian ambassador to India spawns administrators for the United Nations in Geneva who in turn spawn young Tamil-speaking, Swiss-educated lawyers who, after study in Cambridge, will seek work in the international nonprofit community as advocates. Perhaps they will do something about East Timor. Or imagine simply the earnest middle-class children of midlevel European executives in multinational companies or civil servants in the national capital or school teachers who seek a profession in law. Perhaps they went to an international school, had been exchange students, or volunteered for Amnesty International. In any event, they might hope to transcend the details of national practice for the broad generalities and courtesies of international affairs; their own capitals too provincial, the role of the metropolitan civil servant too banal.

For all of these, international law may be an arena of desire and fantasy, a trajectory of self-development. With all its shallow narratives of autonomy from politics, its heady pretenses to public service, its gestures to modern pragmatism, law seems the stuff of identity. Who was sitting in that lovely dining room but lawyers, professionals, spoken by the law, comfortably identifying ourselves through the rituals of shared legal narratives. A new society was being built in Spain and we were part of it. Our contribution may simply have been to tell one another one clichéd banality after another—and that would be enough for modernization, for participation in the cosmopolis. In a sense the law we shared was repository for dozens of incompatible dreams and obscure yearnings.

We might better think of law and the everyday as a rhetorical background to our conversations, appearing only as vague recollections, promises, fickle hints, flirtatious gestures of mutual recognition—how things really were, harumph, what we knew as a matter of course, chuckle, where law was going, starry-eyed gaze. Fragmented into a dozen small exchanges, we were each pursuing our own ambitions, struggling for earnest assimilation, for amusement and interest, for riches and power, for recognition or conflict, at least in part by invoking and following the narratives of law and its twistingly ambivalent relations to the everyday, calling on a tool kit of rhetorical tidbits that could be strongly asserted or knowingly assumed.

Of course, such rhetorical tidbits are not just the fantasies of aspiring cosmopolites. They are also the institutional practices of the cosmopolis itself. Here, in Spain, I was more than a postcolonial agent for the center prospecting in the periphery. I was building a graduate program for a world law school, promising options opened, purveying credentials, contacts, connections. At once a symbolic and constitutive function, returning an identity in the reflection of their ambition. If the center, the metropolis exists to order, the cosmopolis exists to recruit, assimilate, proliferate.

Mostly, these dreams would remain obscure, for all those who came to law were learning how difficult it was to put law's sovereign and activist promises into play in any literal way. To work in an American law firm, to return to your uncle's office in Bombay, to teach at Complutense, to work for IBM. Somehow nothing seems up to the cosmopolitan dream, remaining enticingly offstage. At other times, a modern cliché could burst in on the cosmopolitan with energy and meaning. If I connected with any of these young cosmopolitans, it was not through empathy with their cynicism nor the seduction of irony as in Lisbon—the scene was too savvy for such a strategy. What worked seemed oddly the reverse: a blunt assertion of the boldest metropolitan banality about their roots, cultural origins, and aspirations.

One night, I had a delightful dinner with a group of young Spanish lawyers. Several had been at Harvard as graduate students and seemed to entertain me both to strut their newly jaded professional airs and to see whether I could ignite their nostalgia for academic idealism and social responsibility. In Cambridge, as in Lisbon, my work is to open a cosmopolitan everyday in what might otherwise be a tiresome imperialism. It took me a moment to see that in Spain, amongst these young graduates, I would find my function reversed. They were always already savvy and postmodern. Could they still be tourists, still awaken to meaningful commitments and authentic experiences?

The three-hour feast, following hot on the heels of a lengthy and elaborate lunch, left me a bit tired. As we left the restaurant shortly before midnight, one of my hosts told me of her love for flamenco dancing and her plan that we adjourn to a flamenco restaurant where we might be able to dance and experience the "real Spain." It was a familiar gesture—like the Timorese dancing two weeks before. In Lisbon I, like most of my little cosmopolitan affinity group, had turned it down—or gone only to feed an ironic sensibility. But I had never seen flamenco and didn't place it as a standard modernist authenticity trope. Maybe I thought only I had papered my high-school bedroom with posters of bullfighters and flamenco dancers. In any event, we went and found the small restaurant filled with young Spanish professionals and Japanese businessmen, enjoying their fantasies with enthusiasm. It became clear after about an hour that this was simply the warm-up act. The waiter promised, with another round, the "best flamenco dancer in the kingdom," and we decided to stay.

Back in Cambridge it may undermine my cosmopolitan creden-tials to romanticize this sort of commercial gesture, and it may have been the light, or the food, even the jet lag, but she seemed a John Singer Sargent portrait come alive: at once sexy, powerful, dramatic. I asked my friends about flamenco. It was truly Spanish, one explained, although perhaps she should say Catalan. Another thought perhaps Andalusian. But the dance seems almost Moorish. Yes, in part because the dancers have always been gypsies. At least the explanation, like her primitivism, was reassuringly indeterminate.

About 2:30 our dancer paused to address the audience. "I know the flamenco can be a difficult dance for you, for an audience. It comes from the emotions, from the heart." Not from Africa after all. "I want you to understand the dance, and to enter into it because for me, the dance comes also from you, from your reaction and enjoyment." I was bummed, my primitive scene a tawdry tourist exhibition. I remembered some dancers near Jackson Hole, and some more at Four Corners, the only place where four states meet. Sargeant faded into a turn of the century Brussels exhibition of Congolese primitives arranged on the palace grounds. "The last dance was loneliness. This one will be love."

As cosmopolitan skepticism returned, I thought about my essay on law and the everyday. Where was law now? Could we really be meant to focus on the restaurant licensing rules? I looked to see if they had a mandatory exit sign, if Madrid required those posters of people choking and being Heimlich-maneuvered back to their plates. Were the waiters making minimum wage? Was my drink a standard half liter? Were the musicians in a union? Maybe I should think about the rules of flirtation, the rules for addressing an audience, for garnering our involvement, or of the life of the lawyers I was with, their pleasures, their enthusiasm for this evening of foreign languages, professional posturings, and dance.

Late that morning, the best dancer in the kingdom paused to accept a small scrap of paper from her guitarist and recognize three dignitaries in the audience. First, she was delighted to welcome the Interior Minister from Bolivia. Applause. Second, from Brussels, the Commissioner of, I think she said fisheries, but it might have been something else. In any event, nationality unknown. More applause. And now she had a special welcome, for she had saved the best for last. We had with us, from Los Angeles, Mr. name-garbled, who was responsible for the special effects in Raiders of the Lost Ark. Very strong applause, some cheers.

Three continents and three eras. And three forms of law in our cosmopolitan everyday. The first a juridical structure, the nation-state, with its bureaucracies, ministries, formalisms. A realm modeled on the desire for a juridical center of power, controlling the interior and authoritative for everyday life. This is a traditional zone, in which law and social life struggle with one another for supremacy. Law may be reason or ideology, the everyday routine or rebellion, but culture and nature can be distinguished and struggle for recognition in one another. To stand with the law is to stand with order, with the center, with reason, with belief.

The second is a more modern realm, detached from nationality, a pragmatic, technocratic metropolis in which law has relativized the everyday, parceling property into bundles of rights to be rearranged among departments, sold, mortgaged, reimagined as futures and institutionalized in secondary markets, in which rights have become things and individuals have become roles. In this scene, thousands of tiny functional calculations have sneaked up on sovereignty and law has merged with commerce. The law and the everyday have become occasional cash payments in an economy of institutional procedures. Life continues in the knowledge that law or the everyday may at any moment be summoned, but they do their best work left in the vault, as reserve for our ongoing and elaborate rhetorical transactions.

The third is a space of culture, fantasy, and fashion. Law and the everyday appear as confusing terms, lapel widths, skirt lengths, as attitudes, tactics, philosophical positions, ambitions, and plot narratives. Sometimes they appear as stereotypes or clichés. And often the clichés are true. They might mark space or count time. They might provide identity, resolve family squabbles, or provide energy to national transformations. They might be simply amusing, standard jokes, or they might be strategies of combat and struggle.

We left just as our dancer had yielded the floor to her male partner. Three cosmopolitan phases, arrangements of law and everyday life contending for deployment. Politics, pragmatism, and play. Tradition, modernity, and the postmodern. Status, contract, and narrative. Identity, relation, and rhetoric. Two weekends and an airplane ride.

Mass Toxic Torts and the End of Everyday Life

George E. Marcus

> A particular problem arises when, instead of being a discourse
> on other discourses, as is usually the case, theory has to
> advance over an area where there are no longer any discourses.
> There is a sudden unevenness of terrain: the ground on which
> verbal language rests begins to fail. The theorizing operation
> finds itself at the limits of the terrain where it normally
> functions, like an automobile at the edge of a cliff. Beyond and
> below lies the ocean.
> —Michel de Certeau, *The Practice of Everyday Life*

While the idea of everyday life has provided an essential reference in
modern social theory and legal discourse, it has nonetheless remained
somewhat intractable. Such an irony is the key concern of this paper,
which argues that it is precisely the reliance of social theory on certain
assumptions about everyday life that has made it unable to encompass
or domesticate for intellectual consumption late twentieth-century
realities. The consequent anxiety about the function and nature of
theory itself is registered (at least, in Euro-American academia) in
renewed discussions about the nature of modernity, posed specifically
as a struggle to define the postmodern.

Contemporary changes seem as unprecedented as were those that
gave rise to the industrial societies of the nineteenth century and that
provided the context for the evolution of present traditions of social
thought across all specialized discourses. In both social theory and
legal discourse, the everyday occupies the space of the moral, the
pragmatic, the accessible, and the commonsensical and is the last
bastion of simple coherence and order. It offers an elusive escape

from abstraction as well as a certain reassurance and complacency about the limits of change, thus inhibiting those working presently within nineteenth-century traditions of social thought from moving too far beyond familiar conceptual terms. In this essay, I am interested in challenges to principled, problem-solving discourses, such as law, that confound the ideological and therapeutic function of the everyday in social thought and language.

There are indeed many calls to revise the available concepts and vocabularies for discussions about the present, emergent realities that defy conventional notions of system. For example, in a recent interview, Fredric Jameson talked about the difficulty of saying things about "the whole" in postmodernist discourse:

> One of the ways of describing this is as a modification in the very nature of the cultural sphere: a loss of autonomy of culture, a case of culture falling into the world. As you say, this makes it much more difficult to speak of cultural systems and to evaluate them in isolation. A whole new theoretical problem is posed. Thinking at once negatively and positively about it is a beginning, but what we need is a new vocabulary. The languages that have been useful in talking about culture and politics in the past don't really seem adequate to this historical moment.[1]

We should probably not look to social theory, as the work of a privileged, detached level of holistic theory building, to provide such new vocabularies. Rather, one might look first to the hesitations, misrecognitions, and anxieties articulated in the discourses of problem-solving institutions and their nurturing professional disciplines that are bent on the technical control of an always unruly world. These are the frontline discourses, so to speak, of institutional practices, such as those of bureaucracy, corporations, diplomacy, and, especially in this essay, the law, in which one version or another of social theory is evolved and applied to the world. They register even more sensitively than the detached debates of academic social theory the inadequacy of current modes of thinking about society.

In the law, and especially in the law of torts, which is the concern

---

1. Fredric Jameson, "Regarding Postmodernism—a Conversation with Fredric Jameson," interview with *Social Text* 17 (1987): 37.

of this essay, the development, articulation, and recording of cases rest on assumptions about everyday life in which injury is conceived as a personal act, done with intention by an autonomous agent—an individual subject or corporate entity—to another. The everyday-life scene of such injury is shaped by linear causality and traditional moral assumptions that apply to standards of interpersonal conduct. The law shares with narratives of social theory a reliance on these mundane, but essential, assumptions about the coherence and integrity of the everyday. Nonetheless, since the late nineteenth century at least, both law and social theory have wrestled with the complexities of macroprocesses in industrial mass society that threaten constantly to overturn these simple assumptions about the everyday.

The history of American tort law during this century has shown the commitment of legal thought to both sustaining the human-scale, face-to-face character of the everyday scene of the "facts of the case" and coming to terms with the systemic, societal nature of individual injuries.[2] Of course, legal theorists and practitioners have long viewed the law as dynamically facing innovative cases—law is always being made in its routine process of facing new challenges—but I would argue that certain legal adaptations to late twentieth-century conditions, such as class-action litigation, have in effect posed a postmodern challenge to habitual ways of thinking about society in legal ideology. Mass toxic torts, especially, challenge the courts and legal scholars to represent and act upon situations that cannot be reduced to the traditional quotidian grounding of run-of-the-mill torts.

In this essay, which takes the Agent Orange case as a key example of the mass toxic tort,[3] I want to register the highly problematic nature of the otherwise essential concept of the everyday in legal discourse. On one level, I am suggesting, with de Certeau, that the everyday is never fully or simply representable in discourse, and that the attempt or need to capture this elusive object therefore plays an important and enabling ideological function in Western social thought by guaranteeing an always present situational and integral world of fallible, commonsense rationality. Yet the presence of the everyday is never fully demonstrated in any particular complex event or case

---

2. G. Edward White, *Tort Law in America: An Intellectual History* (New York: Oxford University Press, 1980).

3. Peter H. Schuck, *Agent Orange on Trial: Mass Toxic Disasters in the Courts* (Cambridge: Harvard University Press, 1986).

of conflict in contemporary society. On another level, I am arguing that in the complexities of mass toxic torts, which defy at least in the legal sphere comprehension by macro systems analysis, the everyday has difficulty even sustaining this ideological "space" in legal discourse. It is with the intractable difficulty of reducing such cases to everyday dimensions in their judicial administration that I am most concerned.

Constructing mass toxic torts as "cases" out of disaster, the law is posed here on the edge of the cliff of which de Certeau speaks. But the focus on the everyday as comprehensible and ordinary can no longer harness for rational discourse the ocean below. Does this mean, however, that the everyday disappears from such cases, that it loses its conventional meaning as the situated here and now of immediate human experience in favor of macroconceptual inventions, such as public law as a policy-oriented sphere, aggregate risk assessment, and the actuarial construction of human subjects?[4] Or are there ways to reconceive the scene of the everyday by fusing the multiple realities and diffuse effects of technology and history in class actions, especially mass toxic torts?

Before proceeding with a discussion of the function of the everyday in social theory generally, I want to position my concerns in this paper in relation to the vital, productive trend of critical social-science research on the law that combines the early 1980s initiative of the critical legal studies movement with the empirical research traditions of social science disciplines, represented by the Law and Society Association.[5] On the one hand, this scholarship, informed by debates among literary and social theorists, has provided sophisticated analyses of legal ideology as discourse and rhetoric.[6] On the other, through its critique of law as a hegemonic and authoritatively self-contained production of universal rationality, this scholarship has probed more saliently than ever before not only the thoroughly social character of legal process itself, but also the diverse discourses

---

4. Jonathan Simon, "The Ideological Effects of Actuarial Practices," *Law and Society Review* 22 (1988): 771–800.

5. See Susan Silbey and Austin Sarat, "Critical Traditions in Law and Society Research," *Law and Society Review* 21 (1987): 165.

6. See, for example, John M. Conley and William M. O'Barr, *Rules Versus Relationships: The Ethnography of Legal Discourse* (Chicago: University of Chicago Press, 1990); and Robert Ferguson, "The Judicial Opinion as Literary Genre," *Yale Journal of Law and the Humanities* 2 (1990): 201–20.

and practices masked by this hegemony. In this latter effort, which depends on the ethnographic gaze upon the micro social situation, the focus on and valorization of everyday life have been essential. It is therefore not surprising that this research has most often been situated where the role of legal discourse and practice in everyday life is least problematic and most accessible to here-and-now, direct-participant observation—the lawyer's office, the small claims court, the welfare agency, and so on.[7]

Perhaps much of the work of the law can be so literally posed and situated. Certainly, blurring the boundaries between the language of legal writing, which is distanced from everyday situations in society to which it refers, and the legal discourses and concepts occurring within social process itself is valuable. But, as against much of this scholarship, I am interested in a kind of estranged situating of the everyday as a crucial artifact of legal ideology, where it is both most problematic as a social referent and least accessible to an easy link-up with specifiable, localized social settings. Removing this obvious dimension of locatable time-space from the assumptions that naturally connect law to the everyday creates a predicament for both the legal practitioner and the social scientist interested in the recuperation of legal discourse to the scene of everyday social experience and practice. Now several removes from any specification of the here and now, the everyday scene as an essential component of a case becomes something in the processing of a mass toxic tort, which, while perhaps understood implicitly by judges and lawyers, remains unspoken and generally evaded in the management of such a class action. As we will see, the evasion of trial, of the multiply situated presentation of a case in court, and, consequently, of the standard tort assumptions (that what is at stake is A's alleged injury to B under specifiable conditions), is perhaps the most salient feature of the Agent Orange case.

There are real, humanly situated experiences of injury, suffering, and greed at stake. Everyone involved knows this, but given the

---

7. Sally Engle Merry, "Everyday Understandings of the Law in Working-Class America," *American Ethnologist* 13 (1986): 253; Austin Sarat, "'. . . The Law Is All Over': Power, Resistance, and the Legal Consciousness of the Welfare Poor," *Yale Journal of Law and the Humanities* 2 (1990): 343–80; and Austin Sarat and William L. F. Felstiner, "Law and Social Relations: Vocabularies of Motive in Lawyer/Client Interaction," *Law and Society Review* 22 (1988): 737–70.

scope, scale, and issues at hand, legal practice currently lacks the discursive capacity to address, at the level of everyday experience, the claims and interests of the thousands of actors involved. Matters of legal administration may pale relative to the engagements of law and society in the closely observed interactions of lawyers, judges, clients, and claimants in office and court settings. However, it has been this relatively insulated sphere of managing mass toxic torts to which the ingenuity of jurisprudence has been devoted, and from which alternative, novel conceptions and deployments of the scene of the everyday might emerge in legal discourse.[8]

The Function of Everyday Life in Modern Social Theory

> The quotidian is what is humble and solid, what is taken for
> granted and that of which all the parts follow each other in
> such a regular, unvarying succession that those concerned have
> no call to question their sequence; thus it is undated and
> (apparently) insignificant; though it occupies and preoccupies it
> is practically untellable, and it is the ethics underlying routine
> and the aesthetics of familiar settings. At this point it
> encounters the modern. The word stands for what is novel,
> brilliant, paradoxical and bears the imprint of technicality and
> worldliness; it is (apparently) daring and transitory, proclaims
> its initiative and is acclaimed for it; it is art and aestheticism—
> not readily discernible in so-called modern spectacles or in the
> spectacle the modern world makes of itself to itself. The
> quotidian and the modern mark and mask, legitimate and
> counterbalance each other.
>   —Henri Lefebvre, *Everyday Life in the Modern World*

I want to clarify the kind of contemporary vision of problems that everyday-life constructions in social theory no longer address. Then, I also want to explain how my own ethnographic work on American dynastic families, which recognizes the very important function that various legal specialists, especially in trusts and estates, had in shaping relationships internal to those families, led me to think about everyday life not literally as "the social" that the law penetrates, but

---

8. See Donald L. Horowitz, *The Courts and Social Policy* (Washington: Brookings Institution, 1977) for an early indication of this potential for social theoretic innovation in the policy aspects of judicial decision making.

rather as the main figure or trope that constructs the essence of the social in the imagination of overlapping sociological and legal discourses.

Everyday life is the seat of order in social life. It provides the setting for human action, the virtues, vices, contingencies, dramas, and themes of life to be closely observed and modeled as the "micro" in social theory, the "event" in history, or the "case" in law. Whether directly treated or only assumed, tremendous weight is born by the commonsensical, ordinary, tacitly meaningful arena of the quotidian in social theory's macroarguments about the systemic and rational nature of culture and society. However momentous are the changes in macrosocial life, they are subtly addressed and registered in the sense-making processes of the quotidian. While several alternative conceptual apparatuses have developed for filling the discursive space of the everyday, crystallizing the most momentous problems of society and culture in the medium of phenomenology seems to be a never quite achievable, but nonetheless alluring, quest of modern social theory.[9] From the rhetorician's perspective, in which all social

---

9. Most of the social theory treatments of everyday life have been dedicated merely to revealing its capacity for creating meaning, sense, and order. This is a complex but limited operation that does not always recognize its normative and ideological significance. Rather, the theorists who have embellished the everyday by explicitly making it theater or narrative or by bringing to bear history upon it, have shown the normative weight that the everyday carries in most of our thinking about culture and society.

Husserl's phenomenology, Heidegger's philosophy of being, and several philosophies of the symbolic, given, for example, a synthetic articulation by Suzanne Langer, have been important stimulants for many of the post–World War II perspectives on everyday life. In sociology, there has been the influential book of Peter Berger and Thomas Luckman on the social construction of reality (*The Social Construction of Everyday Life*, New York: Anchor Books, 1967), inspired by Weber and the then little-known phenomenological writing of Alfred Schutz. There has also been the writing of the symbolic interactionists, and the writings of the ethnomethodologists, especially those of Harold Garfinkel. In anthropology and linguistics, everyday-life perspectives have focused on the use of language in social context, inspired from the later 1960s on by the philosophy of Wittgenstein. The resulting subfields that probe everyday life are sociolinguistics (or in linguistics, the study of pragmatics) and the so-called ethnography of communication. In economics, the effort to model everyday life has largely been developed as game theory, characteristically reductive in theorizing a radically individual-focused vision of situations, events, and transactions. And the effort to assimilate these various microperspectives to ongoing Western traditions of social theory which, especially in the period immediately after World War II, had not been inclined to focus on the order of everyday life, has been, for example, the project of Anthony Giddens in the Anglo-American tradition as crystalized by

discourses can be understood as narratives, ordinariness—the discursive space most fully explored by phenomenology and philosophies of subjectivity—is the moral ground that allows cultural norms to emerge as stories, or as accounts of everyday life. In legal discourse, among others, the normative weight of the everyday authorizes the case of determinable facts as the narrated object, upon which courts and legal treatises operate.

Provocative contemporary notions of social process explode this construction of the everyday as the situated, sense-making essence of social order. The postmodern vision of the disembeddedness of

---

Talcott Parsons.

Now beyond these efforts to explore the secrets of the sociological coherence of the everyday have been numerous contemporary theorists who have attempted to imagine the everyday in more vivid and critically committed terms. These writers have tended to place the everyday in more embedded historical contexts or in terms of their committed notions about the condition of contemporary society. They want to do more with the everyday than to theorize its capacity for meaning and sense making. For them, the everyday becomes the grounds of cultural critique. In the United States, one thinks of the distinctive writings of Erving Goffman, who with the use of dramaturgical metaphors most effectively communicated that the order of everyday life was indeed the moral order in which values were most consequently transacted. In Germany, Jürgen Habermas has attempted to revive critical theory by anchoring notions of liberation on the everyday site (however idealized) of speech acts. In France, the work of Michel Foucault came finally to focus on the microsphere of everyday life, the ground upon which a theory of power embedded in practices could be most profoundly imagined. Originally remaking the notions of exchange in French sociology and ethnology, Pierre Bourdieu, too, came to focus on the consequentiality of the everyday in his use of the notions of habitus, disposition, practice, strategy, and economy.

These theorists have been especially important for shaping the terms in which contemporary ethnography is written. Ethnography, of course, has been the one social science genre that has always depended intimately on the construction of everyday reality and the "local knowledge" to be understood in its midst as its objects of inquiry. Now especially through the influence of Bourdieu and Foucault, the everyday is the site in ethnography at which the micropolitics of resistance and accommodation to larger structures is to be uncovered and communicated as the "weapons of the weak," to cite the title of a recent book by James Scott on how the relatively powerless, the victims of large structures, remake in their own interests and through the commonplaces of everyday existence such structures that impinge on them. In such studies, the order in everyday life takes on a certain virtue and politics that finds hope in the quotidian against fears or an unflinching recognition of "a totally administered and commodified world." The very construction of argument or position in contemporary social theories is thus a question of making "the quotidian and the modern mark and mask, legitimate and counterbalance each other," in Lefebvre's terms, and the site for this task is almost always now that of everyday life where the most abstractly conceived issues can seemingly be resolved in concreteness and the virtues of simple, unreflected upon existence.

contemporary institutions, of processes that are not fixed temporally and spatially in situations—but rather exist in fragmented, discontinuous, and simultaneous time-space—and of social identities that disseminate in multiple social contexts of unexpected interconnection, absorbs the classical and commonsensical notion of the everyday.[10] Contemporary systemic, global phenomena that cannot be known by available theories make specific this vertiginous quality. If the everyday is conceived in cultural analysis not only as the "here and now," but simultaneously as the "elsewhere" as well, institutional discourses such as the law, which draw on the intellectual capital and assumptions of social theory, must solve a descriptive problem— a problem of determining the facts of the case.

The solution to this problem offered by prominent sociological theorists, such as Anthony Giddens and Pierre Bourdieu, during the late 1970s and 1980s was to preserve the integrity of "the local," the sphere of everyday, while conceptualizing ways in which "the global" penetrated it and was in turn modified by it (through the notions of structuration proposed by Giddens, and habitus proposed by Bourdieu). In my view, such a solution has indeed been entirely theoretical, and any attempt to render an account of it empirically runs up against aspects of postmodern reality already mentioned. The absence of a sociological account that deals with the disjunctive, simultaneous space-time of phenomena like toxic disasters radically challenges dualistic terms such as the global and the local and, of course the everyday as coherently local. It is in this sense that we lack the vocabularies Jameson mentioned.

And it is in this sense, also, when the law is faced with a phenomenon of a quintessentially postmodern nature, such as the Agent Orange case, that judges and lawyers are left to improvise. Whether this improvisation tends to refuse, by means of certain procedural manipulation, the substantive development of a case that is incommensurate with the modern legal conceptions, or whether it tends to reinvent discursive space, is of the utmost import not only to the functioning of legal institutions, but to social theory itself. This is because the postmodern challenge to social theory can no longer be addressed only by "social theory"; instead it can only be

---

10. George E. Marcus, "Past, Present, and Emergent Identities: Requirements for Ethnographies of Late Twentieth-Century Modernity Worldwide," in *Modernity & Identity*, ed. by Scott Lash and Jonathan Friedman (Oxford: Blackwell, 1992).

dealt with in a piecemeal way, by the frontline social discourses of the law and other institutions of state and economy. This is why I believe that both ethnographic study and rhetorical analysis of institutionally located discourses, in all their variety and complexity, must replace modern social theory as a discrete academic practice, or at least relativize it. In this radical shift of privilege and position, the end of everyday life as it has been constructed in theory—which has sustained distinctions like the local and the global, the micro and the macro—is a key development.

One of the most interesting challenges for legal sociology or anthropology has been to understand the way law influences ongoing social life outside its own institutional confines. The anthropology of law had until the 1980s been focused primarily on processes of dispute management, that is, on social life, brought into the arena, more or less institutionalized, where it is constructed as a special kind of problem-oriented discourse. In societies without formal legal institutions anthropologists sought to establish the widest possible cultural and social contexts that dispute cases concern. Here the focus was on the social moving into the legal, so to speak, rather than the opposite.

As anthropologists of law repatriated their research,[11] its focus has moved from the legal to the social. This is particularly so in late modern or postmodern society, since one of the key characteristics of modernity is the degree to which all social relations are, first, pervasively penetrated by the operations of expert systems and technologies, of which the law is one of the most important and the most long-standing, and, second, are conducted and monitored through the movement and exchange of symbolic tokens such as money, electronic credit accounts, and commodities.

Dynastic families provide an excellent site to observe the (post) modern constitution of the internal human relations among family members. The face-to-face medium of such anthropological subjects cannot be understood without also giving attention to the way several different spheres of specialized activity—parallel to, yet discontinuous in space with, the day-to-day interactions of family members—also

---

11. For example, as I have done in recent years with my study of the late twentieth-century fate of American family fortunes, George E. Marcus, *Lives in Trust: The Fortunes of Family Dynasties in Late Twentieth-Century America* (Boulder, Colo.: Westview Press, 1992).

construct the family and its wealth. Such a human family is tied to its "unseen worlds"[12] in ways that are difficult to define through the imagery of linear, continuous relationships to which most social theory is accustomed. Here indeed is a specific problem that requires reenvisioning our conceptual apparatus to understand constitutive processes like "the family," already thought to be well understood as largely separate from, say, the state or the economy. What we are perceiving, then, in discrete research projects, is "a loss of autonomy of culture, a case of culture falling into the world," as Jameson says.

In my dynastic family project, of all the expert systems constituting conventional social relations in the family, I found the law most salient, pervasive, and monolithic, not only in its obvious function for a wealthy family through trusts and estates, but in the way that it shapes and mediates, both as regulation and as a form of paternalistic discipline, many other aspects of family life (e.g., banking, investments, education, servants, leisure time, and the consumption of luxuries). In fact, based on my understanding of how the contemporary American middle-class life course is more generally shaped and scheduled by being enmeshed in expert systems and systems of symbolic tokens (e.g., think of how the considerable complexity of long-term saving for a child's education among middle-class families in significant ways defines what it is culturally to be middle class), relating the law directly to the sphere of the social outside of court contexts is a direction in which the sociology and anthropology of law might move even more concertedly.

However, when "the social" is specifically conceived as "everyday life" in relating law to society, then one immediately confronts the limits of representation of contemporary social theory. The law as an expert system among and within others shapes the here-and-now conditions of sociality in very indirect ways for which there is not yet a very good language of description. So while law is certainly part of everyday culture and society, it tends not to be intimately present except in very banal ways. There have been many studies of how specialized discourses, like those of anthropology, sociology, and the law, eventually reenter their subject matters, but once such specialized discourse is assimilated into everyday life, it becomes commonsensical, and enabling of order in the everyday (e.g., complex

12. George E. Marcus, "The Problem of the Unseen World of Wealth for the Rich: Toward an Ethnography of Complex Connections," *Ethos* 17 (1989): 114–23.

normative and theoretical discussions of citizenship and travel in the law sort out as the routine use of passports in the everyday sphere). Thus, one hopes to show how law and legal concepts work their way into the home, office, or shopping center and subtly and significantly shape the content of everyday life. But this is not likely to be fruitful, because law in modernity apparently does not work so powerfully in any direct or simple way on the level of embedded cultural cognition. Once the law is related directly to everyday life, there suddenly seems very little to talk about.

Further, as I have suggested, it is chimerical to think that the social can be understood effectively as merely situated face-to-face relations. The global and local collapse in the multiple determination in heterogeneous spaces of even the most intimate and private of actions or the most public of events. The parallel, simultaneous work of law is important in demonstrating this, but such a demonstration is not exactly about revealing how the specialized discourse of law penetrates and becomes registered as culture or local knowledge outside its confines. While everyone is aware of the law in various forms and expressions, people still don't seem to think legalistically or in terms that are derived from law.[13] This leads to the second problem

---

13. What I am saying here and in preceding paragraphs about the very indirect relation of law—as a set of discursive forms and habits of thought as well as a body of expert and specialized practice—to the everyday life of middle, working, and lower-class people in contemporary society may seem to be contradicted by the important body of law and society research that shows that various sorts of clients and subjects, whom the law touches or regulates, think in very sophisticated "folk" terms about legal matters in their everyday lives (Merry, "Everyday Understandings"; Sarat, "The Law is All Over"), and further that the terms of legal discourse within its institutional settings is itself always being negotiated between practitioner and client or interested party (Sarat and Felstiner, "Law and Social Relations," 737–70). However, as I stated in the introduction, much of this research is directly focused on those aspects of legal process and discourse that are unambiguously relevant to the everyday affairs of persons in society. I am concerned rather with the more indirect, mediating, and specialized domains of law that address the institutional and, especially, the technological forces that shape everyday lives. Legal process, here, has very important effects on everyday life, but unlike the law of small claims courts, family courts, and welfare bureaucracies, it is often far removed from these impacts both in cognitive and actual social distance. It is precisely these realms of law, estranged from everyday life but having great implication for it, that show what everyday life can mean in legal ideology. This is a very different situating of the question of the relationship between law and everyday life than in most of the research that locates itself within disputes that are in turn unproblematically lodged in the "everyday" facts of the standard form of the case.

of relating law to everyday life, the problematic nature of the everyday in social theory with which I began this paper.

Taken quite literally, the practices of everyday life as phenomenology are intractable to theorization as performed in social theory or legal discourse. This point has been most cogently made by Michel de Certeau, especially in his critique of Foucault's and Bourdieu's efforts to operate theoretically on the level of the quotidian:

> Foucault and Bourdieu situate their enterprise on this edge by articulating a discourse on non-discursive practices. They are not the first to do so. Without going back to ancient times, we can say that since Kant every theoretical effort has had to give a more or less direct explanation of its relationship to this non-discursive activity, to this immense "remainder" constituted by the part of human experience that has not been tamed and symbolized in language. An individual science can avoid this direct confrontation. It grants itself a priori the conditions that allow it to encounter things only in its own limited field where it can "verbalize" them.[14]

Once the space of the everyday becomes filled by the conceptualizations of social theory, its basic phenomenological character is violated. So, if the idea of relating the law to the quotidian is to be taken rigorously, following de Certeau, it cannot be done without certain rhetorical sleights of hand. The everyday, while putatively the site of the most basic and radical representation of social life, has, under this illusion, performed quite different and quite ideological functions in the production of theoretical knowledge. Therefore, in addressing the topic of law's relation to everyday life, I have decided to move from a literal treatment of the everyday, say, in the context of a dynastic family, to an examination of the significance of the everyday in the construction of the contemporary legal discourse of torts, facing at its cutting edge the postmodern challenge of cases like Agent Orange.

There can be no simple or literal sense of the everyday in this discourse—it always gets rhetorically transformed by some metaphor

---

14. Michel de Certeau, *The Practice of Everyday Life* (Berkeley and Los Angeles: University of California Press, 1984), 61.

of social theoretic vision. In light of this, the everyday to me is most meaningful as a base theoretical metaphor in this process of representation. How it changes at various sites of discourse and theorization when faced with the present incommensurability of the reality it attempts to represent is the problem I address in this paper. The everyday is thus not something outside the law—reality, simply— but a key figure of the representation of reality within ongoing legal discourse.[15]

Everyday Life and the Case of Tort Law

> From the industrial revolution onwards . . . there has developed a
> type of society which is less interpretable from experience. . . .
> The general problem which has exercised many producers—
> perhaps more often in plays than in novels—is whether to break
> with the realist tradition altogether or try to extend it. . . . That
> has produced extreme complications for the traditional form
> because it did depend, in my view, on the idea of a knowable
> community, and now we are faced with the fact that this cannot
> be called a community and is not knowable in former ways.
> The result is an extreme crisis of form.
>   —Raymond Williams, *Politics and Letters*

> A tort suit was no longer a two-party affair, whose costs were
> imposed on one or the other of the participants, but a "three-
> party affair," in which the third party was society at large. Such
> a conception of tort law assumed that American society was an
> interdependent entity in which the misfortunes of one person
> affected others. That assumption was fundamental to early
> twentieth-century reformist thought.
>   —G. Edward White, *Tort Law in America*

---

15. This problematization of the everyday pursues the vision of anthropology that Mike Fischer and I developed in *Anthropology as Cultural Critique* (George E. Marcus and Michael M. F. Fischer, *Anthropology as Cultural Critique: An Experimental Moment in the Human Sciences*, Chicago: University of Chicago Press, 1986). In making this shift, I am also leaving behind the areas of law and society that I know best from firsthand research on family fortunes and moving to an area that I know only from secondary reading (although, it should be noted, that tort law has been perhaps the most relevant area of law informing the development of the old anthropology of law focused on mechanisms of dispute management in traditional societies by such writers as Max Gluckman in England and Laura Nader in the United States). Consequently, anything that I argue specifically about tort law and mass toxic torts must be tentative, to be refined by actual scholars of these areas.

Torts as an independent common law subject emerged in the United States only after the mid-nineteenth century. Its emergence also coincided with and was one of the most important media for the development of an applied social theoretical discourse in the law, since it parallelled and had complex relationships to the development of the modern social sciences in the United States.[16] For G. Edward White, the history of tort law in America since the 1870s has reflected the broader intellectual dialectic in the law between two originary trends. The first is the legal science movement, which sought to extract systems of coherent rules from the stuff of cases. The second, legal realism, was a reaction against scientism. Recently, theoretical commentary on torts, as in the influential writings of William Prosser and Roger Traynor, has been a matter of sythesizing or counterbalancing the intellectual legacy of these two movements.

Historically, tort law arose from the complications of the conditions of an industrializing, modernizing society. The theory of torts addresses ways of conceiving of such conditions as the events of everyday life for the purpose of adjudication. The creation of rules about negligence, duty of care, and causation was used to establish doctrine and consistently attribute blame in what were conceived as two-party situations. The optimistic source of social change in the late nineteenth century was science and technology, and law was seen to be an integral part of this development. Problems posed by social change, from instance to instance and case to case, could be also dealt with by scientific practices, which sought general principles controlling social action and then introduced and rigorously applied them within problem-solving institutions such as the courts.

Legal realism suggested the need to move beyond blameworthiness and strict liability, and it was the early findings of emergent social science itself that undermined the notion that the law could generate scientific doctrine in the matter of torts. For the realist, the purpose in adjudicating each tort case was not to establish doctrine but to carry out the policy providing just compensation for the harms generated out of the complex social processes of modernity. The realist position was based on the recognition of the difficulty of establishing the facts of an increasing number of tort cases, and as a result, judges had no choice but to be applied social scientists.

16. Thomas Haskell, *The Emergence of Professional Social Science* (Urbana: University of Illinois Press, 1977).

Realists had not lost faith in the ability of the social sciences to provide secure knowledge about modern society—to the contrary— nor did they challenge conceptually the way tort issues were framed as cases, but they did recognize the "third party," society, which now intruded on the everyday-life grounds from which tort cases were ordinarily constituted in legal discourse.

The 1970s witnessed the return of a neoconceptualism in tort law and the reappearance of comprehensive, abstract, generalized theory. As White observes, "The significance of neoconceptualization in torts literature thus far lies in its reaffirmation of the value of abstract theorizing itself, not in the seminality of any of the theories its proponents have advanced."[17] In this move, which resembles the legal science of the late nineteenth and early twentieth centuries, the return to general theory looks for "true" grounds or foundations of tort law decisions outside law itself, in the principles, say, of economic theory. And like the reaction of legal realism to the ambition of legal science brought on by the recognition of the intractably complex worlds that "case" discourse tried to encompass, a parallel reaction has set in during the 1980s, a postmodern challenge if you will, to the optimism of neoconceptualism, this time brought on by the appearance of cases of overwhelming complexity. Not even social science now offers hope or comfort that the "third party" in some tort cases, especially in class actions, can be distinguished from the classic two parties in situated contention. Now thousands of everyday lives are encompassed in tort cases, and those lives must be understood totally and systemically if the classic notion of tort itself is to be sustained. Thus, the everyday has lost its grounding function in constituting the tort case.

Since my focal concern in this paper is with how legal discourse has depended on constructions of the everyday, most important for me in the history of tort law is the genre that has shaped its expression, and this is of course the construct of the case. We learn from White that the emergence of the case method of instruction in American law was coincident with the rise of legal science: "Its original advocates such as Christopher Columbus Langdell, dean of Harvard Law School from 1870 to 1895, supported the case method because they believed that law should be studied through first-hand exposure to

---

17. White, *Tort Law in America*, 212.

original sources, that 'appellate cases' were the original sources of the legal profession, that cases were sources of general rules and principles, and that the articulation of rules and principles would make law more 'scientific.'"[18] While the case method is certainly not limited to tort law, it is nonetheless in torts that assumptions about the social, particularly about everyday life, are most clearly coded into the notion of the case. In torts, as opposed to, say, contracts or property law, cases arise from the naturally occurring grounding of everyday life in events that make the everyday suddenly problematic and a matter for law.

Even legal realists were confident that reality could be harnessed by the case form for law to do its work. Despite radical social changes, the idea of the case carried along with it the rhetorical baggage associated with traditional society—in Raymond Williams's terms, that torts continued to arise from communities that were knowable in the immediacy of situations, and that the facts and identities of parties to cases were easily determinable by their location in relatively simple social structures. However, because legal realists at least recognized the role of the third party, society, present in many cases, the idea of everyday life as the firm ground of tort determination was thus problematized without being overturned. So far, then, the nonlocal, nonquotidian, systemic embedding of torts could be managed by conceptual revision and artifice; the rhetoric of the case as a framing for the social reality that the law addresses—mostly a reality focused against the everyday lives of specifiable plaintiffs and defendants—remained intact. But the question in the present moment is whether the whole dialectic of debate between doctrine and policy that has governed the intellectual history of tort law is still sufficient to deal with the challenge to the management of torts, which is now felt most deeply in the inadequacy of the conventional case framework to constitute a discourse about certain disputes, like the mass toxic tort. The postmodern cases of the 1980s have thus finally brought to the consciousness of legal theorists and practitioners alike the extreme crisis of form or genre to which Williams alludes.

Throughout the twentieth-century history of torts, the most difficult cases have been those in which the connections between the injured and the injurers have been the most difficult to establish. It

18. White, *Tort Law in America*, xiii.

was such cases in the heyday of legal realism that most strongly prompted the shift from the doctrine to policy, and they do so again, but much more strongly, in the late twentieth century. For instance, *Palsgraf v. Long Island Railroad* became a favorite case in legal education and scholarship precisely because of the indirectness of action and the complexity of the relationships among the parties associated with the relevant event of injury.[19] While the issues at hand in this case never escaped the conventions for containing the relevant social facts within the case framework (save for the free-wheeling criticism of Noonan), discussions of *Palsgraf* certainly verged on defamiliarizing the quotidian grounding of tort cases and moving toward the broader systemic issues that were at stake in what seemed a freak accident, but in which negligence could be argued and eventually found. It was only in the 1980s, in a general intellectual atmosphere of skepticism, and with the appearance of mass conditions of injury with indeterminant plaintiffs allegedly perpetrated by indeterminant defendants, that representing and determining the facts of the case became a major problem in the law of torts.

Class Action in Product Liability, Public Law, Risk Assessment, and the Actuarial Subject

> . . . [I]ndividuals, once understood as moral or rational actors, are increasingly understood as locations in actuarial tables of variations. This shift from moral agent to actuarial subject marks a change in the way power is exercised on individuals by the state and other large organizations. Where power once sought to manipulate the choices of rational actors, it now seeks to predict behavior and situate subjects according to the risk they pose. The effects can be discerned in the way we understand ourselves, our communities, and our capacity for moral judgment and political action.
>
> . . . Actuarial classification, with its de-centered subject, seems to eliminate, in advance, the possibility of identity, of critical self-consciousness and of intersubjectivity. Rather than making people up, actuarial practices unmake them.
>   —Jonathan Simon, "The Ideological Effects of
>   Actuarial Practices"

---

19. See John T. Noonan, Jr., *Persons and Masks of the Law* (New York: Farrar, Strauss, and Giroux, 1976), 111–51.

The notion that reality is complex, almost unbearably complex, as it constitutes the "stuff" of legal cases is nothing new in American social or legal thinking. From the end of the last century to the end of this one, *society* has been a term in the discussion of personal circumstances of injury. What seems to be salient now in this fin de siècle period is both the heightened sense within legal institutions of being stretched to the limit by certain kinds of diffuse, global cases, and the consequent need for solutions that are practical and legitimated by rational, scientific techniques. Facing the literal disaster of mass toxic torts, as well as their figurative disaster for judicial administration, the situational scale of the everyday tort seems to require some sort of conceptual and methodological leap into abstraction and aggregation. At the same time, traditionalism, commonsense perception, habit, and a basic committed humanism in judicial discourse staunchly, but sporadically, resist attempts to move beyond the legally framed circumstances that define the everyday scene and experience that constitute cases.

The evolution and advocacy of class actions in product liability cases have created the discourse for aggregation, for the truly collective appropriation of the tort understood commonsensically and in everyday terms as an affair of individuals. The massive number of persons and businesses frequently involved in product liability cases, the consequent difficulty of proving causation in any particular instance of injury, the indeterminacy of those who occupy the role of plaintiff and/or defendant, and the substantial cost of litigating such cases on a case-by-case basis all have stimulated a literature calling for changes ranging from the elimination of torts as a branch of the law to the redefinition of torts as a field of "public law."[20] Even though the public/private distinction in legal thinking has been subject to much critique, writers such as Rosenberg and Huber see it as the only solution to the management of mass torts.[21] A public-law approach would entail routinely making product liability cases class actions and would establish principles of adjudication based on quan-

20. See Peter Huber, "Safety and the Second Best: The Hazards of Public Risk Management in the Courts," *Columbia Law Review* 85 (1985): 277; Peter Huber, *Liability: The Legal Revolution and Its Consequences* (New York: Basic Books, 1989); and David Rosenberg, "The Causal Connection in Mass Exposure Cases: A 'Public Law' Vision of the Tort System," *Harvard Law Review* 97 (1984): 851–929.

21. Gerald Turkel, "The Public/Private Distinction: Approaches to the Critique of Legal Ideology," *Law and Society Review* 22 (1993): 801–23.

titative assessments of risk and liability, drawn from available techniques and practices in fields such as economics, demography, and the insurance industry.

For example, Rosenberg argues that mass-exposure cases should proceed as class actions and should employ remedial techniques such as damage scheduling and insurance fund judgments.[22] He further argues for replacing the preponderance-of-the-evidence rule in "private law" adjudication, where causation is impossible to prove, by a proportionality rule, which would hold manufacturers liable for the proportion of total injuries attributable to their products. However, Rosenberg believes that judges themselves will be the main opponents of this approach, and he points to lack of expertise as the reason:

> Despite the productivity gains that proportional liability and public law process promise, courts seem reluctant to adopt these approaches. Given that judges usually lack expertise in using and evaluating scientific information, their retention of the preponderance rule and private law process in mass exposure cases raising complex medical and epidemiological issues may be a subtle admission of institutional incompetence.[23]

However, from the perspective of traditional social theory, much more is at stake than the failure of judges to appreciate the power of quantitative techniques in the social sciences. Thus, Jonathan Simon asks what happens to the human subject, comfortably situated in everyday life, in the traditional construction of the tort, when finally taking account of the social in aggregate terms requires the statistical, or as he says, actuarial, construction of the person.[24] Influenced primarily by the work of Michel Foucault, Simon seeks to connect new strategies of social control emerging in the late nineteenth century and the pervasive use of actuarial techniques in the operation of state and industry. The relatively recent actuarial construction of the legal subject, which is itself entailed in class-action and public-law approaches, has in fact been heavily dependent on disciplines

---

22. Rosenberg, "Causal Connection."

23. Rosenberg, "Causal Connection," 925–26.

24. Jonathan Simon, "The Ideological Effects of Actuarial Practices," *Law and Society Review* 22 (1988): 771–800.

and fields like economics, demography, and insurance that have long been operating in these terms.

Simon indicates, however, that the law has been a site of contestation and struggle over the use of these methods. The image is of judges, comfortable dealing first-hand with everyday situations, resisting the utopian methods of totalizing analysis suggested by legal and social science scholars:

> In America, because of the central role of law in maintaining ideological structures, struggles over the imposition of actuarial practices are often fought out on a legal terrain. There have been local resistances to actuarial practices, although we rarely understand them as belonging to a critical struggle over who we are.[25]

In the discussion of a specific case (City of Los Angeles Department of Power and Water v. Manhart, 435 U.S. 702 [1978]), Simon poses this contest in the law as that between what he calls the "insurance-oriented critique" and the "legal-rights-oriented" defense of Manhart. More generally, one could say that the coming of actuarial techniques to law has provided, in one sense, a needed antidote to the strong strain of individualism in American social thought—the notion that the individual is separate from, and even prior to, the social order in which he or she lives. These techniques are the outcome of more than a century of debate about the intrusion of the social into the scene of the everyday.

But in its dehumanizing rationality, the actuarial, while thoroughly submerging or even dispersing the individual as a whole person and moral subject, has perhaps gone too far. Aggregation, while radically collectivizing, is in fact achieved at the cost of the social and the historically specific. As Simon argues:

> The kind of groups whose formation is encouraged by actuarial practices are aggregates; conglomerations of people whose belonging together is unrelated to any significant traditions, discourses, or action. Actuarial practices define as groups assemblies of people which are singularly sterile in their capacity for political empowerment. Where they locate divisions along dimensions of

---

25. Simon, "Ideological Effects," 789.

traditionally recognized difference (e.g., gender) actuarial practices tend to separate this difference from the political and moral
significance that history has built up.[26]

We turn now briefly to an instance of judicial resistance to the
actuarial.

A Judgment for Everyday Life in Texas

We are also uncomfortable with the suggestion that a move
from one-on-one "traditional" modes is little more than a move
to modernity. Such traditional ways of proceeding reflect far
more than habit. They reflect the very culture of the jury trial
and the case and controversy requirement of Article III. . . .
    . . . Texas has made its policy choices in defining the duty
owed by manufacturers and suppliers of products to consumers.
These choices are reflected in the requirement that a plaintiff
prove both causation and damage. In Texas, it is a "fundamental
principle of traditional products liability law . . . that the
plaintiffs must prove that the defendant supplied the product
which caused the injury." These elements focus upon individuals,
not groups. . . .
    . . . Texas has made its policy choices in its substantive tort
rules against the backdrop of a trial. Trials can vary greatly in
their procedures, such as numbers of jurors, the method of jury
instruction, and a large number of other ways. There is a point,
however, where cumulative changes in procedure work a change
in the very character of a "trial." Significantly, changes in
"procedure" involving the mode of proof may alter the liability
of defendants in fundamental ways. . . . A contemplated "trial"
of the 2,990 class members without discrete focus can be no
more than the testimony of experts regarding their claims, as a
group, compared to the claims actually tried to the jury. That
procedure cannot focus upon such issues as individual causation,
but ultimately must accept general causation as sufficient,
contrary to Texas law.
    —Judgment, Fifth Circuit Court of Appeals, re Fibreboard
    Corporation and Pittsburgh Corning Corporation petition
                            for writ of mandamus, 1990

The above are fragments of a judgment granting a petition for a writ
of mandamus by the defendants in an asbestos case, in which Judge

---

26. Simon, "Ideological Effects," 775.

Robert Park of the Eastern District of Texas had given pretrial orders for the consolidation of 3,031 cases. This judgment merely serves here as a useful illustration of the kind of judicial resistance, noted by Rosenberg, to the transformation of the judicial process engendered by innovative moves toward public-law approaches, with their reliance on class actions, on statistical methods in aggregation, and finally, on the asocial, actuarial construction of plaintiffs in torts.

Most important for us is that the judgment is strongly sympathetic in its rationale to the pervasive ideology of individualism in American society even as this ideology is given specific cultural inflections in terms of what the region has declared as its desires (through Texas law). And it is through such specific instances of arguing for the priority of individual rights that the scene of the everyday is also being retained in legal discourse and culture. The judgment makes no practical suggestions about how, while respecting the individual, everyday realities and diversity of the cases, the undeniably "social," interconnected character of the cases is also to be recognized, especially with regard to how the courts are to manage the formidable administrative task of considering each case in its own terms. Of course, the judgment on the petition at hand is not obliged to do so, and it stands therefore more clearly as a statement of principle and valorization of the sacred ideological ground of everyday lives and situations with which legal process must keep in touch. Thus, what is missing here is a sense of compromise with the inherently social character of mass toxic torts. Just as the public-law approach as developed so far is seriously flawed in totally excluding the scene of the everyday, so is the ideology of rights-bearing individualism as the version of everyday life offered in resisting public-law approaches.

If not the rights-bearing autonomous individual, Texas-style or otherwise, then what is the person to be in the mass tort? If not the actuarial, then what is the social to be in the mass tort? Such are the questions for the reconceptualization of the everyday. Before taking this issue up again in the conclusion, I will survey one intensive treatment of perhaps the most famous (or rather infamous) mass toxic tort case. Here, manipulative judicial management (the sort rejected by the Fifth Circuit) of a particularly complex case embraces neither high-tech social science solutions nor commitment to doing justice to each and every instance of injury. Rather, in moving toward settlement, such management evades any authoritative mode of representing the

disaster. Despite scholarly debates about alternative solutions, prag-
matically muddling through, with the aid of a charismatically reinforced exercise of judicial authority, seems to be the only way out of
such cases within the frame of tort litigation.

Mass Toxic Torts and the End of Everyday Life

> [T]he nominal representative plaintiffs in class action are only
> names" [Weinstein, the most prominent Agent Orange case
> judge]. When Yannacone [the most prominent Agent Orange
> case plaintiff attorney] protested that "Michael and Kerry Ryan
> are not just names," Weinstein disagreed. "This is what Rule 23
> envisions," he said. "There is no possible way for the named
> plaintiffs to participate in the details once the case is turned
> over to the lawyers.
> —Peter H. Schuck, *Agent Orange on Trial*

Schuck locates his account of the Agent Orange case within a corpus
of contemporary tort cases of unprecedented character:

> Today, the law books abound with tort cases, especially in the
> product liability area, that involve not a few individuals but large
> aggregations of people and vast economic and social interests.
> These cases are not preoccupied with corrective justice between
> individuals concerned solely with past events. Instead, they con-
> cern the public control of large-scale activities and the distri-
> bution of social power and values for the future. The court and
> jury in these cases do not simply prescribe and apply familiar
> norms to discrete actions; they function as policy-oriented risk
> regulators, as self-conscious allocators of hard-to-measure ben-
> efits and risks, and as social problem solvers.[27]

---

27. Schuck, *Agent Orange*, 4. I have chosen to rely heavily on Schuck's study
in this paper, because in the absence of my own primary research on mass toxic
torts, I have found his the most detailed and extensive treatment of such a case. Also
because of the media attention given to Agent Orange, there are a number of easily
available sources in journalism and scholarship on this subject to offer me comparative
perspectives other than the legal. Unfortunately, I have not been able to compare
here the overlapping treatments of Agent Orange in law, press, and memoir (e.g.,
Elmo Zumwalt, Jr., and Elmo Zumwalt III, *My Father, My Son* [New York: Macmillan, 1986]) as a complex postmodern phenomenon variably assimilated to or
evading the scene of everyday experience. A mapping of such an ecology of discourses
on this subject would seem ultimately crucial to the consideration of the law's capacity

What is so congenial about Schuck's study for my argument is that his primary interest in the Agent Orange case is in the opportunity it offers to test the limits of the assumptions and framing rhetoric on which tort law has traditionally been based.[28] It is a case that obliterates the situated everyday grounds as the assumed "scene" of tort cases. It challenges the theorist of law and society to rethink the everyday as something other than a concrete, person-to-person situation, and to see it as a *mass* condition with a complex ecology of effects (as in the long-term and deep effects of toxicity, the apocalyptic harm wrought by the complex processes of modernity). The routine, ordinary, and quotidian is to be understood as much in global as in

---

in and of itself to evade the concept of tort and the scene of the everyday, or to transform completely the evaluation of such mass torts in terms of a doctrine of scientific risk assessment and the actuarial construction of subjects.

I should note that the other candidate for focal attention in this paper might have been the asbestos cases, and as my brief treatment of the Texas judgment in *Fibreboard Corporation* shows, these cases in particular have raised the issue of the validity of assimilating a diversity of individual situations and experiences to class action. But given the prominence of centralizing judicial administration in Agent Orange (in the person of Judge Weinstein) as well as the more thoroughly problematic indeterminacies as to defendants and plaintiffs associated with it, I have found the use of this case both more convenient and apt than asbestos in the illustration of my argument.

Finally, while finding Schuck's account congenial to my own purposes and perceptions (he rightly emphasizes, I believe, the sheer difficulty in managing the case as an empirical phenomenon, as paperwork and records—this is its most surreal quality—which seems to be the strongest motivation for evading climax hearings or trials of the "facts"), I do not do so uncritically or with a complete commonality of scholarly interest. As an ethnographer rather than legal theorist, I would have given more attention to the diffuse and diverse voices in the case that are finally assimilated to Judge Weinstein's powerful, overbearing administration. I tend not to have the same confidence in scientific analytical tools to answer certain macro questions involved in such cases, nor do I think that the micro, everyday situations of those affected by such technological disasters can be effectively dealt with by administration outside torts, especially when there are a number of overlapping (and sometimes competing) accounts of the same issues in other media that are heavily moralistic and seek to establish blame and liability. Still, Schuck's account cogently explores the difficulty of the scene of the everyday, as conventionally constructed in tort law, in finding a venue in the legal discourse on Agent Orange, which remains my prime rationale for giving it focal attention here.

28. While the Agent Orange case does indeed combine numerous features that make it especially complex, and Schuck's arguments do depend on his own rhetorical accentuation of the singularity of the case, it is by no means unique: see, for example, Sindell v. Abbott Labs, 26 Cal. 3d 588 (1980); Ayers v. Township of Jackson, 189 N.J. Super. Ct. 561 (1983); Duke Power v. Carolina Environmental Study Group, Inc., 438 U.S. 59 (1977); and Sierra Club v. Morton, Secretary of the Interior, 405 U.S. 727 (1971).

local terms. Society finally becomes more than just a third party to the local, quotidian ground of the tort, but is an integral part of that ground itself.

The adjudication of the Agent Orange case required either taking up the challenge of reconceptualizing the scene of torts as occurring in global heterogeneous space, or evading this overwhelming challenge of representing the facts, conditions, and causation of the case by settlement strategies. The case, in the broad ethnographic sense of the total corpus of discourse that constitutes it as a social event and process, is so rich because it, in fact, takes up both options. It thus serves as a valuable object to probe the emergence, misrecognition, and blocking in the law, functioning as applied social theory and trying to preserve the rational in the face of the incommensurable. In this, yielding the security and confidence provided by the assumptions about the bedrock, human-scale, sense-and-order-making nature of everyday life is the crucial issue to register in the analysis of what lawyers, judges, and other actors involved in the case say and do.

As an ethnographer of grounded social practices as well as one concerned with representations and their production as the primary object of cultural analysis, I was most struck by Schuck's introduction to the extreme complexity of the Agent Orange case in terms of its sheer, massive materiality:

> Apart from its locus in a courtroom, it bears little resemblance to traditional tort adjudication. Its magnitude and complexity beggar the imagination, as a few crude numerical indicators suggest. The case is actually a consolidation into one class action of more than 600 separate actions originally filed by more than 15,000 named individuals throughout the United States, and almost 400 individual cases not included in the class action ("opt-out" cases). The parties in these consolidated actions consist of some 2.4 million Vietnam veterans, their wives, children born and unborn, and soldiers from Australia and New Zealand; a small number of civilian plaintiffs; seven (originally twenty-four) corporate defendants; and the United States government.

In a typical case litigated in the federal court in which the Agent Orange case was heard, the docket sheet is one or two pages long and contains perhaps sixty thousand entries, each representing a filed document. The Agent Orange docket sheet in the district court alone is approximately 425 single-spaced pages long. It contains over 7,300 individual entries, many representing documents that are hundreds of pages long. The files of briefs, hearing transcripts, court orders, affadivits, and other documents in the case were so voluminous that the already cramped clerk's office had to take the unprecedented step of devoting an entire room, staffed by two special clerks, to house them.

The financial and personal demands of the case are even more staggering. The plaintiffs are represented by a network of law firms that numbered almost 1,500 by May, 1984, located in every region of the country; the documented cost of their activities to date certainly exceeds $10 million and increases daily. It has been estimated that the defendants spent roughly $100 million merely to prepare for the trial, utilizing hundreds of lawyers and corporate staff in their Herculean effort.

The court has also bourne [sic] an enormous administrative burden. The current district court judge—the second to preside over the Agent Orange case—has to create a considerable bureaucracy within his chambers simply to enable him to run it, employing additional law clerks and paralegals. And although it is highly unusual for a judge to appoint even one special master to handle particular aspects of a litigation for him, this judge used no fewer than *six* special masters (four or five of them simultaneously) plus a federal magistrate, and they in turn sometimes hired consultants to assist them.[29]

This passage serves a function that would be rhetorically quite congenial to anthropologists. It is an act of defamiliarization, common to traditional ethnography, which establishes the bizarreness of one's subjects. This is clearly Schuck's intention—to set up the Agent Orange case as a radical break with the past of torts. Having thus recognized what amounts to a postmodern challenge to the law, Schuck's account then focuses on how legal discourse, developed in the commonsense frame of lawyer-judge negotiation, tries to tame the behemoth. The everyday has been relegated to the uncomprehending

---

29. Schuck, *Agent Orange*, 4–5.

vantage point of the veterans who are left on the sidelines, far from the discussions that argued and settled the case. The scene of "torts" is focused in the "Rule 23" status of those veterans as "mere" names, despite the anachronistic crusading attorney Yannacone's attempt to remind Judge Weinstein that "Michael and Kerry Ryan are not just names." Only if the case had come to trial might the everyday have reentered it through the voices of plaintiffs telling their stories to a jury. But the legal practitioners on all sides, and especially Judge Weinstein, worked to prevent a trial and the return of the everyday. Why?

Schuck's account comes to focus on the work and thinking of Judge Jack B. Weinstein, who took over the case after the first judge, Pratt, had been elevated to the Court of Appeals. It was only Weinstein, according to Schuck, who finally had intellectual mastery of the case and thus provided a holistic frame of reference. The overwhelming complexity of the case thus came to rest conventionally nonetheless on one man's comprehension, the traditional position of the judge. While Judge Weinstein clearly saw the plight of the plaintiffs in the human-scale terms of their everyday lives, he also understood the impossibility of recognizing their claims under traditional tort rule. The "scene of the everyday" was banished from the structure of this class-action case in which there were indeterminant plaintiffs, indeterminant defendants, and no way to show preponderance, scientific or otherwise, in causation. Weinstein was in the ironic position of having systematically to deny the everyday-life situations of the plaintiffs in the framework of tort law in order to achieve the effect finally of providing them with compensation:

> "We are in a different world of proof than that of the archetypical smoking gun," Weinstein insisted. "We must make the best estimates of probability that we can, using the help of experts such as statisticians and our own common sense and experience with the real universe." Furthermore, he added, the classwide solution might in fact be "the only practicable way to secure a remedy" for plaintiffs because of the high administrative costs, risk of inconsistent verdicts, and other incidents of individual litigation. "Particularly during this period of rapidly changing scientific approaches and increased threats to the environment,"

he concluded, "we should not unduly restrict development of legal theory and practice" by dismissing the class action.

With this analysis, Weinstein had thrust forward the frontiers of mass toxic tort law. At each point, he had manifested a general readiness, even eagerness, to abandon or adapt traditional tort rules that would otherwise bar "statistically injured" plaintiffs from recovering. Because particularistic evidence was hard to come by in mass exposure situations, he had opposed placing "too heavy a burden . . . on plaintiffs by requiring a high percentage or incidence of a disease to be attributable to a particular product." This led him to endorse the weak version of the preponderance rule, another innovation. And to overcome the indeterminate plaintiff problem, he had both rejected an individualized burden-shifting solution in favor of a classwide one and endorsed the previously untried ideas of proportional liability and probabilistic causation. Under this novel approach, not only were class actions permissable in mass exposure cases, notwithstanding Rule 23; they must henceforth be regarded as indispensable, at least in *indeterminate* plaintiff solutions.[30]

Once Judge Weinstein enters the case, Schuck's account is an admiring compendium of such maneuverings. Indeed, Judge Weinstein's power to coerce and persuade derived, in part, from his explicit recognition that legal discourse could not encompass the facts of this case or even determine them: "As we saw earlier, the very notion of a 'claim' was undeniably difficult to define in the context of the Agent Orange case. His overriding argument, however—his frequently played trump card—was that plaintiffs' case, particularly with regard to causation, was so weak that it would not have been entitled to go to a jury. Plaintiffs, that is, were legally entitled to zero. In that view, *any* settlement amount . . . covering *any* number of claims and *any* distribution of that amount . . . were more than they were entitled to. . . . This argument was Weinstein's ultimate conversation stopper. Only an appellate court could compel him to resume it."[31]

The incommensurability of the case to traditional tort law and

---

30. Schuck, *Agent Orange*, 188–89.
31. Schuck, *Agent Orange*, 206.

the inadequacy of the latter were the weapons or levers that Judge Weinstein so skillfully wielded. He "made law" in his decisions, but he did not theorize.[32] The ultimate question of the dispersion of the everyday ground of tort cases and the way that it dissolved into the heterogeneous global space of a mass toxic tort is left to Schuck. Is the everyday grounding of tort law gone for good in cases like this, or does it return in another radicalized form? Is it salvageable in the social theory that legal scholars create in contemplating cases, or is law bound to lose this bedrock sense and scale of the personally human?

Schuck surveys three ways in which legal discourse might adapt to mass toxic torts. He starts with an analysis of the traditional tort approach consonant with the argument of this paper: "The traditional tort approach, one must conclude, is not so much a serious response to the special problems posed by Agent Orange–type cases—the problems of proof of causation, scale, spatial dispersion, time span, and cost—as an ostrichlike avoidance of them"[33]

Schuck then considers the public-law approach, which encourages the kind of managerial judging Weinstein had exercised in the Agent Orange case. This approach works on systematic exclusion of the everyday grounds of traditional torts and considers most issues like causation in social, aggregated terms. Schuck seems to think that the valorization of the macrosociological conception of mass toxic tort cases in the public-law approach is a move in the right direction: still, as a form of *policy*, this approach does not go far enough. The issue in mass toxic torts is as much about risk, developed in a totalistic assessment of the worth of a certain agent, as about an instance or type of demonstrated injury. That is, in public-law torts, the specific injury brought by plaintiffs should be balanced against a judicial/ social scientific inquiry into the totality of harm and the otherwise risk-reducing potential of a particular substance or process.[34]

---

32. For Weinstein's similar style of centralizing judicial administration in his more recent entry into the controversy over the Manville Trust, set up in 1988 to settle all future claims against the company that was for decades the world's largest asbestos manufacturer, see Stephen Labaton, "The Bitter Fight over the Manville Trust," *New York Times*, 8 July 1990, sec. 3. The mismanagement and early exhaustion of this trust's resources demonstrate the vulnerabilities in practice of what seem like workable collective solutions to class actions in the area of product liability.

33. Schuck, *Agent Orange*, 41.
34. See Huber, "Safety."

This suggests an approach that is outside the concept of torts, whereby massive toxic tort cases would be dealt with beyond the realm of litigation among a set of risk-regulating institutions. This is the approach that Schuck finally seems to favor, and it is the one that definitively marks the end of everyday life in these cases, in favor of technology-minded systems analysis, in which tort issues are resolved and subsumed under the focused consideration of risk. As he says: "By taking the giant step to a wholly aggregative, distributive justice approach—one in which individual A is compensated by company B even though A may not have been harmed by B or indeed by any responsible actor (other than Mother Nature)—the public law structure might well destroy whatever residual moral justification remains for shifting A's loss to B through tort adjudication. If so, we might be wise to acknowledge candidly any changed assumptions that exist and to pursue their implications for institutional and doctrinal change. We should not pretend that we are still operating in the moral universe of tort law when mass toxic exposure problems render it anomalous."[35]

Schuck then goes on to consider the trade-off between compensation and deterrence; he suggests decoupling compensation and deterrence and providing the former through insurance schemes and the latter through administrative regulation. Thus, the representation of the everyday in Schuck's favored move beyond torts becomes thoroughly rationalized and translated into the machinery of expert systems and the ideology of risk analysis—the worlds of actuarial subjects—and the imagined connection of law and grounded everyday life bound historically to the idea of the case becomes finally and radically effaced in legal discourse.

The only thing that Schuck obscures in this solution is the decisively nonhermetic nature of the law in contemporary society: it is pulled by as much as it pushes the popular media of journalism, where the power of mass, collective representations of unimaginable phenomena are daily reduced to the images and stories of everyday lives. Finally, it is the mass belief in and interpretive power of the human-scale scene of the efficacious quotidian that will limit any definitive end to the moral ground of the everyday within abstracting discourses about complex postmodern events that challenge the propensity to social theorizing within the law.

---

35. Schuck, *Agent Orange*, 276.

The End of Everyday Life?

> By the late twentieth century, our time, a mythic time, we are
> all chimeras, theorized and fabricated hybrids of machine and
> organism; in short, we are cyborgs. The cyborg is our ontology;
> it gives us our politics. The cyborg is a condensed image of
> both imagination and material reality, the two joined centers
> structuring any possibility of historical transformation.
> —Donna Haraway, "A Manifesto for Cyborgs: Science,
> Technology, and Socialist Feminism in the 1980s"

Given, then, that the scene of the everyday can never completely
pass from legal discourse even in the most radical departures from
the traditional tort framework, and given also the inadequacy of the
everyday that is already available and deeply embedded in conventional legal discourse, the important issue is how the everyday might
be rethought, how the terms in which it is generated in legal discourse
might be modified to incorporate the presence of the most global,
systemic forces operating within the most intimate and most quotidian
circumstances of personal experience. How might we develop a discourse of the everyday in the law that gives access to complex global
and technological processes in a way that would be every bit as
powerful as, and even complementary to, the mathematical modeling
and actuarial tendencies of public-law approaches?

What might be expected here is not the creation of a new vocabulary or typology, a set of comprehensive neologisms, or even a new
epistemology by a single stroke (or competitive strokes) of scholarly
or judicial genius, but rather the gradual remaking of legal cognition
and modes of representing social reality. Thus, one would not expect
a wholesale replacement of "rights" discourse in the law, since so
much of the ground of value and morality is communicated by it.
Rather, as new social conditions and realities are perceived through
the evolution of class actions and other quite pragmatic and
incremental innovations in legal procedure and administration, the
entities—the legal fictions such as the person as autonomous agent,
as mind more than body—to which rights adhere might profoundly
change. This is the challenge of mass toxic torts to traditional assumptions about what terms like the individual and society have meant.

Thus, an important task of contemporary ideology critique is
reading for quiet, but radical, transformations in the understanding

of social and cultural phenomena in the frontline discourses that I evoked at the beginning of this paper as a framework for thinking about the law. Schuck's work and that of numerous others like it are produced under assumptions that we are living through a watershed period of social change. However correct or relatively accurate these perceptions may prove to be, writing and thinking within the law according to them are bound to produce marked changes about basic, taken-for-granted terms that have defined the social in legal cognition.

To my knowledge, there has not yet emerged in the discussions of legal studies an explicit self-conscious registering of such subtle, yet radical shifts at so basic a level of conceptual reference. But certainly the space for such discussions has been cleared in attempts to suggest comprehensive solutions to the management of mass toxic torts and in the contesting of these solutions by putting the scene of the everyday at stake. And the everyday has been the linchpin, as I have argued, in social theory as well as legal discourse for postulating order and normalcy both within society itself and within the nineteenth-century apparatuses for apprehending it. The treatment of mass toxic torts begs for some new assumptions about the nature of the everyday that address the specific circumstances of rights-bearing persons, which are as global or systemic as they are local, and for ways to confront a mass of specifics and contexts—the traditional specifiable facts of the case(s)—to counterbalance public-law approaches. These assumptions are likely to emerge with the evolution of procedures for treating such cases, but because of the threat of dissolution or evasion of the everyday that we have seen, alternatives for rethinking the everyday deserve some special pleading and provocation.

In this, I can only end on a note of visionary musing drawn from the example of a particular strain of feminist thought, particularly concerned with the social construction of scientific knowledge (not unrelated, of course, to the sort of technological and systemic issues of causation at stake in mass toxic torts). Incidentally, feminist thought in its most cogent expression has operated through the metaphor of "stealing the language"—that is, in offering provocative remakings and retellings of conventional narratives such that the reader or listener would never receive them in the same ways again.[36]

36. Alicia Suskin Ostriker, *Stealing the Language: The Emergence of Women's Poetry in America* (Boston: Beacon Press, 1986).

I would like to key on Donna Haraway's construct of the cyborg, drawn from science fiction, but wielded by her to provide an alternative way to think of the unified subject acting situationally.[37]

Haraway's specific interest is in breaking the nature-culture, animal-human, machine-man divide as a habit of thought and cognition in the production of scientific knowledge.[38] The cyborg has its own local, everyday life and situated identity, but it is always wired simultaneously into the operations of more global systems, patterns, and technologies. Human actors conceived as cyborgs block an analysis in terms of our traditional categories of segmenting the human naturally into the cultural, the social, the psychological, the emotional, the political, and so on. The cyborg is used as a provocation to construct different sorts of stories about humans that are recombinant of our standard classifications in ways both that seem persuasive in terms of our sense of emergent late-twentieth-century phenomena and that ultimately would revise deeply essentialist thinking, especially about the nature of gender and race. However useful the evocation of the cyborg might prove to be as counterdiscourses are developed in the work of different natural sciences, it is a powerful opening gambit in disrupting deep-seated notions about the person and the social.

My own interest here in Haraway's critical stratagem of posing the cyborg is merely to suggest the need for a similar sort of provocation in areas of law such as mass toxic torts, where the scene of the everyday is at stake not because it is incommensurable with the "mass" character of the phenomenon that the law addresses, but because the everyday, when it is posed, is not conceived in a way that has much relevance for or relationship to the global, systemic factors at issue in such torts. Referring to the epigraph of the preceding section of this paper, what if the nominal representative plaintiffs in class actions were not only names, but were to be represented as or like cyborgs—victims and products of certain complex conjunctions of technology, politics, and history? What, then, if Michael and Kerry

---

37. Donna Haraway, "Situated Knowledges: The Science Question in Feminism and the Privilege of Partial Perspective," *Feminist Studies* 14 (1988): 575–99, and "A Manifesto for Cyborgs: Science, Technology, and Socialist Feminism in the 1980s," in *Feminism/Postmodernism*, ed. Linda J. Nicholson (New York: Routledge, 1990).

38. Donna Haraway, *Primate Visions: Gender, Race, and Nature in the World of Modern Science* (New York: Routledge, 1989).

Ryan are not just names, not just conventional human agents in the scene of the everyday, but rights-bearing cyborgs? At least then the legal discourses in any specific case might open up to explicit consideration and representation of the social, organic, and personal conditions of those in litigation. These conditions—the old scene of the everyday—would not, however, be strictly localized accounts of injury and hardship, but would show the continuous relationships of humans to technology and its risks. Through collective, multiply situated ethnography or microsociology, a set of connected persons, corporations, technological processes, and political decisions would be introduced as an object of judicial inquiry to be juxtaposed to current public-law approaches. Only in this way would the everyday reenter with relevance and power the development of mass torts in contemporary legal process.

Appendix

A Note on the Historic Link between Tort Law and the Development of Ethnography in Anthropology

When Section 165 of the *Restatement of Torts* was presented at the May 1929 meeting of the members of the American Law Institute, Cardozo's opinion in *Palsgraf* appeared in this form as an illustration of Clause b of the rule.

> A, a passenger of the X and Y Railway Company, is attempting to board a train while encumbered with a number of obviously fragile parcels. B, a trainman of the company, in assisting A does so in such a manner as to make it probable that A will drop one or more of the parcels. A drops a parcel which contains fireworks, although nothing in its appearance indicates this. The fireworks explode, injuring A's eyes. The railway company is not liable to A. Matthew Wood, Joseph Keany, and William McNamara, adventitious figures, had disappeared. The judges no longer disputed. Helen Palsgraf had become the injured A and the Long Island Railroad the A and Y.
>
> It was not only the eyes of A which had been blinded. (John T. Noonan, Jr., *Persons and Masks of the Law*)

Ethnography and the law, especially tort law, share the case as a mode of representing their subjects in common. In fact, historically, there has been a close relation between the development of theory in social anthropology and legal concepts and training. Sir Henry Maine, John McLennan, and Lewis Henry Morgan, for instance, were all legal scholars who became nineteenth-century theorists of tribal societies and whose framing concepts, derived from the Western legal tradition, lasted well into the twentieth-century paradigm. In ethnography, especially as promoted by British exemplars of this discipline-defining practice for anthropology, everyday life as closely observed in fieldwork has always been the medium in which knowledge has been produced. The case became one of the primary methods of ethnographic presentation and writing, a means of circumscribing and reducing the complexity of everyday reality—the data recorded in field notebooks—to illustrations of orderly process so that the basic combined ethnographic task of theory-in-description could be accomplished.

The case method in legal education and discourse became a direct inspiration for the presentation of cases in British and American ethnography. In Britain, this connection was made primarily through social anthropology at Manchester under Max Gluckman, a lawyer by training, who pioneered both the anthropology of law, primarily focused on African societies, and the more general use of the case to illustrate and analyze social processes in the sphere of the quotidian with which anthropological knowledge was customarily concerned. In the United States, the direct connection was made by E. Adamson Hoebel, who worked closely with Karl Llewellyn to develop an anthropology of law based on the constitution of data in the form of cases.

Beyond the confines of the subspecialty of the anthropology of law, which initially developed through the study of informal mechanisms of dispute management, the presentation of ethnographic material as cases or extended cases, usually of conflict, to illustrate and argue about the diverse claims that ethnographers make about their subjects became a favored genre for presenting and analyzing data. Victor Turner's 1956 study *Schism and Continuity in an African Society* is perhaps the key crossover work, in that while coming out of the legal anthropology tradition at Manchester, it nonetheless developed an extended case method as "social drama," as a vehicle of description that enabled the incorporation of a greater variety and richness of detail than that permitted in the usual "facts of the case" when these were specifically directed to the interests of law or dispute management.[39] In general, then, what are indeed cases of torts in tribal societies have been converted by anthropologists into circumscribed narratives of principle and process of social and cultural structure at the core of ethnographic description.

There are indeed great differences between what the case means and encompasses in ethnographic research and what it means in legal discourse. The differences can be most easily understood when the legal case itself is in part the object of anthropological inquiry. What does the ethnographer want from a case and what does a legal practitioner want, particularly with regard to the level and understanding of everyday life that the case is made to encompass and represent? For the ethnographer (or for the historian of law like Schuck, or a maverick critic like Noonan), a legal case like *Palsgraf* or Agent Orange should be understood as broadly as possible, in the most human of terms, and from the multiple perspectives and interests that compose it. When it is discourse that is focused upon by the ethnographer or historian, a case is the total corpus of representations, associations, commentaries, popularly expressed opinion, and documents of which it is constituted in language and social action. In other words, it is a totally embedded and graded cultural phenomenon.

For the legal practitioner and scholar, a case is of course much more structurally limited and bounded for particular purposes. Official productions of a case for presentation in a court context, and subsequently only certain authoritative and official versions of the cases tied to matters and purposes of law, are the ones focused upon by most legal scholars. Noonan, as critic, takes the ethnographer's view in demonstrating how the humanity is leeched out of cases in the course of this development within legal discourse and cognition. Schematically, cases remain tied to the everyday conditions out of which they are presumed to arise, but what is at stake in cases is very sparely constituted and described on behalf of established rhetorics of legal treatment. The ordinariness of life is presumed to background the cases without being represented in them. It takes the

---

39. Victor Turner, *Schism and Continuity in an African Society* (Manchester: University of Manchester Press, 1956).

development of certain kinds of contemporary cases, such as class actions, to move toward the effacement of the assumption of everyday life operating within the abstract representation of legal cases. But at this point, the notion of the case as a containing wall in which legal discourse and work can be done is also in jeopardy. The law is forced to broaden its vistas to events that cannot be encompassed by a restricted view of the case held to focus by the assumption that facts are everyday, here and now. At this point, the ethnographer's or historian's broad view of the case in terms of its heterogeneous global dimensions and the law's would converge.

Contributors

David M. Engel is Professor of Law at the State University of New York at Buffalo.

Hendrik Hartog is Professor of History at Princeton University.

Thomas R. Kearns is William H. Hastie Professor of Philosophy and Professor of Law, Jurisprudence, and Social Thought at Amherst College.

David Kennedy is Professor of Law at Harvard University.

Catharine A. MacKinnon is Professor of Law at the University of Michigan.

George E. Marcus is Professor of Anthropology at Rice University.

Austin Sarat is William Nelson Cromwell Professor of Jurisprudence and Political Science and Professor of Law, Jurisprudence, and Social Thought at Amherst College.

Patricia J. Williams is Professor of Law at Columbia University.

Index